MW01248496

It's Not About the dEvil

True Stories About Fighting Evil in the Modern World

John DiGirolamo

ISBN 979-8-89112-274-1 (Paperback)
ISBN 979-8-89112-276-5 (Hardcover)
ISBN 979-8-89112-275-8 (Digital)

Copyright © 2024 John DiGirolamo
All rights reserved
First Edition

Previous books by John DiGirolamo
It's Not About the Predator: A Parent's Guide to
Internet & Social Media Safety (2022)
It's Not About the Sex (2022)
It's Not About the Badge (2021)

All rights reserved. No part of this publication may be reproduced, distributed, or transmitted in any form or by any means, including photocopying, recording, or other electronic or mechanical methods without the prior written permission of the publisher. For permission requests, solicit the publisher via the address below.

Covenant Books
11661 Hwy 707
Murrells Inlet, SC 29576
www.covenantbooks.com

Testimonials

All of life is spiritual warfare, whether we know it or not. The world is full of dark forces, and John DiGirolamo provides the reader with three gripping stories about individuals who stand up to evil forces. I've seen firsthand the insidious nature of the occult and diabolical in the streets of LA while working in law enforcement, and this book reveals the devil's playbook. Clement's experiences are a vivid reminder of how the ultimate predator, the devil, seeks to ruin lives and destroy souls, but more importantly, how he assists an exorcist priest to liberate one man from a life of sin and demonic affliction.

The book's authentic portrayal of the rite of exorcism will captivate the reader from start to finish. This book is timely because this is the greatest evil of our time—child-human sex trafficking.

—**Jesse Romero**, retired Los Angeles Deputy Sheriff, host of the "Jesus 911" podcast, and author of *The Devil in the City of Angels: My Encounters With the Diabolical*

***

Evil comes in many forms. DiGirolamo's latest book quickly immerses the reader in three compelling stories about fighting the darkness in our modern world. The stories weave in perils of society such as teen sexting, online predators, and pornography. Within the final chapter is a powerful story about angels and demons and one man's fight to take back his soul. The devil is very real, and DiGirolamo's book sheds needed light.

—**EMAC**, author of *Life Letters*

***

This book, *It's Not About the dEvil,* is like reading the headlines from today's newspapers. It's hard to think about our country turning its back from being a Christian nation to what it has become today. Even our children are indulging in things that were unthinkable a few short years ago.

—**Charlotte Burrous**, editor-in-chief of the *Fremont County Crusader*

***

John DiGirolamo is a noted expert in his field. The success of his previous books are testimonials to his ability to provide simple actions to confront and prevent evil while celebrating the heroes who have done so. I applaud him for expanding our knowledge and wisdom in a way no one else has done before.

—**Eugene F. Ferraro**,
CPP, CFE, PCO, SPHR

***

This book highlights the undercurrents of our twenty-first-century digitized world. However, the author shines the light of hope into each situation.

—**Cynthia L. Simmons**, author
of the *Southern Gold Series*

***

Dr. Wheeler's story reminds us that all our lives are journeys. We make decisions along the way, considering different factors, but most importantly, the moral dimension of each choice must be weighed. We must not justify our actions but recognize there is an ultimate authority that determines right and wrong.

Dr. Wheeler's vivid and accurate depictions of abortions, both as a participant and as a friend to those who have been affected by them, remind us of the pain and harm inherent in this action that affects so many women, men, and families around us. Ultimately, she found her way to healing in Christ, a path we will all hopefully follow.

—**Ingrid Skop**, MD, FACOG, vice president and director of medical affairs, the Charlotte Lozier Institute

***

A compelling journey of faith through three intense stories of God vs. the devil: Child trafficking, abortion, and an epic battle with Satan for a man's soul. You will not be able to put this book down. An inspirational work that will help us all in our journey with Christ. The author has reached a new level in his writing.

—**George Gramlich**, editor of *The Sangre de Cristo Sentinel*

***

It's Not About the dEvil helped me wrap my brain around the evil I see in this world and the troubling times in which we live. Through its insightful narratives, the book is rich with resources that bolster its themes. Whether it's practical tips for responsible online behavior, navigating discussions about killing our unborn children, guidance on addressing cyberbullying, or profound prayers that resonate through the ages, the book serves as an invaluable toolkit for readers seeking guidance and empowerment.

One of the book's most crucial messages revolves around the legal implications of certain digital behaviors. With candor, the author underscores the potential legal consequences for minors who engage in sending explicit images, enlightening readers that such actions may inadvertently create child sexual abuse material (CSAM) and open them up to prosecution. This frank discussion is a powerful wake-up call for both young readers and their guardians, highlighting the importance of informed decision-making in a digital era.

The most impactful feature of this book is its use of real-world stories that resonate deeply with readers. These stories illustrate the harsh realities of our generation and the spiritual realm in which we fight, making the book not only a call to awareness but a call to action. It's a testament to the power of knowledge, faith, and the human spirit in the face of modern challenges. I'm grateful for these stories, these resources, and John DiGirolamo!

—**Sabrina Stratford**, human trafficking abolitionist, www.SabrinaStratford.com

***

Whether you are a mother or father, grandfather or grandmother, brother or sister, aunt or uncle, single or married, or cousin—*It's Not About dEvil: True Stories about Fighting Evil in the Modern World* is must-read. This book will take you from being angry to rejoicing, from being scared to relief, from being confused to understanding. This book is an absolute must-read for middle schoolers to great-grandparents and everyone in between.

Being a very active and involved praying grandfather, I did not expect reading a book that would so alarm me to the depth and seriousness of the evil DiGirolamo writes about. And for those of us who would say, "That does not go on in my town!" We are grossly mistaken! DiGirolamo has interviewed three people on the front line of serious issues facing us today and then weaves the stories into compelling, "cannot put the book down" writing that intrigues, informs, and educates in such a way as to compel the reader to action. Sitting and doing nothing is no longer an option!

—**Brad Tuttle**, author, speaker, and host of a joint TV prayer program sponsored by Colorado Prays and Rocky Mountain Christian Television Network

***

John has really put a lot of time and effort into the research and writing of this book. Readers' eyes will definitely be opened to the evil and darkness of the world as well as the light from the heroes that fight it each day. While it reads like fiction, the scary part about John's book is that it is 100 percent real. We've all heard about kids getting conned online; however, in the first chapter, "The Equalizer," John illustrates just how easy it can be for a young person to be sucked into the web of an online predator.

It's Not About the dEvil grabs a hold of your attention, making it hard to put down. Whether you are a parent, senior, community leader, teacher, married, single, or anyone with a pulse, this is a must-read.

—**Tamara Markard**, Go+Do reporter/
managing editor *A&E Spotlight and MyWindsor* magazines, Greeley Tribune

***

Many people struggle to understand how teens can fall victim to sex trafficking and sextortion crimes. Once again, author John DiGirolamo has shown us exactly how it happens. Using real-life scenarios from teens in Meridian, Idaho, as well as the experience of a former school resource officer, DiGirolamo masterfully dissects the insecurities and vulnerabilities that make teens easy prey for predators. These intertwined, real stories also delve into the perverse callousness of the predators who view humans as nothing but commodities. It's a fascinating and engaging read as well as a cautionary tale that all can learn from.

—**Jennifer Kocher**, journalist

***

As in his previous book *(It's Not About the Sex)*, John writes about complex moral and ethical dilemmas that face us in today's world. In these stories, John graphically relates the struggles of three individuals who found themselves confronting the Deceiver face to face, sometimes in terrifying circumstances. Each must choose between life and death. Dr. Wheeler's chapter is especially appealing to us in the pro-life ministry.

This is a book about courage. Each of the three characters must do the spiritual hard work to save his own life and, in some situations, the lives of others. It is also about hope. These individuals appear very ordinary on the outside and yet each is a hero in his/her battle seeking truth. Their successes offer courage and hope for the rest of us!

—**Judy Ann Fender**, RN, MSN, MBA; Salida Pregnancy Resource Center executive director and nurse manager

***

What could be more redemptive than a former abortionist who realizes the destructive effects of abortion? Catherine Wheeler's story in chapter 2, "A Pebble in My Shoe," describes her journey from performing abortions because she truly thought she was supporting women to realizing, over time, the pure evil of it. In the horror she experiences at this realization, she encounters "the grace of God, unveiling the reality of abortion," and it changes her forever. She now influences others humbly and boldly, speaking life into every conversation, whether personally, professionally, legislatively, or regarding the church's role in overcoming abortion. Catherine is a real person with real-life struggles, and God uses every part of her story for His glory, proof that no matter what a person has done in the past, God can and will redeem it all when they choose Him and His ways!

—**Joni Williams Shepherd**, executive director of Hope and Grace Global

***

The author shares critical facts and dispels and discredits the classic lies and rhetoric in our society's battle against life and "women's choice" in a captivating and unique storyline.

—**Naomi Allen**, executive director of Buena Vista Pregnancy Center

***

One of the most confusing things to understand about human trafficking is the complicated social situations that our youth are experiencing through social media and peer pressure. This first chapter puts you in the middle of reality, so you feel what it is like when a person is coerced into victimization and abuse. It is really easy to picture these situations happening in real life, and it terrifies me to think how my life would have been affected if I had gone through adolescence with a smartphone screen 24-7.

As a parent, I would want every person who considers an Internet connection to have read this book. I spend a good part of my day trying to get people to understand that people are going to try to trick you and take advantage of you; you need to learn some tools to acknowledge it and know what to do to avoid it happening to you or others as much as possible. This chapter in particular should be a wake-up call. Thank you for bringing this into existence for all of us!

—**Billy Joe Cain**, cofounder
of PBJ Learning

***

The book highlights the dire consequences of teenagers' desperate need for attention and affirmation in the digital world. Their innocent intentions can quickly turn into criminal and life-altering actions, as exemplified by the handled situation involving Officer Gomez. The story serves as a stark reminder for parents, who often underestimate the true dangers their teenagers (and even younger children) face in today's pornified digital society. This dangerous and misguided parental perspective needs to be rectified. As a recovering sex addict and the founder of a proactive nonprofit organization focused on parental education and assisting those battling porn addiction, I hear daily accounts from men, and a few women, who struggle with uncontrollable sexual behaviors and parents who are shocked by their "innocent" children's actions. I strongly urge readers, especially parents, to deeply consider these stories and not underestimate the prevalence of such behaviors. This is not an isolated issue.

—**Dann Aungst**, president and founder of Road to Purity Inc. Road to Purity is a nonprofit organization with the core mission of awareness, recovery, and formation around pornography and sex addiction.

***

I did not need to read John's book to learn about the evil in this world. After working for almost a decade in the antihuman trafficking movement, I see and hear about the evils that traffickers impose on their victims. John's book is an eye-opening read about the evil that is around us. It will make you want to join forces with others to fight back for the many innocent victims affected by evil so they can recover their lives.

—**Beth Ritchie**, director of
Bringing Our Valley Hope

***

In his book, *It's Not About the dEvil,* John DiGirolamo paints a vivid picture for us of the influences of evil that masquerade in our culture as freedom and choice. The real-life experiences of ordinary people illustrate the dark powers present in our world and how the mercy and grace of Jesus, the embodiment of truth and love, are our best weapons against those powers. These stories inspire hope that no matter the nature of the evil encountered in our society, God is stronger.

—**Julie Bailey**, director of Respect Life
Apostolate, Diocese of Colorado Springs

***

One of the best books I have read on spiritual warfare published in the past decade. The third chapter is both bone-chilling and transformative.

—**Brian E. O'Connell**, Colorado District
Deputy #20, Knights of Columbus

***

Dr. Wheeler bravely and honestly tells us what it is like to live a life tossed around by the shifting opinions of society and the pain and disorientation that result. This is surprising because we would think that a highly successful OB-GYN specialist would never suffer. But Dr. Wheeler also bravely and honestly shows us how she listened to the "voice of truth." She learned that a living human being is in the uterus of a pregnant woman. She learned that God Himself puts those babies there. And she lets us know of the joy, peace, and life direction that came to her as she learned and listened and shows how each of us can have that gift of peace also—and if we follow her lead, we can avoid lots of wrong paths and the pain that result.

—**Joe S. McIlhaney**, MD,
board-certified OB-GYN and CEO/
founder of the Medical Institute

***

I found myself cheering (praising God) when evil was stopped and lives were saved. Through the shared stories, there was a message of redemption, and how individuals following God's will in their lives made a difference in the kingdom. There also was sadness that brought me to tears when confronted with how evil destroys everything in its path. People are not inherently good, but with Jesus's saving grace, along with God's Word, they can achieve the good that was intended. These personal stories remind each of us that we are in spiritual warfare and our great need for confidence in our relationship with Jesus. Amen, John! This book can help us in that journey.

—**Tad Harrison**, member of
the board of directors of the
Pregnancy Resource Connection

***

For Julianna and Jackson

PREFACE

All the stories are based on actual events. The author collaborated and reviewed the contents with each person profiled in the chapter to ensure accuracy and authenticity. Details for context and illustrative purposes were added where necessary. Some dates and locations have been altered to shield identities. Also, the names of the accused, criminals, and witnesses were changed in some instances to protect both the innocent and the guilty, and any resemblance to any living or dead person is purely coincidental.

Some of the material in this book is for mature audiences.

Contents

DAVID GOMEZ: CHAPTER 1— *THE EQUALIZER*

PART 1: *THE TIP OF THE ICEBERG,* DECEMBER 2013

Sidney stomped with *purpose* toward the cafeteria table, slammed down her tray, and spilled the bowl of chili. She didn't care about the mess. Instead, she scowled at her best friend.

"What?" Ariana responded, as if she didn't know what was going on.

"Why did you do it?"

"Do *what*?" Ariana sheepishly answered, but couldn't keep a straight face. Her brow creased, and her lips involuntarily created a slight smirk, which forced her to look away for a second. But that would not hide her guilt. Ariana anticipated this conversation, but she didn't expect it to happen so soon.

"I overheard a couple of the boys talking in the hallway. Your picture!" hissed Sidney, who tried to keep her voice to a loud whisper.

"Oh, *that.*" Ariana rolled her eyes and shrugged it off as inconsequential. But when you text a topless photo of *yourself* to your best friend's *boyfriend*, it's anything but inconsequential.

"Why did you send it?" Sidney confronted her friend.

"I don't know. He asked for it, so I sent it this morning," Ariana admitted.

"But he's my boyfriend," Sidney croaked, the hurt noticeable in her response. "Why would you do this to me?"

"He's not officially your boyfriend. You only have a *thing* going on," she casually remarked, as if surprised by Sidney's reaction. But she knew why it was wrong.

"Because he's mine," Sidney retorted and stated the obvious. She folded her arms, glared at her friend, and asked the next logical question. "Are you trying to steal Jake?"

"No, I don't want Jake. It was just a joke," Ariana answered, but Sidney failed to see the humor.

"But you're *supposed* to be my best friend. You could have said no, couldn't you? That's what I would have done," Sidney pointed out and crossed her arms in scorn.

"Whatever," Ariana scoffed back in a snotty tone and purposefully dismissed her point. "Don't be such a drama queen."

Jake became Sidney's sole focus for weeks, causing a strain on their friendship. Ariana was weary because that's all Sidney talked about. Jake said *this* and Jake did *that*; it was all so annoying! Ever since Jake became smitten with Sidney, Ariana was in a crabby mood.

"You're not supposed to send a topless picture of yourself to *my* boyfriend. Go find your own," Sidney sniped. It didn't matter whether or not her *girlfriend* status with Jake was official.

However, Ariana quickly grew tired of the lecture, so when Sidney reminded her that no boy was interested in her, any guilt was immediately replaced with frustration and anger. Her patience evaporated, and it was time to put Sidney in her place.

"I'm sure Jake's bored with looking at *your* pictures," Ariana taunted.

Ariana has always envied her best friend's naturally curly brown hair and cute face with the *right* number of freckles. Sidney wasn't limited by her looks, for she was also an excellent student and a genuinely friendly person.

Sidney got along with just about everyone. Most of the middle schoolers liked her and considered her a friend. She was also a favorite student, a teacher's pet who constantly received compliments and praise throughout elementary school. The trend continued into middle school.

On the other side, Ariana was constantly comparing her looks and popularity to her classmates and knew she came up short. She was a good student too, but who cared? What mattered was this: Sidney was now getting noticed by the boys.

And Ariana wasn't.

Ariana didn't consider whether her negative and cranky attitude was off-putting to both adults and classmates alike. All Ariana knew was that in almost every circumstance, she was second fiddle to Sidney. It sickened Ariana that *she* might be the *tagalong* friend in their relationship; you know, the friend who is lucky to hang out with a popular kid.

Ariana had one advantage over Sidney for now, so she should use it to her advantage. Ariana's wandering thoughts stopped when Sidney spoke.

"I haven't sent him any nude pictures," Sidney divulged.

"Maybe that's why he wanted *mine,*" Ariana clapped back.

"Well..." Sidney trailed off, unable to think of a snarky response, and awkwardly stood at the lunch table. She huffed in frustration, for Jake did in fact ask her for a topless photo, but she'd refused. At least for now. If anyone was going to send a picture to her boyfriend, it was going to be her, not her best friend, or anyone else, for that matter. And certainly not without her approval, not that Sidney would have given it! Her mind was reeling.

"He asked me because he didn't get *anything* from you. Besides, why would he want *your* picture?" Ariana dared with sarcasm, purposefully trying to hurt her best friend and knock her down a peg or two.

Ariana's face was rather plain, framed by dark and straight black hair that she never could do *anything* with. Her cuteness peaked in the fifth grade, and three years later, she turned into a gawky adolescent. She wasn't ugly, but *pretty* wasn't a word that was ever used to describe Ariana.

However, she had two things going for her: trendy designer clothing and her development on top. *Much* further along than her friend. Sending the photo was Ariana's way of flirting with him, and she wished Jake would forget about Sidney. One thing she learned in her short thirteen years of life, it was to accentuate the assets she had. If you've got it, flaunt it, right?

Ariana admitted to herself that she wanted *something* with Jake. This was her first actual competition for a boy's attention and affection, and Ariana lost to her best friend, who was too clueless to notice that there even *was a competition.*

When Jake picked Sidney over Ariana, her reaction was all emotion, and that emotion was *jealousy.*

"What I send to Jake is none of your business," Sidney declared with a raised voice and finally sat down. She didn't want to bring any further attention to the conversation.

Other students stared at her, trying to figure out what was happening.

"I don't know why he'd want your picture, anyway."

"What's that supposed to mean?"

"You're flat as a pancake. Where's the fun in that?" Ariana snickered.

Sidney was stunned and couldn't think of a comeback, so Ariana continued to put down her friend. "Who knows, maybe he'll dump you and want to go out with me!" she mocked and then added, "not that I would go out of my way to be with *him*."

Ariana wrinkled her nose and pursed her lips, which indicated that having Jake was no big deal, which contradicted her genuine feelings. He had a dangerous smile and was one of the hottest boys in the eighth grade.

To Sidney, it implied the worst possible situation: her friend could easily steal Jake away from her. The next thought that popped into her head was even worse: *Jake was only going out with me until he found someone better.* A tear formed in one eye.

Ariana sensed blood in the water and a chance to dominate the relationship and add another dagger cut into Sidney's heart, so with a sarcastic tone, she asked, "How solid is your relationship, anyway?"

Sidney clearly overestimated her control over the direction of their argument. She suddenly felt extremely self-conscious about her feminine growth pattern and attractiveness. *Of course,* she noticed she was underdeveloped compared to her classmates.

Sidney learned in health class that everyone grows at a different rate, and puberty wasn't the same for everyone. She couldn't make herself grow faster. *So what* if she had the body of a fifth grader? She'd develop eventually, right? But why did it have to take so long?

Sidney couldn't convince herself that no one noticed her lack of curves. It looked like every other girl was ahead of her. Boys developed at different rates too, but no one cared about that! She was smart enough to understand that bodies change at their own pace. But that didn't alleviate the nauseating feeling that she was in last place in the race to womanhood.

Sidney wasn't sure what it meant to be in a *thing*. In what way was it different from being his girl? *Girlfriend* had a decidedly better sound to it, versus being in a *thing* with a boy. Who needs fancy labels anyway?

Either way, Sidney knew they had *something*. But what exactly was it? She'd hoped her best friend would be there to help, listen, and be supportive. Maybe to provide each other advice as they navigated the eighth grade *together*.

Ever since they were five years old, Sidney and Ariana were best friends. The bond was unbreakable until now. They knew each other's secrets, personality quirks, hopes, fears, and dreams. They talked incessantly from the moment they got to school and ended each evening with texting past their bedtime.

Teenage girls never stop talking, do they?

Sidney squealed in delight when she told her friend about her first kiss ever with Jake. She naively expected Ariana to be happy for her, but she appeared indifferent. She now wondered if Ariana also liked Jake. When did their friendship change? Too many questions bounced around Sidney's young brain.

Sidney relished Jake's attention and enjoyed holding his hand while they walked down the hallway at school. Everyone noticed, and she *loved that*. She had so many new feelings, and her thoughts of Jake preoccupied her mind throughout the day. This was her first crush. Sidney knew that for a fact because she saw an article in *Teen Vogue* that described her feelings perfectly.

Sidney *was* excited about having a *boyfriend*, but unsure if Jake felt the same. He said he liked her, and that was good enough for now. Her head swirled with too many questions without any answers. Yes, they shared a first kiss, and repeated it several times by now, but where was it leading?

So many questions, and no real way to figure out what to do. What was expected? What *should* she do? What *shouldn't* she do? She certainly wasn't going to be asking Ariana for any advice *ever again!*

It was all new to her, since they had only been a few weeks together in *whatever* their relationship was. She spent hours each day trying to figure out what a *relationship* looked like in the eighth grade.

Sidney was clueless about how to handle another female targeting her first boyfriend. Why would Jake ask for Ariana's picture? Was it because she didn't give him one? *Aren't I pretty enough?* Sidney wondered. Obviously not, she concluded, and despair permeated her mood. She let out a sigh of defeat.

Ariana brought her back to reality and told Sidney with authority, "It's probably not going to last."

"That doesn't make it okay to send him your boobs," she quipped back with all the logic in the world. But it had no impact on her friend.

"It's no big deal," Ariana insisted, thought for a second, and added, "he said his last girlfriend sent him a picture, so I was just trying to help you."

"Help me?" she cried out in full disbelief.

"Yeah, so he'd stop asking for *your* picture," she explained with the reasoning of a thirteen-year-old, then mocked, "who knows, maybe he'll enjoy looking at my picture and forget about you." If Ariana expected her friend to be beaten into submission from her ruthless snub, she'd underestimated Sidney.

Sidney recoiled from her friend's insult, which pushed her over the line. Now it was her turn to react with raw emotion. "You slut!" she attacked.

"I didn't *do* anything with him," Ariana truthfully replied and added with smugness and a simple indifferent shoulder shrug. "Not yet anyway."

Ariana knew she was hurting Sidney, but her words came out without thinking, and sometimes fears and insecurities shared among friends can be used as a weapon. "It's not my fault that guys find me more attractive," Ariana countered with a fake smile, as if she had said, don't hate me because I'm beautiful.

Whether or not that was true was irrelevant.

Whether or not Ariana believed it was beside the point.

Ariana said it because she knew exactly where Sidney, like every teenage girl, lacked confidence.

"Are you saying I'm ugly?" Sidney gasped, torn up by her friend's betrayal.

"If the shoe fits...," she answered without finishing the sentence, tilted her head, and rolled her eyes. She couldn't wipe the smirk from her face.

So much for counting on your best friend to build up your self-esteem. Sidney once again went down the rathole, wondering if she was worthy of having a boyfriend. *Any boyfriend*, that is, let alone Jake, whom she considered a pretty good catch. But what kind of *catch* wants a picture of his girlfriend's BFF? It only brought her insecurities to the surface, and Ariana was an expert on what buttons to push.

"I thought you were my best friend," Sidney reminded her.

"I am. Best friends are supposed to be honest, right?"

"What kind of *best friend* stabs me in the back?" Sidney asked and wondered what possible excuse Ariana could come up with.

The question *stumped* Ariana. She realized she had gone too far but didn't feel like apologizing. So she responded to make Sidney forgive and forget. Ariana played it off as trivial, waving her hand as if she had brushed off a pesky fly and involuntarily smiled.

Sidney wasn't amused and became more frustrated with her friend's cavalier attitude. She would have forgiven her eventually, but Ariana didn't apologize. Not even half-heartedly. Ariana dismissed her concerns, which prompted Sidney's momentary rage.

"I hate you!" Sidney screamed, getting the attention of several students nearby. It already embarrassed her that her boyfriend practically cheated on her, but now other students would ask questions. Her humiliation fueled the anger, and she didn't want to continue the argument, so she stood up out of the chair too fast and bumped the table hard enough to knock over her drink. Her surprise clumsiness only angered her further.

Sidney knew eyes were watching her, and she couldn't think of anything else to do, so she grabbed a piece of corn bread and threw it at Ariana, wildly missing, and it splattered on the floor.

The teacher in the cafeteria noticed the ruckus and headed toward them. Ariana's guilt transformed into her own anger from being disrespected *in public* by her normally good-natured friend. She also quickly stood up with little control and knocked into the table, took two steps toward Sidney, and pulled her hair so hard that she fell to the ground in a cry of pain.

The teacher picked up her pace and ran over to the two girls, who were now screaming obscenities at each other. Luckily, the teenagers listened when instructed to stop, and Mrs. McFerrin immediately escorted them to the principal's office.

It didn't take long for Sidney to spill her guts. She wanted the principal to know she wasn't to blame for the fight. The last thing she needed was to stain her spotless record. All the teachers liked her, and she was afraid they'd think she was a *loser*. The possibility of getting a detention and having to explain everything to her mom stressed her out.

After successfully pointing the finger at Ariana, the principal confiscated both their phones and referred the matter to the school resource officer.

Thirty Minutes Later

Thirty-nine-year-old Officer David Gomez had been a police officer for three years, his entire career with the city of Meridian, Idaho. He started the semester as the school resource officer for 1,200 students at Lewis & Clark Middle School. Meridian, a suburb of Boise, was a city of about 90,000 people, and the police chief thought it'd be a good fit for the calm and easygoing Gomez.

So far, he was enjoying the SRO role. A scuffle in the cafeteria wasn't unusual, but this time it was for an unexpected reason. Perhaps the principal was mistaken, or the girls were exaggerating. This was middle school, after all.

Gomez occupied a small interior office and requested Ariana be excused from class so he could get to the bottom of the argument. Officer Gomez had both phones on the desk but hadn't reviewed their contents since they were password-protected. Ten minutes later, Ariana showed up and knocked on the door. He gestured for her to enter the office and occupy one of the two guest chairs.

"Do you want some candy?" he asked and pointed to the bowl of M&Ms on his desk.

"Sure," she mumbled and scooped up a few pieces.

"I've been updated by Principal Rhodes. Do you want to tell me what happened?" he asked more as an instruction than a question, and he focused his eyes on Ariana's facial expression as she sat down.

"I sent a picture to Jake, but that's it," Ariana answered as if this was a problem that didn't need to be solved.

"An inappropriate picture of yourself?" he asked and ran his fingers through his dark hair.

"Yes, I guess."

"From the waist up? Nude, is that correct?"

"Yeah," she answered, hoping that the line of questioning would soon come to an end. It wasn't.

"Just so we're 100 percent clear, in the picture, it was all skin, right?" Officer Gomez asked and cringed with discomfort on the inside. Outwardly, he appeared relaxed and made his inquiry in a professional manner, seeking the facts. He continued, "Not in a bra or bathing suit?"

"Right," Ariana admitted and squirmed in her seat, for when he put it that way out loud, she sounded reckless. It never occurred to her that her actions might result in a trip to the SRO office to be quizzed by a middle-aged male police officer. *Sheesh*, he was as old as her dad!

Gomez was expressionless on the outside. He wouldn't dare reveal his awkwardness from talking to a thirteen-year-old about her naked body. *What's going on here?* There was a moment of distressing silence, and Ariana attempted to fill the void with, "I guess I shouldn't have sent it."

"Did you only text it to Jake?"

"Yes."

"What was the reason?"

She hesitated and then answered, "He asked." Even Ariana recognized it sounded ludicrous when she verbalized the simple and true answer.

"When did you send it? Were you threatened by Jake or someone else?"

"Oh no, he didn't force me or anything like that," she quickly answered, initially pleased that the situation didn't sound as nefarious as what she guessed the officer must be thinking. "He sent me a text asking for a picture. So I took it when I was getting dressed this morning," Ariana casually recalled.

Gomez noticed she seemed *too* comfortable about sending the picture as if it was the equivalent of sharing her homework. This prompted a follow-up question, "Have you ever sent a similar picture to anyone else?"

It was a routine type of question, and he expected an emphatic denial and explanation that this was the first time, and she'd never do it again. Her lack of serious embarrassment was unusual in his mind. Ariana appeared indifferent that her topless photo was on a teenage boy's phone. She hesitated with her answer, so Gomez repeated himself.

"Does anyone else have your picture?" he inquired and sensed that he wasn't getting the full story. His hope for this girl's innocence was dashed.

"Yeah, just a couple of pictures to Marty and Keenen. Dylan too, I think," she confessed and now showed some of the embarrassment that Gomez had expected. It never crossed her mind that a police officer would find out. "But that was a while ago," she clarified and hoped a time gap would make her actions seem less concerning.

Her admission that three more boys had her picture was totally unexpected. Officer Gomez couldn't hide his surprise this time, and her response brought his shock up to another level.

"I don't send them *that* often," she countered and instantly became defensive and added, "I don't know why you're making such a big deal about it."

Gomez cleared his throat and asked, "Do you realize you created child pornography?"

"No, that can't be right! I'm the one who took the photo," she argued.

"Exactly! Creating a nude picture of anyone underage is the simple definition of child pornography or CSAM, child sexual abuse material."

"But I didn't *do* anything in the picture. I'm not *abused.* It was only a selfie," she argued.

"That doesn't matter," he stated with authority, but not in an accusatory tone. He noticed the surprised expression on her face as the seriousness sank in. "And now Jake and the other boys have child pornography on their phones too. You're only in eighth grade. What are you, thirteen or fourteen?"

"I turn fourteen in January," Ariana answered in a defeated tone and slumped in her chair when she realized her troubles weren't over.

"So, very much underage. This is broader than the legal issue."

"What do you mean?" she asked with honest confusion.

"Sending these types of pictures is against the law."

"Hold on. Am I in *that* kind of trouble?" she gasped.

"I don't think any charges are necessary, but I don't understand why you'd do this. You're a good student and haven't been in trouble before. I'm very concerned that you sent pictures to several boys."

She added unconvincingly, "I get it."

"I'm not sure that you do. Aren't you worried someone could post your picture on the Internet?"

"Jake would never do that. He promised not to show anyone," she objected.

Gomez considered Ariana's actions irresponsible and her understanding of a teenage boy's mind inadequate. Showing someone else is a nearly inevitable temptation for a boy. "You can't control where the picture will go or who will see it. We don't know what's going to happen. I still don't understand *why* you sent it."

"I don't know."

"Come on, give me some insight," Officer Gomez appealed in a friendly manner and leaned back in his chair in a casual way to provide the girl additional space. Was Ariana *that* desperate to be noticed?

"I don't know," she repeated, paused, and finally revealed. "Jake asked, and it was *kind of a rush* knowing that it'd probably shock him. I wish I was there to see the look on his face."

Officer Gomez slightly shook his head in astonishment and thought, *It was the thrill of doing something a little dangerous.* Why did she choose to do *that*? He cleared his throat and commented, "There's a digital recording of this, so I'll be opening up a case file."

"I didn't realize this was gonna be such a big problem," she complained.

"I'll need to talk to your parents, Jake, and the others about this."

"What? You can't do that," Ariana protested with panic. "I don't want to get them in trouble," she pleaded, knowing that if Officer Gomez talked to them, word would get out, and her social status would be shattered. All her effort to fit in would evaporate.

Instantly.

"I'll need to investigate. This is serious."

"No!" she moaned and quickly stressed out.

Her face contorted as if she were in physical pain. Ariana's growing young teenage brain could only focus on one thing. *What will this do to my social life?* Her biggest fear could come true. She could soon be a pariah and labeled a *narc* for getting the other boys in trouble. This was the worst day of her life!

Ariana's stomach tightened with anxiety, knowing this would be the death sentence to her social standing. She'd forever be branded as an ugly snitch *before* she even made it to high school. In her gut, she knew that her life was ruined. Ariana couldn't see the larger picture, that her nude image could be passed around to multiple students. Bullies could use her image to torment her and even upload it to a pornography website, making it permanently accessible on the Internet. She exhaled a loud sigh in despair.

Officer Gomez brought her back to the present situation. "Okay, maybe this is obvious, but don't send pictures to anyone else."

"I've already deleted them."

"That's fine, but I'll still need your phone for the investigation," the officer informed her and picked up the phone off the desk.

"What? You can't have my phone. I swear I deleted those pictures."

"I'm sorry, but I have to take it."

"My whole life is on that phone!" Ariana recoiled with even *more* panic. How could she possibly live without social media? How would she be able to post and update? How would she know what's going on with everyone else? Her *fear of missing out* heightened to new levels. "Why are you doing this to me? Do you want to wreck my life?" she asked.

"I'm trying to protect you. And unfortunately, your phone is evidence, so that's why I've confiscated it."

"But—"

"I'll be seizing the boys' phones too."

"Are you kidding me?" she asked incredulously as the dagger in her heart plunged deeper. Her world was in a downward spiral, for it was bad enough to lose her own phone, but if she was the reason the boys had their phones taken away, she shuddered at a fate worse than physical death.

Social death.

"You can't do that. My mom's a lawyer, and I'm sure she won't allow this."

"Well, she doesn't have much of a choice," he stated, put his hand out, and added, "I'll explain it to her."

"Wait, are you going to look at that picture of me?" she panted with *complete horror*. She hung her head in despair as her situation became worse than she could have possibly imagined.

He clarified, "I only need to verify what was taken and who it was sent to."

"Are you serious?" she gasped and cringed in pain as if her body was being ripped apart by a zombie.

"I'll be quick about it, and the phone will go into an evidence locker, and no one will see it."

"Okay," she resigned in total surrender.

"What's your password?" Officer Gomez asked and then calmly told her she could go back to class after she wrote her password on a piece of paper that he taped to the back of the phone. "I'll be setting up a meeting with your parents soon."

"*Great,*" she replied, dripped with sarcasm, as she expected her homelife to crater as much as her social life. Ariana stared at the floor and dejectedly walked out of the office.

Officer Gomez quietly stared at the ceiling and wondered whether the situation was an anomaly. Ariana was a typical eighth grader, so if she was sending explicit pictures, he wondered how many others were also engaged in this risky behavior.

Two Hours Later

Officer Gomez sat in his office, shook his golf ball snow globe, and watched the ball float and land on the tee. *What's happening here?* Ariana was truly still a child, and he couldn't comprehend her thought process. She sent a picture of herself on purpose.

She readily admitted her actions but wasn't as regretful as he expected. He still couldn't believe that she created explicit pictures. Ariana sent images of herself to *four* boys. It was unfathomable to Officer Gomez.

But it was worse than he imagined.

Jake Michael Jensen reluctantly knocked on the door to his office, and the SRO waved for the student to enter. After probing for details, Jake admitted that he'd asked Ariana for a picture and still had it on his phone. He then casually admitted that Ariana's topless selfie wasn't the first nude picture he'd received. He possessed snapshots of three other eighth graders and one seventh grader. The situation became worse when Jake further explained.

"I didn't ask for the seventh grader's picture. I got that from Manny," he clarified, trying to divert some of the blame.

"What do you mean that you *just got it*?"

"We traded a few," he answered and thought it was a very reasonable explanation and didn't expect the officer to see a problem. But Officer Gomez saw a problem.

A big problem.

"You sent and received nude pictures without consent."

"But the girls sent them voluntarily," Jake countered in a justified tone, his voice slightly rising and cracking. The boy was too young to speak consistently in a deeper and more mature voice.

"I bet they didn't give you permission to trade pictures with a bunch of other boys."

"Well, they didn't say we *couldn't*," Jake pointed out. "Besides, she's not even ranked that high."

"What do you mean *ranked*?"

"It's how we figure out which girls are the hottest," he replied nonchalantly.

"That doesn't matter. Did you send a picture of yourself?" Officer Gomez asked.

"No, of course not," he quickly answered and then attempted to look less guilty than the other boys, so he blurted out, "but I know Manny sent a picture of himself to Jodi."

Officer Gomez once again slightly shook his head in further disbelief and alarm. "I'll need your phone," he informed Jake and received a similar reluctant response as he did with Ariana. Taking a smartphone away from a teenager was worse than pulling teeth.

He individually brought in the other three boys, and they all confirmed receiving the picture of Ariana. They later admitted to also having pictures of several other classmates.

Manny admitted he sent a picture of himself to Jodi. The incident at lunch exploded and eventually led to twenty phones confiscated, all middle schoolers involved in creating and sharing nude photos.

Officer David Gomez received an unrequested crash course in teen sexting and let out a low groan. Tomorrow wasn't going to get any better; he wasn't looking forward to the numerous appointments with the parents.

Viewing the pictures made him nauseous. Most of the images appeared to be simple selfies. But others were more insidiously explicit. They were posed in a specific way, at certain angles to display genitalia graphically and erotically. Simply put, they were *pornographic.*

The Next Evening, 5:05 p.m.

"I don't understand. You made it sound like Ariana sent a picture of herself to some boy," Ashley scoffed, flipped her dirty-blond hair, and scrunched her thick eyebrows when she noticed a ukulele in the corner of the office.

"That's right," Officer Gomez answered as he made eye contact with Ariana's parents.

"There must be some misunderstanding here. I'm sure it's a fake picture downloaded off the Internet," she offered.

"No, what I told you on the phone was correct. She took a picture of herself from the waist up, with no clothes on, and sent it to Jake. It looks like it was taken in a bathroom. She did this on her own, and unfortunately, it's not the only picture that she's sent."

"It must be a vicious rumor! I hope you're investigating it," Ashley responded, clearly perturbed with the officer.

"My investigation confirms it's not a rumor."

"I don't believe you," Matt chimed in. "My daughter would never do something like that. We're a good family, and Ariana knows right from wrong."

"I'm not saying she's a bad kid. She made a mistake."

"She's a straight A student and doesn't get into trouble," Matt added. He had a difficult time believing the accuracy of the officer's investigation and was eager to defend his child.

"Kids make up stuff all the time," Ashley insisted.

"As her parents, I asked you here to explain the situation. I'm sure you're in shock, but you need to know the facts so you can make sure it doesn't happen in the future," Officer Gomez stated with a compassionate directive.

"Trust me, she's in trouble, but we'll deal with this at home," Matt reassured.

"We need her phone back," Ashley asserted in her most lawyerly and stern voice. She was used to having things go her way. She stretched her arm out for the officer to give up the device, but he didn't react. She shifted in her seat as if she expected the conversation to end right there.

It didn't.

"I can't do that. The phone will be placed in an evidence locker. No one will have access to it," Officer Gomez explained.

"Wait, you're not saying that she committed a crime, are you?" Ashley quickly challenged.

"Yes, given your daughter's age, this obviously meets the definition of child pornography with someone as young as Ariana. She knowingly distributed multiple pictures with other students," he clarified and noticed Ashley's face tighten.

Officer Gomez anticipated a vigorous rebuttal, so he quickly spoke before she could, "We have no plans to charge anyone. We're not looking to ruin anyone's life."

"Good, that's a relief!" Matt reacted, and Ashley nodded her head once she heard his acceptable answer.

"But Ariana needs to stop this behavior. That's why you're here, to be aware so you can parent her about this problem and guide her," he courteously suggested.

"But what about her phone?"

"You won't be getting it back anytime soon."

"That's unacceptable," Ashley pushed back, but the look on Officer Gomez's face told her that their conversation wasn't a negotiation.

"This is a disaster," Matt added, and it wasn't clear to Officer Gomez whether that was because they couldn't accept that Ariana sent nude pictures of herself or the hassle and cost of getting her a new phone.

In a last-ditch effort, Matt demanded, "Well, I don't believe you. I need proof. Let me see it."

"You might want to think about that for thirty seconds. Do you really want to see a naked picture of your teenage daughter?" Officer Gomez asked in the most calm and professional manner.

Ariana's father realized that a normal person wouldn't want to see a picture of his topless thirteen-year-old, or any other child for that matter. Matt gritted his teeth from frustration, anger, and embarrassment. He stiffened his jaw, unsure of where to direct his anger, but then he turned and eyed his wife.

Ashley's lawyer façade broke down when she couldn't remove the thought of her daughter sending a naked picture to several students.

"This is awful. It's a catastrophe for our family. How can we show our face in this school again?" Ashley asked in a pained voice and wiped a small tear from her eye. She was uncomfortable showing emotion in a situation that she initially approached like a hostile confrontation with another attorney.

"I was shocked too, if that's any consolation," Officer Gomez offered. But no words could soften the harsh reality of Ariana's actions.

"Ariana said there were other kids doing this too?" Ashley asked and hoped to deflect the attention from her daughter onto other students. Her attorney brain was still working, somehow looking to make an argument that if other kids were exhibiting destructive behavior, then maybe Ariana's actions weren't abnormal.

"Yes, I've had kids and parents in and out of my office the last day and a half, so unfortunately, you're not alone in this situation. I found twenty students involved in varying degrees of sending or receiving pictures. Of course, that doesn't make the behavior any less harmful. Most of them are good kids, like Ariana, who made the wrong choice. But I'm afraid these aren't isolated incidents."

"What do you mean?" asked Matt.

"It might be the tip of the iceberg," Officer Gomez stated flatly.

Two Months Later, January 2014

It'd been a wake-up call for Officer Gomez. None of the kids involved with the picture exchange were charged with a crime, but there were many tough conversations with kids, parents, teachers, and the school administration. Afterward, it looked as if it eliminated the behavior. But it didn't last. Two months later, he discovered another nude selfie sent by a different student.

The digital citizenship training for middle schoolers were cookie cutter presentations and obviously didn't address all the issues. Officer Gomez observed the students tuning in and then phasing out when he would say things like "Don't give out your address" or "Don't share your password."

The absence of training and infrastructure made it impossible to educate kids about the hazards of sexting and online predators. He would create his own materials for educating the kids and staff. He thought of how he and his wife, Tamera, sought to protect their three teenage boys when they were in high school. But stranger danger was now digitized. His mind drifted to his own childhood and how sexting wasn't an issue when he grew up. But there were plenty of challenges being raised by a single mom in San Diego, with the occasional visit to Mexico to spend time with his father.

During his childhood, they frequently moved from city to city when his mom changed jobs or followed various boyfriends around southern California. He attended too many schools to count and now relished the roots he created, settling nicely in the Boise area in his early thirties when he was still an engineer.

He chuckled inside and remembered when he told his mom and wife that he wanted to quit his high-paying engineering job to become a police officer. He was thirty-six years old in the prime of his high-tech career when he entered a new profession that both his mom and wife didn't respect.

Tamera's first husband was a cop who was involved in shady circumstances. The ex-husband's friends and associates were just as crooked, which left Tamera with the impression that most cops were dirty. And then David, her husband of ten years, told her he wanted a midlife career change and became a police officer!

His mother wasn't excited about the career switch either. But he reminded her that ever since he could remember, she constantly helped people. She was always giving of herself, even though they were a poor household, living paycheck to paycheck.

This was *his call* to help people. Tamera's doubts lingered into his rookie year, and only when she observed the colleagues that Officer Gomez brought around did she see police officers in a different light. She soon developed respect for the profession and quickly became an ardent supporter of her husband and the police.

Gomez took a significant pay cut from his civilian job to enter law enforcement, which was unique for any police department. The chief considered him a risky hire because of that, but he made the cut and eventually proved himself. Once on the job, Officer Gomez impressed the police chief with his ability to talk people down and deescalate situations. But make no mistake, he possessed a warrior's heart under the calm demeanor projected to the outside world.

Although he had a technical background, previously working for Micron, a semiconductor company in Boise, those skills differed vastly from what he needed as a school resource officer. Technology significantly and quickly impacted society, especially teenagers, and the SRO needed new abilities in the rapidly developing online world of social media.

He understood the importance of mastering both the technology and programs that children used as well as the role of social media in their lives. He wasn't going to fully assess the danger until he also understood *why and how* the teens used social media.

It was his responsibility to alert middle schoolers about potential online exploiters. Who they think is an online friend may be a wolf in disguise. And trading nude pictures, well, there were so many ways that could go wrong. These kids were at least one step ahead of their parents from a technological perspective. No adult seemed to have the needed expertise. It compelled him to educate as many people as possible. But first, he needed to find out what exactly that danger was and how the predator operated. It was time to do a little research.

Part 2: *Delete Me,* One Month Later, February 2014

"It's too easy with a smartphone. Some kids are obsessed with taking selfies," Dave exclaimed.

"If they stopped to think for a moment, it'd never get sent. Imagine if they had to ask a friend or a parent, 'come here and snap a naked picture of me so I can send it to another student'"—Tamera pointed out and leaned back in her chair and added—"if they said that out loud, the image would never get taken."

"I agree. It's not simply the girls sending pictures of themselves. The boys are a big part of the problem too. They create the peer pressure," Dave stated to his wife after dinner in their home.

"They spend more time in the digital world than in person. It must disconnect them from reality. It wasn't an issue when our boys were growing up. I still find it unbelievable," Tamera commented.

"Me too. The parents were also surprised. These teens are living with the negative aspects of technology like no other generation. Research about pornography usage shows that the average first-time viewer is getting younger, and now it's about ten years old."

"That's just a child," Tamera protested, slightly shaking her head with her blue eyes reflecting a touch of sadness.

"They haven't even started puberty," Dave responded in a measured tone. "Watching pornography makes creating graphic content seem normal. That sets up the pressure to ask other students for explicit pictures or videos."

"Afterward, the bullying takes on a life of its own," she said.

"Yeah. Students at school often experience teasing, name-calling, and nasty comments from strangers."

"Bullying has shifted from school hallways to social media," she stated.

"People are much meaner behind a keyboard," Dave acknowledged. "Kids can be cruel. Most times, the sender is told the picture won't be shared, but that's not what happens."

"And it can get around the school in a matter of hours," she exclaimed.

"That's the difference with this generation. If we made a dumb mistake or did something embarrassing at that age, you had to physically witness it," Dave attested. "It didn't live forever in cyberspace and viewed by strangers."

"Today, every stupid thing a teen does is captured on a phone, most of the time by themselves!" Tamera said in an agitated and frustrated voice.

"Adults too, they're not much better."

"*Everyone* wants attention and affirmation."

"The digital image lasts forever, and it's way too easy to send to anyone," Dave pointed out.

"The sheer volume of people that could see the picture has to be high," Tamera observed.

"Right. The picture doesn't have to be sent to someone else. You can pass your phone around and show people that way," he said. "I've seen it happen at the school."

"They think it's a big joke," she grumbled with more irritation and shifted her position in the chair, trying to relieve the tension in her back.

"And don't forget, parents, teachers, and administrative staff may find out too."

"Sure, once it's out there, it's no longer controllable," Tamera concluded. "It's a quick way to ruin your reputation."

"That's true, especially initially. I've talked to several students, months after an incident, and they get past it. However, it's difficult to see beyond the distress when it's happening in the moment," Dave explained. "You have to be mentally tough."

"That's easier said than done, especially in middle school," Tamera reminded him, remembering what it was like to be a teenager. "Most girls have body image issues, and everything is *so dramatic* at that age!"

"*This* drama is real. The kids and their parents don't understand the danger," Dave offered.

"Because they have no idea how someone will use it?" she asked.

"Yes, you've hit it on the head. It's so easy to make a fake profile, and it only takes a second to click the button to accept a new friend. No one takes the time to determine who the *new friend* really is. It could easily be a predator in disguise, trying to fit into the school scene through social media."

"They try to befriend somebody online. Most applications and games have chat rooms, don't they?" Tamera inquired.

"Exactly. That's how these predators are going after the kids. They become part of their social network, and then it's only natural to have a chat or private message with your *friend*. But they've never met that person and usually don't check the details of their profile."

"Or their motivation." She cringed and adjusted a strand of her blonde hair behind her right ear.

"Yes, there are a lot of bad people on the Internet. Just yesterday, a parent came to my office because she saw the chat room messages in a game that her seventh-grade daughter was playing. She didn't recognize the other person and became concerned after reading what the *friend* wrote to her daughter. I'm glad she brought it to my attention."

"The kids and parents are getting to know and trust you. So who was she chatting with?" Tamera wanted to know.

"I'm still investigating it, but it looks suspicious. Someone outside the country seems to have generated it.

The parent gave me her daughter's password and username, and I took over the chats with the supposed *friend*, a fourteen-year-old boy from another middle school. He was asking for a picture."

"I hope she didn't send any."

"Nope. The girl found it strange the boy wanted a picture of her feet. He offered $10, and she thought that was odd, so she told her mom. The mom started asking more questions and eventually looped me in. The daughter was messaging with this other profile on and off for the last few weeks."

"Why did he want a picture of her feet?"

"That's a predator tactic. They'll offer a small amount of money for a seemingly innocent picture. The money is transferred digitally, or they provide them with a gift card so the kid can buy stuff online. It starts out innocent and perfectly legal, but they eventually ask for more revealing pictures and pay more money. The higher the price, the more explicit the content," Dave explained.

"Oh, I get it, the kid will become comfortable receiving money for sending pictures, and then it eventually gets more and more sexual, but by then it's too late," Tamera noted.

"Yes, the child thinks they're getting something, like an Amazon gift card. They don't realize they're being used."

"These guys need to be stopped," she responded.

"Right. It's my mission to warn the kids and the parents. When I present more training at school, I'm going to bring up this example. But I need to get their attention and hammer home that they're clueless about their digital *friends*."

"How will you do that?"

"I'm going to set up my own profile," Dave announced.

Three Months Later, May 2014

"There's a rumor going around that you're posing as an eighth grader. Is that true?" Sidney asked.

Officer Gomez looked around the classroom, and the students stopped murmuring, for the question caught their attention. Class had begun, and they were now curious. He stood at the front of the class by the teacher's desk and couldn't help but smile at the thirty students.

"Yes, it's true," he answered.

"But why?" Ariana asked without raising her hand.

"I wanted to see how easy it'd be to get into your social network. If I can do that, then how easy is it for someone who doesn't want to be your actual friend? I guarantee at least one of you has a predator in your friend's network," Officer Gomez declared.

He had them listening closely, momentarily. He expected concern and additional questions from the students. They *were* concerned, but the students saw a different danger.

"Have you been secretly chatting with us and being nosy in our business?" Ariana asked, horrified that Officer Gomez might again know what she's been up to.

"No. I've shared some posts and memes on my news feed, but that's all. I didn't have any direct contact."

"Wait, so you're seeing all the stuff going on?" Keenen asked when he realized that his middle school gossip wasn't limited to the other students.

"Yes, whatever comes up on my phone," he answered.

"So you're spying on us?" Ariana accused.

"My point is not to spy on you, but yes, I've seen all the drama," Officer Gomez admitted.

"But that's spying on us!" Ariana complained.

"I suppose that's one way to look at it, but if you've accepted someone into your social network, then it's not really spying, is it?" Gomez countered.

"Well, that's not fair," Ariana huffed and folded her arms, still upset and blaming Officer Gomez for taking her phone away and causing her social status to plummet.

"Would you be surprised to learn it only took a couple of months to get about 450 students in my network?" Officer Gomez asked and looked around the classroom, but none of the students spoke. "Aren't you concerned about who's on your phone? I bet you haven't met all of them in person. Of course, even if you had, that doesn't guarantee they're a true friend."

But the students were instead alarmed that an adult snuck into their middle-school inner circle. "That's a lot of students," Sidney agreed after a few seconds of awkward silence.

"I didn't have to try that hard. I initially sent requests to twenty students with a large number of friends."

"You mean the popular kids?" Ariana snapped in a snarky manner.

"Oh, are there some of those in this room?" Gomez grinned, knowing that Ariana was proud when she crossed the one-thousand-friend threshold in seventh grade. But she wasn't the only one to join that club, and the kids based some of their popularity on who had the most friends and followers.

"I still don't like the idea of you spying on us," Ariana argued.

"There's a simple solution," Officer Gomez replied and held out his phone. He paused a second for the effect, then challenged the students, "Delete me."

"I will," Ariana quickly agreed.

"Me too," Keenen jumped in, also motivated to remove the officer from his social network.

But Officer Gomez wasn't finished; he upped the ante. "I have a $20 gift card to Dutch Brothers Coffee for the first student who figures out which profile is mine." The offer wasn't missed by anyone.

"For real?" Sidney asked.

"Yes, part of today's training is to give you fifteen minutes to see if I'm in your network. Looking around the class, I'd say I'm *friends* with about 85 percent of you."

"Challenge accepted. This won't be a problem at all!" Keenen bellowed. Officer Gomez sat in the teacher's chair and watched the students busily work on their phones.

"Let's see how easy it is with some of you having over five thousand profiles in your network."

He didn't dare guess how many students would find his account. He'd set up a profile with a picture of an athletic fifteen-year-old boy rock climbing. It was at an angle which obscured the person's face. He sent it to the popular kids in seventh and eighth grade.

He was stunned that within an hour, almost all of them had accepted his friend request, without question, without wondering who he was or trying to obtain additional information. They simply thought about it for two seconds and clicked the button. That's all it took.

Officer Gomez surmised the teens had a simple goal: to get as many friends and followers as possible. They built their always-temporary self-esteem on how many pictures were *liked,* or how many stories were *followed,* and how quickly the numbers grew. It was addictive for some.

He warned the students that having thousands of friends wasn't a worthy goal but, instead, was a problem. He'd talked to the students about predators online, but their behavior didn't change. They believed they were *safe* behind their screen and didn't think *they* would be the ones targeted by a predator. It was a typical teenage belief in their invincibility.

He didn't anticipate that his fake profile would connect so quickly with hundreds of students. Once he became friends with the popular kids, everybody else jumped on board. The social media account constantly recommended new friends to request, which only required a simple *click* to send. Once he was friends with the popular kids, the suggestions kept coming, and the number of students in his network easily increased.

"I found you!" Keenen announced, laughed heartily, which was quickly followed by several groaning students who were motivated by the $20 gift card. "That wasn't so hard," he boasted with an arrogant smile.

Officer Gomez walked over to the student, looked at the profile he was showing on his phone, and laughed. "Sorry, that's not me," he answered truthfully.

The students immediately returned to their phones and scrambled to find his profile. Several more students called him over, confident they'd solved the mystery, but none found the teenage rock climber. Eventually, the fifteen minutes ran out.

"Okay, times up," the officer told the students, who were surprised that no one could find his profile.

Officer Gomez told the students about the girl who received a request for a picture of her feet from a supposed teenage boy she'd only met online. "I set up a profile to show that it's easy to blend in as another student. If it was easy for me, it's also easy for someone with evil purposes."

Officer Gomez made eye contact with several students. He'd captured their interest, so he continued, "A predator could seek to exploit you or get information to steal your identity. There are many bad people on the Internet and a lot of potentially negative outcomes. If you don't know who they are, don't recognize the name and the profile picture, don't accept the friendship."

Several students nodded their heads in understanding and agreement, but Officer Gomez wondered if they took him seriously. However, there was a question which ate at the officer. How many predators were out there, and could he stop them?

Part 3: *Pretzel Logic*, July 2014

Authors Note: This section incorporates text/private messaging as part of the story and dialogue between the characters. The text and private messaging in this section do not include slang, acronyms, or other verbiage commonly used by teens and predators, which was a deliberate choice. The author chose to use easily understood language and grammar to make it clear to readers what was being communicated, as texting slang and other communication styles change rapidly and may not be familiar to readers over the age of twenty.

Dat1Kooldude:	I'm feeling alone. I'm so happy you're there.
Socon99:	Really?
Dat1Kooldude:	Always.
Socon99:	I'm feeling empty too.
Dat1Kooldude:	You're a true artist. I see it in your drawing.
Socon99:	That's how I feel today. Dark.

She loved creating art, mostly in pencil and usually of people. She especially liked to draw faces. He was the only one who asked about her drawings and how they reflected her mood that day. It was her way of connecting with him.

Dat1Kooldude:	You're so talented.
Socon99:	I am?

Dat1Kooldude:	Yes! I tell you every time. You must believe me.
Socon99:	Okay.
Dat1Kooldude:	We're good for each other.
Socon99:	You're the only person who thinks I'm an artist.
Dat1Kooldude:	I'm the only one that loves you.
Socon99:	I know.

At least *somebody* loves me.

Dat1Kooldude:	I need you.
Socon99:	I need you too.
Dat1Kooldude:	I wish you were here.
Socon99:	I'm sad that we live so far away.
Dat1Kooldude:	It's okay to be sad. Depressed girls are the prettiest.
Dat1Kooldude:	It's a powerful emotion and girls with emotion are hot.
Socon99:	Me?

I'm hot, she thought to herself. They'd chatted for over a few weeks, and he recently started asking for pictures of her. That quickly morphed into more revealing and sexy poses. It soon became explicit, and she was happy to give in. He sometimes sent Amazon packages with new clothes and underwear that she would pose in. He always asked about her drawings, which proved that he wanted *her*, and not just the nude images.

Dat1Kooldude:	You're my beautiful sad girl.
Socon99:	I am your girl.

Dat1Kooldude:	You're the only one in my life who can make me happy.
Socon99:	Me, too.

She beamed inside and could never get enough of his compliments. And he always listened to her problems. He was real and genuine!

Dat1Kooldude:	I need you here with me.

She knew how to cheer him up since they couldn't be together. It was awkward and embarrassing at first, but it became easier. She found it *incredible* that she had the *power* to make him happy.

Socon99:	You want a new picture, don't you?
Dat1Kooldude:	Yes! It's our thing.
Socon99:	You promise not to show anyone?
Dat1Kooldude:	I haven't shown anyone the other ones.
Socon99:	For real?
Dat1Kooldude:	Yes! It's our secret. You trust me, don't you?
Socon99:	With my life.
Dat1Kooldude:	You're a woman now, right?
Socon99:	I guess.
Dat1Kooldude:	I want the 20th picture of my beautiful woman. YOU!
Dat1Kooldude:	This time, I want your smiling face in the picture.

She hesitated for a moment and looked in the mirror. Maybe *I am* beautiful?

Dat1Kooldude: I'm waiting.

She interpreted his response as impatient and curt, so her stomach tightened. *He's my best friend.* I can't let him down.

Dat1Kooldude: ???

That was his signature move, a little of the carrot and a little of the stick.

Socon99: One sec.

She looked in the mirror, flipped her hair around, and took the picture. This one was different, not from the neck down or a certain body part. This was the first time she was completely naked, from head to toe. She zoomed in on the photo. *I am beautiful, and my smile looked real!* Her eyes shined, and her expression didn't appear forced or faked because in that brief moment, she had confidence. Then she pushed the send button.

Dat1Kooldude: You make me so happy!

And that made *her* happy.

***

He was living out his username persona and beamed with pride. *I am that one cool dude*, Marty smiled to himself. He finally had the all-important full body picture and quickly delivered the good news to the website's owner via a text message. He received instructions to upload the new picture, and they will evaluate it for clarity and pose.

Socon99's stood for *Solitary Confinement (since) 1999*, making her fifteen years old. She appeared young and innocent enough to pass as thirteen, despite being too old for the club. She could be lying about her age too. Who knew? He certainly didn't care.

His *friend* Socon99 had a naturally pouty face, which was a popular pose in the club, but her true uninhibited and easygoing smile in this picture should easily get him accepted. He was singularly focused on one goal, and now he'd achieved it, an image explicit enough to *get him in*!

Maybe it would be enough. But maybe he'd have to find other girls? He could do that. He was always going to need fresh pictures. *Either way, I have to find more girls,* Marty concluded. But would the twentieth picture be enough?

Ding! He received a text with the four words he was working so hard for: *LEVEL ONE ACCESS APPROVED*. He clicked the blue hypertext link and gained admittance to the child pornography group that he had been working so hard for. He held his breath. A wide and wicked grin formed on his face upon seeing the images. He practically jumped out of his chair and had to bite his tongue to stop his squeal of delight.

He looked around the office, and no one was staring at him. Everyone was busy working. He was working hard too, but not for the company. His efforts focused on corrupting innocent children. His wages fed depravity, spoiling the essence of humanity.

After an hour of viewing, he realized it wouldn't be enough. He ignored the chatter from the office and cherished his good fortune that nobody came to his cubicle to talk to him. Sure, he had plenty of new e-mails, but that could wait. He needed to access the higher levels within the group, the ones with video content. The only way he'd acquire access was to create some of his own. The thought was alluring, for something sinister and malevolent stirred deep inside. That feeling was getting stronger.

Merely watching something on his screen left him unsatisfied. No, it was worse than that; it left him *wanting more*. Something that a screen could never satisfy. He craved to touch young flesh. He *had* to live out what he saw on the screen. His next move was mandatory.

He needed to meet the girl in person.

The Next Day (Saturday)

Dat1Kooldude:	Hi beautiful! Do you have any drawings for me today?
Socon99:	No, sorry!
Dat1Kooldude:	What's wrong, my love?

What's her problem? Is she *so* stupid that she forgot? Forgot about *him*?

Socon99:	I got into a fight at school.
Dat1Kooldude:	Are you okay?
Socon99:	Nobody likes me.
Dat1Kooldude:	Everyone hated me when I was in school.
Socon99:	Really?
Dat1Kooldude:	Yes. Now you have me to love you. And I have you to love me!
Socon99:	Yeah! ☺
Dat1Kooldude:	You are the only joy I have in my miserable life.
Socon99:	I feel the same.
Dat1Kooldude:	Can you keep a secret?
Socon99:	You know I can.
Dat1Kooldude:	I want to come for a visit.
Socon99:	For real?

Dat1Kooldude:	Yes. I am going on a business trip.
Socon99:	You're coming to Ohio?
Dat1Kooldude:	Yes, I need you so badly!
Socon99:	I'm scared.
Dat1Kooldude:	Why? It will be awesome!
Socon99:	What if you're disappointed when you meet me?
Dat1Kooldude:	I won't. You're my beautiful teen girl.
Dat1Kooldude:	We can cuddle and hug. I can't wait to kiss you.
Dat1Kooldude:	And more.
Socon99:	Am I the only one?
Dat1Kooldude:	Yes. This could be us going to the next level.
Socon99:	I'm still scared.
Dat1Kooldude:	I know you won't disappoint me.
Socon99:	I'll try not to.
Dat1Kooldude:	Try hard.
Socon99:	Okay.
Dat1Kooldude:	It's you and me against the world.
Socon99:	I like that.
Dat1Kooldude:	I will take care of you. Always.
Socon99:	You're the only one who does.
Dat1Kooldude:	That's because I'm your man.
Dat1Kooldude:	You're perfect. And perfect for me.
Dat1Kooldude:	Do you have a picture for me?
Socon99:	Of course.
Dat1Kooldude:	Chatting with you is the best part of my day.
Socon99:	Me, too.

Dat1Kooldude:	We will soon be together, and I can touch you.
Dat1Kooldude:	I want to be your first.
Socon99:	I'd like that.
Socon99:	I love you. Here's my picture.
Dat1Kooldude:	I can't wait to show you how much I love you.

***

Marty Bradford McKibben reviewed the pornography video for the eleventh time. He put his phone in his pocket and went into the kitchen to help bring food to the table for Sunday night dinner. Rachel made some sort of chicken pot-pie. Bland and boring, just like her personality.

But her thirteen-year-old daughter. Well, she was *anything* but dull to Marty.

"I have to go on a business trip," Marty stated casually.

"So close to our wedding?" Rachel asked with sudden concern.

"It's an emergency, and it's just overnight."

"You work too hard. I hope they appreciate you," she commented.

"They don't, but it pays the bills," Marty responded, involuntarily curling his lip in disgust. They sat for dinner in the two-bedroom condominium.

"Where are you going?"

"Ohio."

"I thought you were assigned to the western region?" Rachel asked, trying not to seem more suspicious than she was.

"One of the other guys is sick, so they asked me to go in his place. Duty calls."

"Is it only going to take one day?" she pressed.

"Um, it should."

"Well, it better. We're getting married this Saturday," Rachel reminded him.

"Oh, I haven't forgotten," he replied and added, "I leave Monday and will be back by Tuesday." He stepped in closer to give his fiancé a kiss. Her cool attitude melted.

"Eww, gross!" Sidney squealed.

"Isn't that what you do with your boyfriend?" Marty teased her.

"Ooh, Jake, you're *so cute*!" both Rachel and Marty teased her in unison. Rachel's thirteen-year-old daughter didn't find it amusing.

"You guys are so weird! You know he's not my boyfriend anymore," Sidney proclaimed. Her relationship with Jake vanished after everyone found out that Ariana had sent him pictures and he had his phone confiscated by Officer Gomez. The last semester of eighth grade was a disaster.

"He was an idiot anyway," he chimed in, lying.

Marty privately admired Jake and wished he were back in the eighth grade again. Jake was *so close* to getting a nude photo of Sidney. Marty was impressed by how he convinced her friend Ariana and a few others to send pictures. He simply needed to ask.

According to Sidney, Ariana willingly sent Jake her picture. Some others were pressured into it, but they eventually relented. Marty wished *he* could be thirteen again, but this time have the technology to receive pictures. *It was almost too easy*, he thought.

His perception was correct. In fact, it inspired him to create an online profile. He used his actual picture but used a fake name when he created *Dat1Kooldude*. He knew he was smart, but he didn't think he'd be able to get pictures of the first girl he encountered online. All he did was tell her how beautiful she was and that sending a picture was *no big deal*.

Once *Socon99* sent the first picture, the next ones kept coming. It was the last thought stuck in his brain before he slept, and it was the first thing he thought about when he woke up in the morning.

Thirty-year-old Marty had watched porn for the past fifteen years, and it accelerated after high school. No matter how much he watched, there was always someone new and exciting to see. He especially liked the genre *wild young teens*. The outfits that some of them dressed in! Wow! It sure made them look twelve instead of eighteen. The actors were listed as eighteen on the website, but it didn't matter to Marty.

The *younger* the better.

The more *wholesome-looking*, the better.

The more *corrupted* they were by the male *actor*, the better.

The more punishment they received for being a *bad girl*, the better.

The more guys in the video that wiped out all traces of her *innocence*, the better.

It went on and on and on. And they uploaded new videos every day. It captured his mind, but he ignored how it corrupted *his soul*.

Even if he could see what it was doing to him, it wouldn't have mattered. Like an additional hit of drugs, he needed more and more to satisfy his urges. It was his daily fix. And not only more time watching, but he needed more deviant and brazen videos.

But videos weren't enough anymore. He needed to experience what he saw on the screen. What he required was nowhere near lovemaking. It was a downward spiral that he didn't want to stop. Marty's challenge was trying to get his work done and avoid getting fired because he spent so much time feeding his habit. This obsession wasn't going to dissipate anytime soon, and it took over his homelife.

He would make excuses to Rachel every night, citing an important customer that needed his attention. He even told her that customers asked for him by name when they needed support, and he was expecting a promotion. She was impressed with his lies. He'd merely shrug his shoulders as a humble superstar employee would and head upstairs to the small desk in the bedroom to check in with *the client.*

Rachel had no idea that there wasn't any client; he wasn't a superstar at work and was getting close to being fired for underperforming. Marty told the lies so often, he was starting to believe them.

This week was a milestone for Marty. He'd received enough pictures from Socon99 to allow access to the child pornography group. His Ohio trip would allow him to do what he had seen other guys do on screen.

He planned to do them all to Socon99. He'd also get the added bonus of videoing everything. That would get him to level two access. He wondered what was required to get to Level Three. But he was getting ahead of himself, as he often did.

Rachel spoke, and he refocused on their conversation, snapping Marty back to the present moment. He had to switch gears and play the part of the loving fiancé and the caring, soon-to-be stepfather.

"He wasn't good enough for you, honey," Rachel chimed in and smiled at her daughter.

Marty couldn't have agreed more. Sidney needed a man, not a boy.

"Yeah, I don't know why I ever liked him," Sidney replied.

"Boys are stupid. Throw rocks at them!" Rachel replied, referring to the book by Todd Harris Goldman.

"Are we going in the hot tub or not?" Sidney asked with her arms folded and frowned because the talk of Jake continued. She wanted to change the subject and forget about the eighth grade.

"Yes, let's go when we're done eating," Marty suggested and then added, "I'll help clean the kitchen when we come back," he promised. He was adept at doing the bare minimum around the house.

"Fine," Rachel gave in and rolled her eyes.

Ten minutes later, they left their condo for the community pool and hot tub, which held ten people. The light was casting shadows from the top of the three-story building. Shady or not, Marty wore his mirrored sunglasses, making it difficult for anyone to catch him gawking.

He stopped staring at Rachel in her bikini months ago. Marty honestly didn't care that she was older than him, although he knew it fed Rachel's ego. She was still an attractive woman at thirty-four years old, with her shoulder-length blonde hair and thin 5' 5" frame.

It was the other female in the family that he *was more interested in.*

When you marry a single parent, it's a package deal. And Sidney was the *whole* package. She was mesmerizing. He wanted to devise a scheme where he'd accidentally walk in on her, taking a shower or changing clothes. But it could actually be better than that!

His marriage would continue his regular access to Sidney. And don't forget the bonus of having close proximity to Sidney's friends. He needed to convince Sidney to invite her friends to a sleepover for Sidney's upcoming birthday. The thought of a roomful of young, sweaty freshman girls in thin fabric pajamas was almost too much to fantasize about. The possibilities were endless.

It completely fascinated him when he heard about Ariana sending pictures to Jake and the other boys. Somehow, he'd have to figure out a way to convince Sidney to repair that friendship. He *needed* to get to Ariana. It shouldn't be that difficult, he surmised. After all, he was that one cool dude! For now, he'd simply enjoy Sidney wearing her one-piece bathing suit. He was awestruck by her youthful innocence and pristine body.

Untouched.

So far.

Three Days Later, Tuesday Evening

Marty viewed the video from his lustful encounter with Socon99 for the sixteenth time. He watched it with a laser focus, and the adrenaline rush which coursed through his veins never diminished. The trip was a great success in his mind. He was confident his two-hour footage would grant level two access.

Excitement and anticipation were bursting inside him. Socon99 had complained about some things he did. Some were painful, and many were humiliating and degrading. *She knew what she was getting into,* he reasoned. It was his way of showing *love*, he told himself.

Marty was honest enough to admit it. He didn't truly love Socon99. In some ways, he detested her. She was too stupid to stop him. He only desired one thing from her, but she was too needy and desperate to recognize it. She was *so naïve,* and he hated her for it. She gobbled up his *love* and attention, and he looked down on her for it.

He came back to Idaho knowing two things for sure: first, Socon99 was totally in his control, and he'd flex his power for his maximum pleasure and gain. And second, he needed to find another Socon99, but this time closer to home.

The Next Day, Wednesday

It took Officer Gomez less than ten minutes to create a profile. He chose a young teen girl with long blonde hair riding a motorcycle. She was wearing a helmet so you couldn't identify the person. He downloaded pictures of girls playing soccer and chose ones where the faces were either turned or far in the distance. It wasn't a deep and lengthy profile, just enough to believably present a thirteen-year-old girl.

He couldn't think of a good username, so he started with Luv_Soccer3303. The "3303" was the last four digits in his assigned police cell phone. That was as creative as he could get, for he was, after all, *still* an engineer even if his paycheck came from the City of Meridian Police Department. At least he had more creativity than an accountant.

At exactly 7:15 p.m., he received his first friend request, which he accepted. At 9:48 p.m., he received his second request from Dat1Kooldude. *Interesting username*, Officer Gomez thought. He clicked on the "accept" button. He didn't realize it yet, but he was about to build a case against Marty McKibben.

Dat1Kooldude:	Hi beautiful!
Luv_Soccer3303:	Hi.
Dat1Kooldude:	It's getting kinda late, can you chat?
Luv_Soccer3303:	Yeah. It's fine. Nobody cares when I go to sleep.
Dat1Kooldude:	You like soccer, huh?
Luv_Soccer3303:	Oh yeah! I'm in a summer league now.
Dat1Kooldude:	That's cool. Where do you play?
Luv_Soccer3303:	At the Jaycee Soccer Complex.
Dat1Kooldude:	In Meridian?
Luv_Soccer3303:	Yeah, you know where it is?
Dat1Kooldude:	Yes. I live in downtown Boise.
Luv_Soccer3303:	Do you go to Boise State?
Dat1Kooldude:	I'm one of the coaches for the soccer team.

Dat1Kooldude:	My other job is with Teen Vogue Magazine.
Luv_ Soccer3303:	You are? Wow, that's so cool!
Dat1Kooldude:	You're very pretty. Maybe I could take some pictures.
Luv_ Soccer3303:	I don't know. What kind of pictures?
Dat1Kooldude:	All kinds. Would you like to be in a magazine?
Luv_ Soccer3303:	That would be awesome!
Dat1Kooldude:	Have you modeled before?
Luv_ Soccer3303:	No.
Dat1Kooldude:	I'd have to talk to my boss since you're new.
Dat1Kooldude:	I'm always looking for fresh faces.
Dat1Kooldude:	I can make you a star.
Luv_ Soccer3303:	You can?
Dat1Kooldude:	And you can get out of this lame town.
Luv_ Soccer3303:	I'd like that.
Dat1Kooldude:	We'll do a makeover.
Dat1Kooldude:	I'll show how beautiful and sexy you are.
Luv_ Soccer3303:	How do I do that?
Dat1Kooldude:	Don't worry. I'll take care of it.

That was so easy, Marty thought to himself. *She thinks I'm one cool dude!* Without a doubt, he could convince her to do anything. The first goal was to meet her in person. Soon! His plan was coming into focus. There were so many obvious advantages with meeting a girl locally instead of having to travel. Merely the cost of a cheap motel room would be his price of admission.

He'd get her sympathy after he tells her that his mom had died. He'd act sad and pretend that he needed to talk to someone about it. It worked so well when he first met his Ohio girl. She would feel needed and naturally would want to *help* make him feel better.

She was so gullible, believing that he was a soccer coach *and* a photographer for *Teen Vogue*! He would buy her outfits from a thrift store, so his new soccer girl would provide a variety of pictures, videos, and Marty's grand prize, a sexual encounter with an innocent soul.

He'd create images and videos of himself with his soccer luv, and he could watch it repeatedly. It flooded his mind with sinister thoughts, and he could hardly contain himself.

The things he could do *for* her.

The things he could do *with* her.

The things he could do *to* her.

The possibilities were endless!

He'd replicate all the scenes he watched from his new pornography club. His soccer girl was his golden ticket to reaching the next level soon. This was his perfect opportunity to experience the depraved pleasure he ruthlessly sought. He would do things to the soccer girl that his fiancé would *never* let him do.

Salacious and malicious.

His mind spun ferociously formulating his plan. He'd convince his soccer luv she was a grown-up, and grown-ups act mature. And what could be more mature than the ultimate physical act? He'd tell her that everyone else was doing it. Eventually, he'd make her succumb to his perverted longings and manipulate her to *want* to do it. He anticipated the day that she would do *anything* to make him happy, just like his Ohio girl.

A wicked smile pasted across Marty's face. He'd control the girls and have them *begging* for more! Marty was very impressed with his abilities. Driven and focused, he was unstoppable. He had to be smart *and* sneaky. He had the skills for that, and Rachel was too stupid to figure it out.

Marty *knew* how to play the game.

His desire morphed into an uncontrollable preoccupation. He needed, and it was *absolutely required*, in a physical and psychological way, to fulfill his fantasies. He imagined building a network of local soccer luvs, one for each day of the week. Marty decided for the rest of the evening that he would find another hundred local middle schoolers to send a friend request.

Two Hours Later

He viewed so many profiles. Such young skin and innocent faces. Some were developing femininity; some were not. It didn't matter. They were all beautiful to him. They were all his potential prey, and, like a predator on the hunt, he enjoyed the pursuit and the ego boost once anyone accepted his friend request.

He likened it to going to the greatest buffet in the world; so many choices, and he didn't know where to start. His perverted desires were spinning out of control. He was getting tired and couldn't wait until morning to see how many accepted his request for a digital connection. He reluctantly headed to bed.

The Next Day, Thursday Afternoon

Dat1Kooldude: Where are you?

Dat1Kooldude:	Are you there?
Luv_ Soccer3303:	I'm here. I was in school.
Dat1Kooldude:	I need you.
Luv_ Soccer3303:	What happened?
Dat1Kooldude:	I didn't want to tell you yesterday.
Luv_ Soccer3303:	Tell me what?
Dat1Kooldude:	My mom died a few days ago.
Luv_ Soccer3303:	What? That's awful. I'm so sorry.
Dat1Kooldude:	I need somebody to hold me.
Luv_ Soccer3303:	I wish you didn't hurt so bad.
Dat1Kooldude:	Talking to you makes me feel better.
Luv_ Soccer3303:	That's good.
Dat1Kooldude:	I'm so alone, but being with you eases the pain.
Luv_ Soccer3303:	I'm glad I can help!
Dat1Kooldude:	You'd probably never go for this, but can we meet?
Luv_ Soccer3303:	Maybe?
Dat1Kooldude:	Do you vape? I can bring you some.
Luv_ Soccer3303:	I've never done that.
Dat1Kooldude:	It will make you feel good. Let's get together.
Luv_ Soccer3303:	I'm only 13, so I don't have a car.

Dat1Kooldude:	That's okay. Can you ride your bike?
Luv_ Soccer3303:	I guess so.
Dat1Kooldude:	Can I be frank with you?
Luv_ Soccer3303:	Who is Frank?
Dat1Kooldude:	I mean, can I be honest with you?
Luv_ Soccer3303:	Yes.
Dat1Kooldude:	Only you can make me feel better.
Dat1Kooldude:	When we meet, can I give you a hug?
Luv_ Soccer3303:	Sure.
Dat1Kooldude:	That would make me happy. Do you want me happy?
Luv_ Soccer3303:	I suppose so.
Dat1Kooldude:	We have this emotional connection, don't we?
Luv_ Soccer3303:	Yes.
Dat1Kooldude:	I'm going to bring champagne when we meet.
Luv_ Soccer3303:	I've never had champagne.
Dat1Kooldude:	You're going to love it.
Luv_ Soccer3303:	Do you think so? Aren't I too young to drink?
Dat1Kooldude:	You don't need to play by the rules.
Dat1Kooldude:	I don't.

***

It was a gold mine for Marty. His child pornography group contained a blog with hints about how to obtain digital content from unsuspecting victims. He was already doing some things *right*. With Socon99, he previously got information about the girl, and she now completely trusted him. Even more importantly, she trusted *only* him. She was a lonely girl, so it wasn't hard to convince her to stop interacting with her family. Marty told her to dump her friends. It required more time from him to feed her fragile ego, but it was worth it.

He thought back to when they met in person at the motel in Ohio. He showed her pornography videos. *See, lots of people do that. She's asking him to do it,* he told her, referring to the female *actress. She wants it!* They spent the first half hour watching videos together. He carefully chose parts where the girl didn't get hurt or begged the man to stop. All that would come later, but he didn't want to scare her off.

These things are delicate and take time.

For Marty, taking time meant a few hours since they only had the motel room for one night. Socon99 resisted initially, but she eventually complied and bent to his will. As he had a lot of explicit content of her, he could blackmail her if she stopped sending him daily images. He didn't want her to become a *problem*, but if necessary, he'd skip the threats and go right to sending her pictures and videos to everyone in her social media connections.

He didn't care if it ruined her, and in a small way, he hoped he could wield his power over her and destroy her. His logic was *twisted*, like a pretzel. Such thoughts excited him. But for now, he was getting ahead of himself. Socon99 did everything she was told.

Marty upped the ante. He told her to find a boyfriend that was her age or younger to secretly record themselves, preferably in her own bedroom. If she managed to take a high-quality video and send it to him, he could get access to level three. A secret recording of two minors engaged in sexual activity was considered high-value content. It was happening fast, although it couldn't happen fast enough. He provided her several tips on how to hide a phone.

He sent her a second cell phone so she could get different angles. She promised to make it happen within a week. She was desperate to make him happy, and Socon99 didn't question why he wanted her to have sex with someone else. The endorphins released into his bloodstream coursed throughout his body. His blood pumped faster when he imagined his first glimpse of Socon99 and her new unsuspecting boyfriend.

I'm a genius, he thought to himself.

Later That Evening, Thursday

Dat1Kooldude:	Let's meet tomorrow.
Luv_Soccer3303:	Okay.
Dat1Kooldude:	We'll make it a spa day in a motel room.
Luv_Soccer3303:	I've never had a spa day. What's that?
Dat1Kooldude:	I'll start by giving you a massage.
Luv_Soccer3303:	That sounds nice.
Dat1Kooldude:	Can you wear something blue? And no bra?
Luv_Soccer3303:	Why?
Dat1Kooldude:	Because that's what I like.
Luv_Soccer3303:	Okay, I guess.
Dat1Kooldude:	Wear a thong too.

Luv_Soccer3303: My mom won't buy them for me because I'm only 13.

Dat1Kooldude: I'll get you one and you can wear it when we meet.

Dat1Kooldude: It will be our secret.

Luv_Soccer3303: Is it far from my house? I'm not old enough to drive.

Dat1Kooldude: I'll find a place close to you. You can ride your bike.

Luv_Soccer3303: Okay.

Dat1Kooldude: I can't wait to hug you and touch your beautiful body.

Luv_Soccer3303: You think I'm beautiful?

Dat1Kooldude: You're my dream girl.

Luv_Soccer3303: I am?

Dat1Kooldude: You're my dream come true girl.

Dat1Kooldude: I'm going to do all kinds of things to you.

Luv_Soccer3303: More than a massage?

Dat1Kooldude: Oh yeah!

Luv_Soccer3303: Like what?

Marty stared at his phone for a minute. He was simultaneously watching another child pornography video while texting with his soccer luv. He went back to the video again, completely enthralled and described in graphic detail what he was watching and typed in each horrifying perversion to Luv_Soccer3303.

He wrote exactly 716 words describing his desires, a step-by-step of what he wanted to do. It was a torrent of graphic lust and sadistic plans. His heart was racing, and his breathing was erratic, just like the devious thoughts which bounced around his brain.

Merely imagining and anticipating the experience for tomorrow was exhilarating. After he sent his messages, he was so absorbed with his plans that he forgot about how his soccer luv would react. Then his phone *dinged* with her response.

Luv_Soccer3303:	Wow, I've never done that before.
Dat1Kooldude:	It will be fun!
Luv_Soccer3303:	I'm 13. Am I too young to do all those things?
Dat1Kooldude:	No, you're the perfect age.
Dat1Kooldude:	Trust me.

Friday

It'd been four years since her divorce, and it genuinely surprised Rachel when Marty popped the question at the Cottonwood Grille in Boise. He'd planned it all out. When the waiter brought champagne, he also carried her engagement ring on a silver platter. She looked at the tray and saw a ring instead of food. He bent down on one knee to ask for her hand in marriage.

He'd secretly asked the waiter to pass a note to the nearby tables to help him out, with instructions to chant "say yes!" repeatedly. Eight boisterous people were energetically encouraging Rachel to accept his proposal. There he was, down on the floor in the classic and romantic position, while total strangers yelled in a sophisticated restaurant.

It caused quite a stir, and much to Marty's delight, several more chimed in. Marty was such a good organizer.

The pressure to say "yes" was high, and all eyes were on Rachel. She was surprised, so she hesitated. She didn't think Marty was the marrying type, someone who would make a commitment to her. Someone who would put the needs of another ahead of his own. That kind of someone, *he was not.*

Her *pause* was about to get uncomfortably long, and she looked away from Marty for a moment and locked eyes with a woman at a nearby table who was encouraging her to *just say yes*! The woman seemed confident. Maybe she admired Marty's good looks and bravado to make a spectacle out of such a personal question. Or maybe she wished *she* was on the receiving end of the outlandish public display of affection. Rachel didn't want to disappoint anyone or embarrass Marty. So she nodded her head and finally *said "yes."*

Marty stood up and pumped his fist like he'd made the winning touchdown and, just like at a sporting event, the crowd went wild! Marty was the handsome hero, exactly where he liked to be. He seemed to enjoy the attention from the spectacle of the *proposal* more than the seriousness of a lifelong commitment.

Rachel was the coveted prize, but in the pit of her stomach, she didn't feel like celebrating. In fact, when he dropped her home later that evening, she decided to wait for *him* to bring up a wedding date. Let Marty show exactly how much he wanted to be married.

Marty again surprised her with his eagerness when the next weekend he showed up with a car full of his clothes. He was moving in. Again, Rachel was taken off guard, *and again* she didn't protest. She also didn't argue when he wanted to get married soon. That was four months ago. She couldn't figure out why he was in such a hurry. But here she was, minding to the final details.

Now, with one day to go before they were to exchange sacred vows, she worked overtime to convince herself that this time the marriage would succeed. Sidney's father was mostly out of the picture, and she hoped Marty would be a good stepfather. But *hope* is not a plan. She poured herself a small cup of coffee before leaving for work.

Marty entered the kitchen, and Rachel exclaimed with excitement, "I can't believe tomorrow is the big day!"

"I'm going to leave work early today and take care of a few things before the rehearsal dinner. I'll meet you at the restaurant."

"Okay, don't be late."

"I won't. I'll be there by 7:30 p.m."

3:45 p.m.

"He's going to text my phone to tell me what room number he's in," Officer Gomez stated to the team in the conference room at the Meridian Police Department. "Officer Mitchell is at the motel already and watching for his arrival."

"I'm in position now," he responded from his cell phone.

"We must be prepared for anything, since we don't know if he'll be armed. I've already talked to the motel manager, and we have a card key to the room," Gomez informed the team.

Sergeant Kiehm added, "We'll assign him to a unit at the end of the hallway."

"We'll have a team in all directions. The room only has a window by the front balcony. No windows or doors in the rear to escape from," Officer Gomez told the team.

"Right," Sergeant Kiehm agreed. "Let's head out," he commanded.

***

Check-in time for the motel was 4:00 p.m., and his soccer luv was due at four-thirty. That would give him enough time to set up the cameras to wirelessly connect to his laptop. He wanted more, of course, but he'd save a full overnighter until after the wedding.

He'd feign disappointment and show anger toward his boss for making him help a client so soon after getting married. It wouldn't be the client he'd be taking care of. He knew Rachel would believe him. This time, it wouldn't cost a plane ticket and rental car. Merely a room at an average motel and cheap champagne. He had a difficult time containing his excitement, for in just a few hours, he'd be meeting his newest conquest, Luv_Soccer3303.

4:25 p.m.

Dat1Kooldude:	Are you getting close? I got us a room.
Luv_ Soccer3303:	Yes. I am looking for a place to leave my bike.
Dat1Kooldude:	You can store it in the room. I'm in #18.
Luv_ Soccer3303:	Okay. I'm nervous.
Dat1Kooldude:	Don't be. You're going to be a woman soon.
Luv_ Soccer3303:	You think so?
Dat1Kooldude:	You will love having sex with me.
Luv_ Soccer3303:	I'll be there in one minute.

It unfolded like it was straight out of a procedural manual, which it was. They opened the door to the small rectangle motel room and surprised Marty, who was working on his computer. In less than five seconds, they had him on the ground, another ten seconds to cuff him, and Officer Gomez was halfway through his Miranda warning by the sixty-second mark. They raised Marty off the floor, and another officer escorted him out of the motel.

Officer Gomez let out a sigh of relief. An arrest without incident or struggle is always the best. Gomez and the team were prepared for anything, for earlier in the summer, they'd met a predator in a local park. When the man realized that police officers surrounded the park, he took out a gun. Within seconds, the man had taken his own life.

But what if he instead had wanted to get in a shootout with the police or tried to escape and direct his anger toward an innocent bystander? Every case was different, and all had the potential to go awry.

Officer Gomez had made his fair share of difficult arrests. He didn't shy away from them, but those which went down without a struggle or a shot being fired were the most gratifying.

With Marty escorted to the police car, Gomez reviewed the contents of the motel room. The first and most important pieces of evidence he found were Marty's phone and laptop, open and unlocked. He called the tech crew to quickly transfer the data to a secure hard drive. The messages Gomez received as Luv_Soccer3303 and what they would eventually find on the electronic devices would be key for the prosecution. The phone and laptop would yield a massive amount of damming evidence but also required hundreds of hours for a thorough investigation.

Although Officer Gomez didn't know it at the time, it would leave many guests wondering why the groom didn't make it to the rehearsal dinner. Most assumed he got cold feet. Few speculated that he'd spend the night before his wedding in a jail cell.

This was a good day, Gomez thought to himself. On one hand, it disgusted him that there were so many predators online, and he could only make a small dent in the problem.

But on the other hand, Marty wasn't going to terrorize any young girls. His days of traumatizing unsuspecting *chil-*

dren were over. Gomez knew that kind of experience would haunt the victim for life. Survivors are never 100 percent healed. They only have degrees of recovery, and Gomez took some satisfaction that, at least when it came to Marty, the pain he inflicted on others came to a cold, hard stop.

Two Weeks Later

"Yes, I'm the lead on the case," Officer Gomez stated. "I can't tell you about the details of our evidence. You'll have to talk to your fiancé's lawyer about that."

"He's no longer my fiancé," Rachel said emphatically. She wanted nothing to do with Marty. She already felt like a complete idiot for letting him near her daughter and almost marrying him.

"Right."

"I can't believe he's a child rapist. But I'm more concerned about my daughter. She's only thirteen."

"Yes, I'm aware. Someone from the department along with victim services will interview her, with your consent, of course."

"I've talked to Sidney several times, and she swears that Marty never touched her, thankfully," Rachel exclaimed.

"But you want to be sure, right?" Officer Gomez asked.

"Yes."

"We want to know as well, and there's a strong case against him, but there's evidence that this wasn't his first attempt to meet someone," Gomez told her, not wanting to get into the details about what they found on Marty's phone and laptop.

"If he touched my daughter, I want him to fry," Rachel coldly announced.

"The people that do the interview are pros. It's an awkward and difficult conversation, and they're trained for these sensitive situations."

"Good. How long will it take?" she asked.

"It depends," Gomez answered, knowing that if something went on with Marty and Sidney, the interview would take a long time, but he didn't want to get Rachel worried unless there was something to get upset about. "Plan on two hours, but you won't know until they see where the conversation takes them."

"I understand," Rachel replied, and her voice cracked, feeling stressed and guilty that she brought a monster into her home. "When I arrived at the rehearsal dinner, I had this bad feeling. I didn't know what it was."

"Hmm," Gomez replied, unsure of what she meant, but he sensed she wanted to explain something.

"I wasn't expecting Marty to get arrested, but I felt that something wasn't right. I was by myself for a moment, and I prayed to God for a sign about my upcoming marriage. Was he the right guy to marry? I guess God spoke loud and clear," she explained and let out an audible sigh.

"I'm sure this has been a painful experience, but someday you may realize that you got lucky."

***

Marty hadn't yet implemented his plan to groom Sidney, so Rachel's worst nightmare hadn't materialized. The forensic review of Marty's phone and laptop revealed he sent over one thousand requests to middle schoolers over several weeks, and 90 percent had accepted his friendship. In mid-December, Marty was convicted and sent to Idaho State prison.

Officer Gomez would use this case as a teaching moment in the years to come for parents, kids, and other police officers. He set up a Facebook account to share what he learned about online predators. He hoped parents would heed his warnings.

PART 4: *FELONY FLATS,* JULY 2019

Officer Gomez transferred from Lewis & Clark Middle School in 2014 to become the school resource officer at Mountain View High School in Meridian, Idaho. The middle school fed into the high school, so he knew many of the students when he started the new SRO position. He created several anonymous profiles and frequently saw trouble coming, whether it was a fight at school, or someone who had run away from home or kids involved with drugs.

Over the years, he built solid relationships with many of the students and earned their respect and friendship, which led to honest and open dialogue. Sometimes, he'd offer Dutch Bros. Coffee cards for any information passed to him about serious situations, including a runaway's location.

The more he investigated runaway cases, the more he saw a common thread: dangerous situations. That *situation* could be the teen's home environment they were running from or wherever they temporarily lived. Couch surfing didn't provide a safe long-term plan and included dangers that most runaways didn't anticipate.

Knowing this, he and Tamera took in runaway teens who needed a safe place to stay. Even in middle America and "nice" communities such as Meridian and Boise, the street was not a place for any teen. Since their boys were grown and out of the house, they had extra bedrooms upstairs. Some runaways would stay for a few days and some for a couple of years.

The runaways that Dave and Tamera took in were not reported to the police or part of the foster system. Most times, their parents didn't notice or care enough to file a report and attempt to bring the teen home. No one was looking for these kids, so they truly flew under the radar and, therefore, were the most vulnerable. Dave and Tamera opened their house and hearts to these kinds of teens.

The Gomez household had few rules, but the ones they established were strictly enforced. The teen needed to attend school, do their homework, and be in the house by 10:00 p.m. There was also a modest dress code. Some abided by the rules, and others didn't want to live with any structure or requirements, so they didn't stay long.

They took in runaways for years, and a sixteen-year-old girl stayed with them in the summer of 2019. The house was available for this girl as long as she could follow the rules. At exactly 10:00 p.m., Lisa returned to their house and walked by the television room.

"Hey," Lisa greeted Dave and Tamera and gave them a slight head nod. Dave watched her movements and mannerisms to detect any drug or alcohol use.

"How was your evening?" Tamera asked.

"Fine," Lisa retorted.

"Were you hanging out with friends?" Dave asked.

"Yeah." Lisa, as usual, was in no mood to reveal the details of her life. She turned and walked toward the stairs, implying she was finished for the night. But before she could get too far, Dave needed some information.

"Hold up a second. Do you know Becky Henderson? She's fifteen," Dave inquired.

Lisa stopped and turned around. "Yeah, why?"

"She's reported as a runaway. I opened her case today and was hoping for a lead."

"Do you remember my ex-boyfriend, Clayton? That's his sister," Lisa uttered.

"I thought I recognized her last name."

"Maybe she's with him," Lisa offered.

"Do you have his address?" Gomez inquired.

"Not anymore. Clayton started hanging out with this lowlife Melvin, so maybe they're both over there," Lisa provided, although more motivated to end the inquisition than to be helpful.

"Is Melvin a drug dealer?"

"Yeah, among other things."

"Oh, what other things?" Tamera asked, wondering what kind of crimes Melvin was involved with.

"You didn't hear any of this from me," Lisa stated emphatically, without providing additional details or answering the question. She marched upstairs, this time with more *oomph*, for she wasn't in the mood for further conversation.

"Have you heard of this Melvin character?" Tamera asked her husband.

"Not much, but I'll talk to some officers on the drug task force to get some background information. Having connections with these kids has really helped in several investigations," he commented.

"That's a benefit of having an SRO in the school. You've mentioned several times how kids have given you a heads-up when another student might be in trouble," Tamera added.

"Most of the time, their tips are spot on. And if one of my profiles is in their network, I dig for more information. The kids realize I'm not bluffing when I know enough details."

"I don't know how many times you've told me that a nude picture is usually involved."

"Absolutely. During my last classroom training, I told the students that my educated guess was that 80 percent of the high school students had sent or received some type of nude picture," Dave stated.

"That's *so* high," Tamera exclaimed.

"I asked the students to raise their hand if they thought it was lower than that. Nobody did."

"It seems to get worse each year."

"True. I've seen it with sixth graders, sending pictures with a smile pasted on their brace face."

"*Sheesh*!" Tamera recoiled in disgust, and her face involuntarily scrunched as she processed what her husband had told her.

"Unfortunately, it's not the exception, it's the norm," Gomez cringed.

"Do you think the parents are clued into what's happening?" she asked.

"If they've taken my training or seen my Facebook account."

"But the parents that need the information the most are the ones who don't bother, so the majority are blindsided when it hits home," Tamera declared.

"And if most of the students send pictures, the kids don't see it as unusual. They downplayed the significance."

"Unfortunately, that's the prevailing attitude until something goes wrong."

"Like bullying and blackmail," he pointed out and added, "there's coercion, where a student will want to break up with someone, and the other person threatens to expose pictures unless they keep dating."

"Geez, that's a nice and *healthy relationship*," she barked with sarcasm.

"It goes beyond the students. The predators are in their social network," Dave pointed out. "Wi-Fi is the great equalizer because if you're online, you are visible to everyone and anyone, regardless of where you're located or who you are."

"The kid could be at home, and the parents think their child is safe, but the predator is in their pocket, where their phone is located. Something could happen right under their nose," she added.

"True. Even if the kid isn't looking for trouble, *trouble* is looking for them."

The Next Day

Officer Gomez knocked on the door of the run-down apartment. Maddie Henderson was expecting the visit but didn't look happy to see him. After introducing himself, she grunted and motioned him to come inside. She looked tired and much older than her thirty-nine years of life as she shuffled into the center of the apartment.

Maddie had long brown hair with streaks of gray and was pudgy. The apartment was sparse but surprisingly tidy. A man sat on the couch and didn't get up when the officer entered. He looked to be in his forties and was watching television.

"I'm Officer Gomez. We spoke on the phone, and I'm investigating the runaway report you filed yesterday."

"Yeah," Maddie answered, "I'm not sure where that girl went off to."

"When was the last time you saw Becky?"

"I don't know, maybe a week ago, maybe more."

"Wow, why did you wait so long to file a report?" the officer inquired.

"I don't know. I thought she'd come back," she answered honestly.

"Maybe she's with your son? Can I have his number?"

"It's possible. He's nineteen now, so I don't keep track of him, ya know?" Maddie explained and plopped herself down at the kitchen table.

Officer Gomez continued to stand. "I understand, he's an adult. Do you think she's with him?"

"They don't get along and never have, so who knows?" Maddie replied with a *who-cares* attitude. She picked up her cell phone from the small kitchen table, found a scrap piece of paper, and wrote down Clayton's number.

"Are there other friends she might stay with?"

"I guess. But her friends are just as flaky as her, so don't expect much help from them," Maddie complained.

Leo found a convenient opportunity to criticize Becky and grumbled, "Yeah, she'd bring around her stupid friends, and you couldn't get them to shut up, unless, of course, they were eating our food! I don't miss that at all."

The officer's attention was redirected to Maddie's boyfriend. "Aren't you worried about her?" Officer Gomez asked.

"Nah, she can take care of herself," Leo stated.

"She's only fifteen. She's not supposed to be on her own."

"I guess," Leo agreed, unconvinced.

"There are a lot of ways she can get in trouble, and—" but Maddie interrupted Officer Gomez.

"I got my own troubles to worry about. I'm tired of getting calls from the school about her skipping class."

"Ah, that's why you filed the runaway report."

"Well, yeah," she said flatly, as if that were the only reason a parent would file a runaway report.

"What about a boyfriend? Is there someone in the picture?"

"Oh, she's got *lots of boyfriends*. That's where she was the last time she ran away," Leo piped in.

"I don't have anything about her running away previously," Officer Gomez informed them.

"I don't think I made an official report," Maddie explained.

"Why not? How long was she gone?" the officer asked.

"About a month."

"She's difficult to deal with, so it was nice having a break from her," Leo added, continuing to reveal his annoyance with Maddie's daughter. "She's got ADD or ADHD. That girl's got *lots of* problems."

"And if she doesn't take her meds, she doesn't listen. You can't tell her *nothing,*" Maddie added to clarify that her daughter was the bad person in their household.

"There isn't a magic pill to *fix* her," Officer Gomez corrected.

"I don't know. What *I do know* is that those pills are expensive," Leo barked with disdain. "I think she tries to sell them."

"I guess you can look for her, but she's only going to run away again," Maddie reasoned.

"So it doesn't matter if I find her or not?" Officer Gomez inquired.

Maddie answered with a shoulder shrug. Many years had passed since she really cared about what her daughter was up to, and she was counting the days until Becky's eighteenth birthday.

"Maybe some nice family will take her in," Officer Gomez suggested, thinking of how he and Tamera have helped kids like Becky.

"Who would want her?" Maddie quickly retorted.

"Not me," Leo sarcastically volunteered and stretched out in the recliner.

Maddie then imagined her daughter in the care of a loving family. *That bothered her.* "I don't want her with strangers," she asserted, forgetting the possibility that Becky could be couch surfing all over the Boise metro area *with strangers.*

"There's lots of people who help troubled teens," the officer pointed out.

"No way, and have Becky turn into a great kid and *they* get all the credit. I don't think so!" Maddie complained.

"Okay," Officer Gomez replied, holding back a snarky response.

"If you find her, you bring her back here. In fact, you tell her she's committing a crime and scare her straight!" Maddie told the officer. The thought of Becky cowering in fear from disobeying her mother had a powerful appeal.

"That will teach her a lesson," Leo echoed, and Maddie nodded her head. As usual, they were on the same page when it came to what Becky's behavior *ought* to be.

"First, I want to make sure she's safe and not in any danger," Officer Gomez replied and thought, *There's no police lecture that would be scarier for Becky compared to living with these two.* He'd only been there five minutes, and their attitude toward her daughter alarmed and sickened him.

It was clear to Officer Gomez that he wasn't going to get help from Becky's mom and live-in boyfriend. He would move his investigation to finding her brother Clayton. Maybe she's with him. When he returned to his patrol vehicle, he shook his head and concluded that Maddie was, unfortunately, like many parents of runaway teens.

She epitomized the five reasons he believed why teens ran away: the parents, parents, parents, parents, and the parents.

***

"I haven't run away. I'm taking a break from my mom," Becky told him from the hallway. Even though Becky didn't get along with her brother, he was the one person in this world who would understand why she wanted to leave home. He reluctantly agreed to *help* her and sent her to Melvin's place, so she was expected.

"Yeah, sure," Melvin scoffed back at the teen. He stood over six feet tall with dark black curly hair that came down to his shoulders. He was lean and carried himself with the confidence of someone with money to burn. Wearing the best designer clothes was his preference, and he was content with having more style than smarts.

"My mom is cool. She won't care if I'm here. She knows I'm mature," Becky boasted but thought to herself, *She doesn't care where I am.*

"I don't want your mom coming here and ruining my party! Clayton has told me some crazy stuff about her."

"Trust me, she won't come here. She wants me to have a good time," Becky promised and shifted her hands to her hip in a flirty manner.

Her naturally wavy dark brown hair was mixed with green highlights that reached the center of her back, making her look taller than her five-foot-two-inch frame. She wore tight jeans and a simple T-shirt that accentuated her feminine qualities.

"Oh, believe me, you'll have a good time around here," Melvin bragged. He still doubted the truthfulness of Becky's story, but that didn't stop him from quickly brushing away any concerns.

"So, can I come to the party and maybe stay a day or two?" she asked hopefully.

Melvin smiled at her response and thought, *I love needy girls*. "Sure! Your brother Clayton says your mom and her boyfriend are a bunch of losers anyway."

"He's right," she admitted, dropping any *my mom is cool* pretense.

"Come on in," he gestured, and she entered his apartment. "I won't tell anyone you're here. I don't want a sweet girl like you to get in trouble. You don't want to get in trouble, do you?"

"No. They want me to have my own life," she countered, not knowing why she was trying to pretend that her mother cared about what she did. Melvin surely wasn't buying it.

"Whatever," he laughed at her, for he'd seen plenty of girls who made up tales of a happy homelife, but he could see through those lies from a mile away.

"Oh crap, are we in a bad cell service area?" she asked after examining her phone for a few seconds.

"No, of course not," he responded in an annoyed tone.

"My phone isn't working."

"Let me see that," Melvin instructed, and she handed him her phone.

"You no longer have cell service," he told her.

"What do you mean? Is it broken?" Becky asked and grabbed the phone back from him. Her heart sank when she noticed the words *no service* where the signal strength should be displayed.

"Your phone's been turned off. Did your mom forget to pay your bill?"

"I don't know!" she wailed.

"Or maybe she *canceled* your service," Melvin teased.

"No, no!" Becky responded, grabbed the phone back, and feverishly pushed the buttons. She frantically attempted to somehow fix it. She couldn't.

"It's obvious she doesn't want to take care of you." Melvin needled her.

"Ugh, what am I supposed to do now?" she asked to no one in particular.

"I have an extra phone. Do you want to use it?"

"You would do that?" she asked incredulously. She didn't expect help from anyone, including Melvin. Maybe he was a nice guy after all.

"Sure. I'll do you a favor, and then someday you can do *me a favor*. How does that sound?" Melvin offered.

"Yeah, that seems *totally* fair," Becky exclaimed with a little too much enthusiasm, revealing her desperation to be back online. *How long has my phone been dead?* She then wondered, *What favor is he going to want?*

"Your first post on the new phone should be at the release party," he suggested with pride, playing up his local celebrity status.

But that's hours from now, she thought to herself. *I have to wait that long to post an update on my social media?* She didn't have a lot of options, so she forced a smile on her face and answered, "Oh, yeah, that'd be cool!"

"Do you have a lot of people following you on Instagram?"

"Yeah, almost a thousand," she bragged.

"Good. You can link a picture from the party to my YouTube channel. I'm sure it will impress your friends that you're going to be in my latest video."

"I've told everyone," she lied.

He promised to put Becky in his new rap video. She wasn't getting paid for it, but Melvin convinced her it was an opportunity. Maybe she could use the video to achieve semi-celebrity status.

"If you're loyal to me, I can make you *famous*!" he exclaimed with hearty enthusiasm.

"Do you think so?"

"A lot of Instagram influencers started this way," he informed her with authority. He had no clue, but then again, neither did she.

"Yeah, that could *work*!" she answered eagerly.

"When you're making six figures as an *influencer*, don't forget who helped you from the beginning," he said confidently and stroked her cheek gently. She successfully stopped herself from recoiling. She forced herself to embrace his attention.

"*You're* not someone I can easily forget," she flirted with him, flipping her hair back and trying her best at a mischievous smile. She already learned how *easy* it was to feed a male's ego.

He nodded his head in agreement. "You got that right!" Melvin laughed at his own humor. He frequently impressed himself with his entertainment abilities.

She instantly imagined making money and living on her own. Look out world, here comes Becky! There didn't always seem to be a rational reason why some online influencers attained instant popularity.

Why *not* her? She *could* get lucky, and the video *could* go viral. Who knows? Luck would definitely have a part in Becky's future, but it wasn't clear yet whether staying at Melvin's would bring good or bad luck. Any chance to make money and stay away from her current living situation sounded fine to Becky. She dreaded returning to her mom's apartment and her scuzzy boyfriend. She hadn't seen her dad in four years and had no clue where he was living, or whether he was alive. Leo wasn't a father figure and was only too happy to have her out of the house.

Melvin was a self-made rapper, about to release his fifth video, hoping to be picked up by a record label, but for now he was content with producing videos and having parties to celebrate his accomplishments. The more people that came to the party, the more potential customers there were to buy his drugs. Hosting parties was a good way to drum up business and make extra cash, even if he didn't profit from rap videos.

Melvin lived in a Boise apartment for the past seventeen weeks, and the landlord was pushing him to make a rent payment. His deposit was already used up, but he wasn't planning to spend any money on rent. When the eviction time came close, he and his crew would move to another location.

He'd put down a new deposit for a different place and later refuse to make any rent payments, waiting for an eviction notice before doing it all over again. With social media, he'd easily tell his friends about his new apartment and, more importantly, the location of his next party.

Melvin was quite happy to have another hot young teen stay at his house, for it always helped recruit more guys to show up to his parties. Becky was an attractive girl with nowhere else to stay, so Melvin knew she would earn her keep around his place, *one way or another.*

That afternoon, they visited a local park to film the dance scenes that would be edited in the video. Becky and three other females were the dancers. Clayton would be behind the camera, and Melvin, of course, would be the center of attention. The females wore matching outfits of bright yellow leather skirts and a button-down half shirt that showed plenty of stomach *and* cleavage to get the attention of anyone watching.

Luckily for Becky, she'd seen some of Melvin's earlier work and knew the kind of dance moves that he typically used. She was confident about her ability to keep up with the other dancers. Two girls were late teens, while the third was about twenty-one years old.

Melvin approached the ladies and inspected their outfits. He rolled the first girl's skirt, raising it higher to be more revealing. Becky was the second one, and he made the same adjustment, and also unclasped a button on her shirt to expose the maximum amount of skin.

During the process of the wardrobe *adjustment*, he copped a feel, and his hand lingered long enough for the others to notice. Becky barely reacted but instead looked at her nineteen-year-old brother who was getting ready to video *the dancing*. She gave him a look as if to say, *Are you going to let him do that?*

Clayton understood her facial expression and simply laughed, "Melvin's the boss. He's in charge, so do whatever he says, loser." He knew exactly what Melvin had on his mind but felt no older brotherly obligation to protect her.

She was on her own. At that moment, it sank in. Becky knew what was required to have a roof over her head. She understood what Melvin valued, and her being merely fifteen was appealing to him.

Clayton scored points with Melvin for offering up his sister. Becky realized she was a pawn and was disappointed by her brother's quick approval of Melvin's intentions. But she shouldn't be surprised, for she and Clayton didn't share a sibling bond.

***

Becky remembered as young kids, they were constantly fighting for their mother's love and approval, which was in short supply. Clayton was a scrawny teen when he entered high school and was constantly getting picked on.

He dared not tell his mom about his school troubles because it was embarrassing, and the last thing he wanted was his *mommy* to talk to the school principal, or worse, confront the boys stealing his lunch money, punching him in the stomach and teasing him for being such a beanpole.

It wouldn't have mattered if he asked his mom for help because she wouldn't have lifted a finger. It wasn't necessarily bad parenting to let kids work things out for themselves, but Maddie could have at least provided some guidance, support, or encouragement.

Clayton was always left to defend himself. At the very least, Maddie could pretend to care, but she was into her own survival and dreams, specifically to find a rich man to take care of her. She was tired of working and being stuck raising the kids on her own. She wasn't concerned if her sugar daddy would take care of Clayton and Becky. But she ended up with Leo, so *that plan* didn't come to fruition.

Eventually, Clayton became frustrated because he was constantly getting beat up. He found Becky and a friend playing with dolls in the living room one day. Seeing her having a moment of fun with another fourth grader infuriated Clayton.

He instantly reacted and kicked the doll out of Becky's hand, hurting her. He grabbed a doll, ripped off its head, and tossed it outside. Becky and her friend instantly started crying. The cruel and unprovoked action horrified them.

"What do you think of that?" Clayton bellowed. "You two are a bunch of bratty little girls! Tell your friend to go home and stop playing with those *stupid dolls*," he growled menacingly, shifted his death stare at Becky's friend, and added, "You're making too much noise."

"But that was my favorite doll," Becky protested.

"I! Don't! Care!" Clayton yelled, scaring the two girls. Maddie wasn't home, so Clayton was *in charge*.

"But...," Becky again pleaded for Clayton to change his mind.

"I told you two to shut up," Clayton countered, now fully enraged, and he quickly stepped into the kitchen and grabbed a knife. Becky attempted to move away as Clayton brought the knife closer to her face, and her friend fled the apartment.

"I'm going to cut you up, so *maybe* you'll remember to do what I say," he told her and moved the blade closer. Becky squirmed to escape, and instead of cutting her cheek, he sliced the top of her shoulder. She immediately started bleeding.

"Now look what you've done!" he screamed even louder. "Don't make a mess, or mom will kill you!" he threatened.

Becky clutched her shoulder and ran into the bathroom. She panicked and grabbed a towel to stop the bleeding. Some blood landed on the bathroom floor, and her mother was furious to see a towel ruined when she returned home.

Becky tried to explain what happened, but Maddie shut her down, telling her she didn't care about *her excuses*. She was less interested in *how* the blood got there but more focused that Becky made a mess. She made Becky scrub the floor as she was weeping while she got on her hands and knees.

Clayton smirked, and Maddie didn't want to deal with Becky's sniveling, so he *volunteered* to ensure that Becky did a good job with her scrubbing. He was pleased to point out any area of the bathroom floor she missed.

However, being the youngest, Becky received some attention and affection from her mother, even if it was on a rare occasion. This infuriated Clayton further. He sought to undermine Becky in any way, frequently hiding her homework and throwing away her favorite clothes. In turn, she would try to get her brother in trouble, so Maddie's wrath would keep Clayton occupied.

It was a vicious circle, pitting the kids against each other with embellished stories of wrongdoings. Their relationship continued to spiral downward, with each sibling actively undermining the other at every opportunity. Maddie couldn't tell the difference between the truth and the lies, so she ignored both her children. But that didn't stop Clayton and Becky's constant bickering. Maddie eventually tired of their games so that neither child received any positive attention.

Once Clayton left the house, their hatred for each other mellowed out, but Becky didn't trust her brother as far as she could throw him. So really, why should she expect her brother to protect her from Melvin?

***

Melvin wanted to capture the content at sunset. The dancers would only appear during the chorus lines, and he didn't think it would take too much time. The four girls were near the park swing and wrapped themselves around the poles like they were at a strip club. They were instructed to spin around the pole fast enough to make their hair fly through the air and blow kisses to Melvin.

Clayton played part of Melvin's new song on his iPhone and gave them instructions on how fast to swing around the pole. Clayton went in close to capture each of the girls individually. Melvin instructed them to look into the camera with a sultry and seductive pose.

"Make love to the camera," Clayton instructed.

"I won't disappoint you," Tina, one of the dancers, answered.

"I know *that*!" Melvin responded with approval and vigorously nodded his head up and down. They knew what that meant. Show more skin and allure the viewer. There were no new moves left to use. The shock value of a sexy music video faded away a long time ago.

Melvin had watched raunchy videos more often than he could count, so he didn't bother to pay attention. He didn't care about the talent level of his dancers, for it wasn't costing him anything, and they'd only appear for a few seconds here and there. Just enough to feed their egos. Over 90 percent of the final video would feature him singing and driving down the street in his convertible Mercedes.

It took less than thirty minutes to shoot the footage needed. The *official* version featured the dancers for a mere thirty-five seconds. Clayton would spend the next two hours editing the video, just in time to play it on the large television in Melvin's apartment for their midnight premiere.

When it was almost 11:00 p.m., the party ramped up. Becky was happily enjoying her fifth margarita and scarfing down the delivered pizza. She hadn't eaten all day and quickly became intoxicated. She hoped the party would go late into the evening and maybe Melvin would pass out, for she'd rather crash in the spare bedroom instead of with him. But she understood it wasn't up to her.

Melvin *certainly* had plans for Becky. He'd have his way with her tonight. There wasn't any doubt. He knew it, and she knew it. But he had plans beyond his own physical desires. He'd force her to visit his landlord and entertain him equal to a weeks' worth of rent. He'd use her to pay off his debts. *This girl will come in handy*, he thought to himself. If she refused, it didn't matter, as another one would come along soon enough.

12:08 a.m.

Becky stared at the television screen in disbelief. It looped to play a second time, and Clayton encouraged the partygoers to take part in certain sections of the video, where they'd mindlessly whoop and holler. Perhaps they reacted as instructed because of their drug-infused numbness.

The video featured Tina's dancing prominently, giving her much more screen time than the other dancers. The only time Becky showed up in the video was from behind when she was twirling around the pole, with her hair flowing through the air. *It was impossible to tell it was her!* Becky was furious at her brother. Her thoughts of being an Instagram influencer evaporated.

Reality has a way of crushing a girl's dreams.

Becky watched Melvin and Clayton receive accolades from the crowd, and he put his arm around Tina's waist and planted a long kiss on her lips. The video ended, and Becky concluded Melvin possessed virtually no musical gifts. His lyrics didn't rhyme, weren't creative or meaningful, and the *music* was mostly a thumping base.

Melvin was many things, but talented and original weren't any of them. It was no wonder he didn't have a recording contract. The exuberance from the crowd was fueled by intoxication, and Melvin and Clayton ate it up. Melvin loved to be the center of attention in *his* video and *his* party. He was the star of the show.

Becky had no choice but to shake her head in disappointment and wondered if this was going to be her new life. *And what a crappy life it is,* she thought to herself. Maybe she would earn her way up to the featured female in the video, but then she thought to herself, *What's the point?* Melvin isn't going *anywhere.*

The next video was one that Melvin recorded a few months ago, and Becky scanned the crowd packed into the apartment, jumping up and down and moving their bodies to the *thump* of the music. She thought to herself, *My whole life is screwed up. How did I become such a failure at only fifteen years old?*

Although there were over fifty people at the house party, Becky felt completely alone. For a fleeting moment, she felt a sense of pride in herself for being featured in a video alongside a *cool* rapper and a number of older girls. She briefly viewed herself as a mature teen who was accepted by Melvin and his crew. But that feel-good moment quickly vanished. The allure faded and was replaced by the knowledge that *she didn't matter*. She downed the rest of her margarita and craved another drink to dull the anguish of her life.

She knew what Melvin wanted to do to her, and probably sooner rather than later. Everyone looked right through her, never seeing a person. They only saw a body that could provide something for them.

She'd have to play up her attraction to Melvin and stroke his ego by declaring how awesome his new video was. Her act could last a few days, but she couldn't plan beyond that. Hoping for courage, she found another margarita.

Tina watched Becky walk by herself, invisible to the crowd, and grab a drink. Clayton noticed his sister too and her empty-eyed expression. He commented to Tina, "That girl has *daddy* issues."

Tina answered him with scorn and a touch of melancholy, "Don't we all?"

The Next Day

Law enforcement used social media to gather information and connect people through their network. Young people post everything about their lives online. Officer Gomez reviewed Clayton's Instagram account and found over forty pictures uploaded as the official rapper's photographer. After looking through half of them, he noticed a picture from the release party that included Becky. He viewed Clayton's prior social media posts, which provided the address of the *big* release party. This led Officer Gomez to Melvin's apartment.

Officer Gomez recognized the address as a high-crime area, which the local police officers referred to as *felony flats*. It was no surprise that twenty-four-year-old Melvin Harris was a high school dropout with a long rap sheet, mostly for drug possession and distribution. Not the worse criminal he'd come across, but not the guy you hoped your daughter would marry. Even low-level drug dealers were dangerous, so given all this, Officer Gomez was cautious when he parked his patrol vehicle and scanned the surroundings.

Although it should be a routine inquiry, he knew any circumstance could go south at any moment, especially since he was by himself. He took the long and lonely walk from the relative safety of his vehicle to the second-floor apartment. It was about noon, and Melvin opened the door. The officer peered inside and saw Becky passed out on the couch. She looked disheveled and hungover.

"I hope you weren't dealing drugs here last night," Officer Gomez stated and expected a denial from Melvin, which he immediately received.

"Nope. Nor do I allow that type of person at my parties. We had a few of my friends over to watch the release of my newest video. I'm sure you've heard of me. You like rap music, don't you?"

Gomez ignored the question and got to his point. "That girl looks like Becky, the teen runaway I'm looking for. Did she have a rough night?"

"I don't know. She's my photographer's sister," countered Melvin with a blank look. He was skilled at deflecting questions from the police.

"You mean Clayton?"

"Yeah, he shot the video and put it all together."

"That's fine, but you know it's illegal to provide alcohol or drugs to a minor, right?"

"I would never *knowingly* do that. She had a small part in the video. Do you want to see it?" Melvin asked and held out his phone to offer proof.

"No, I believe you, but I need to get her out of this situation and back home," Officer Gomez informed him.

"Not a problem. You can take her," Melvin quickly offered. He was happy to get rid of Becky so Officer Gomez would spend the least amount of time in his apartment.

Gomez approached Becky and explained the situation to her. She was groggy but cognizant. Although she didn't feel like going home, she lacked the energy to argue against it. She gathered what little possessions she owned and followed the officer back to the patrol vehicle and didn't realize that getting away from Melvin was in her best interest.

Ninety-Eight Days Later, October 2019

"I have three stories I want to share with you today," Officer Gomez told the students. He was doing a presentation in the health science class. "I know we've talked a lot about the perils of sending nude pictures and the dangers of online predators. Some of that happens in our high school. There are lots of predators out there, and they'll try to exploit anybody, and they don't care whether you're a boy or a girl, rich or poor, tall or short, fat or skinny. It's what these people do."

"I wanted to bring up a new trend," Gomez continued, and as he looked around the room, he saw the students were paying attention, so he added without missing a beat.

"They want *more* than just your picture. I've investigated a few of these cases, and here's what I learned. If you think because you're a male that no one will try to take advantage of you, think again. Boys are targeted too."

The officer let that sink in a moment.

"For example. I had a case where someone created a profile of a good-looking college-age girl. *She* connected on social media with a teenage boy," the officer stated and heard several boys snicker, as they would enjoy having a sexy college girl part of their social network.

"I know you all think it's funny, and that's exactly what they're counting on. This *college girl* is usually a fake profile trying to get your attention. They're going to suggest exchanging pictures. Now keep in mind this other profile isn't real, so they're going to use downloaded pictures, probably from some pornography site."

Officer Gomez noticed the snickering continued. "They will send the boys a nude picture and say, *I've shown you, now you show me*. Many teenage boys have sent their own pictures. This is a trap, so what do you think happens next?" The snickering stopped, but no one raised their hand to answer his question.

"Well, the good time is over because as soon as he sends the picture, she is going to ask for money. That's called sextortion. And if he pays, what do you think happens *after that*?" The classroom was silent. The officer had everyone's attention.

"They ask for more money?" a student finally spoke.

"Exactly. As soon as anyone pays, they want another payment. And if the boy doesn't pay, the *attractive college girl* will threaten to send his picture to everyone in his social network," Officer Gomez told the class. "And of course, if they're your friend or follower, they can see everyone you're connected to. You're in a no-win situation."

"Do they really send the picture?" another student asked.

"Many times, yes. Remember, they don't care about you. They're not an actual *friend*. This is very real, and I'm telling you this story because I don't want you to get fooled."

"Has this happened to someone at our school?" a student inquired.

"You know I'm not allowed to go into details about a student's case, but I can tell you I've personally investigated cases of sextortion. This is a crime, and many times, it happened fast in less than twenty-four hours."

"Questions?" Officer Gomez asked, but nobody wanted to come forth. "You can always see me in my office if you want to learn more, or if you know someone that this happened to and might need some help," he offered. It was always easier to get a student to tell the officer about a problem that happened to a *friend*.

"Okay, let's switch gears and talk about two cases with runaway teens. I know things can get crazy at home sometimes, but you need to know about the dangers of running away," Officer Gomez explained. He paused, saw the students were listening, and continued, "Most of you know the obvious. If you're living on the street and are homeless, that's a dangerous situation. But even if you're couch surfing with friends, that usually doesn't last too long, and many times the runaway ends up at a party looking for a place to stay.

"I know many of you think the party scene is fun, but there's a lot of risk to your safety. Not only are there drugs and alcohol at those parties where somebody might overdose, but I'll be honest, there's a good chance that if you're intoxicated, you'll be sexually assaulted. That's what happened in one of my cases over the summer. Some are trafficked."

"Trafficked?" a student asked, and he saw confusion on her face.

"A person pressures someone into a commercial sex act through force, fraud, or coercion," the officer explained. "Most sex trafficking victims are underage." Again, the officer was met with silence from the students.

"Going through high school is a tough time. I get it. But if you are having issues at home and you're thinking about running away, please come to my office, and we can talk further. There are alternatives, and you don't want to get involved with these low-level rappers and parties. They may try to charm you, but they're not the kind of person who you want to end up with."

There weren't questions, so he continued, "I know they seem popular and cool because they get a lot of likes and followers, but that's not how you should value yourself. When you become adults, and maybe eventually get married, you need to realize that *tens* don't marry *twos*. I'm married to a *ten,* and I know she's worth it. So I'm going to put a lot of work into keeping my relationship with a *ten*. But if you are a *two*, you're not going to attract somebody who is a *ten*. What a *ten* means to you may be different than the person sitting next to you. You'll want to create the best version of yourself. Let's say you're a *five*. How do you become a *ten*? Anyone?"

"Get good grades," a girl suggested, and Gomez was grateful for the student interaction.

"Absolutely a start. You're not going to take drugs, and you'll go to school and do your homework. Focus on developing your skills beyond school grades. Acquire life skills too, which can be anything. You could learn a language, music, art, poetry, or how to fix a car. All kinds of things."

"Learn how to arrest criminals!" somebody shouted, and the class laughed.

"Yes, you could even go into law enforcement, and there are different things besides being a school resource officer or on patrol. I know a lot of you watch CSI, and you need to learn a lot of technical and scientific things to be that type of person.

If you build yourself up to be the best that you can be, you're going to be a *ten* and probably attract another *ten,* so you'll have a better chance at a great life. There aren't any guarantees, of course. But if somebody is married to a *two,* that marriage isn't going to last long. And if you're with a *two* and they leave, well, no big deal, because you can easily get another *two*."

A few students nodded, and he guessed several kids weren't receiving parental guidance at home, so he used the opportunity to give them something to think about. The officer decided that the relationship portion of the class was finished. "Okay, no more from Ann Landers."

"Who?" a few students asked.

"Never mind. Listen up, the last story is a case I had over the summer. I was investigating another teen runaway. I found her at a party with several other minors. Normal police protocol is for the parent to come get the juvenile from the scene. We could not contact her mother, so we transported her to juvenile detention, where she'd be safe until her mother could come pick her up. In this situation, police procedure is to handcuff the juvenile so that they don't run away again."

"Is it a crime to run away from home?" a student asked.

"Some juveniles have strong reasons for not wanting to go back home, and I understand that. But most states consider running away from home against the parents' wishes a crime, a status offense, even though some juveniles have valid reasons for not wanting to return home. A status offense is anything that they charged a juvenile with that they wouldn't be charged with if they were eighteen or twenty-one, such as purchasing alcohol or cigarettes," Officer Gomez explained.

"This was complicated because her mom was homeless, and the young lady ingested hard drugs while at the party. I wasn't sure if it was an overdose situation, so I took her to the hospital to get checked out. I spent the next three hours at the hospital while she was being examined. When she was with the doctor and nurses, I learned that she and her mother were living at a local homeless shelter. The girl told me she didn't have any other family."

"Did her mom have a cell phone?" a student asked.

"Yes, but we couldn't reach her, and she wasn't in any of the shelters. I was very saddened that I, the arresting officer, was the only person at the hospital to care for her," Officer Gomez recalled and paused a moment. "I made the best of it and treated her like family. By police policy, I had to keep this young lady handcuffed while I was with her. I switched the handcuffs to the bed railing in her hospital room, so it'd be easier for the doctors to look at her. My point is that going to this party, she got out of control and probably didn't know what drugs she was taking. She could have easily overdosed but got lucky this time."

"Did her mom come to pick her up?" a student wondered.

"No. That's the sad part. After three hours, she was cleared medically, so I moved her to juvenile detention. As we were leaving the hospital, she gave me a giant hug while still in handcuffs. She thanked me for caring about her and being there at the hospital. I was glad that I didn't leave, but it got to me that there wasn't anyone else to provide comfort. I felt like I needed to be there for her at that moment."

Two Months Later

Officer Gomez was invited by Mountain View High School student, Sarah VanDam, to an art gallery in Boise. Sarah attended the class when Officer Gomez recalled his story about the homeless runaway. Sarah sketched a moment from the story and entered the drawing in an art competition and received second place. This was a complete surprise to Officer David Gomez, who had never felt so honored in his life.

(Reprinted with permission by Sarah VanDam)

Part 5: *The Edge of Seventeen*, Late November 2021

The *Waldorf Astoria*, located on Park Avenue in New York City, is so famous that it doesn't need the word *hotel* at the end of its title. The historic establishment has hosted celebrities and dignitaries alike. Its signature suite is 550 square feet, and there are over 300 restaurants within a quarter of a mile of the hotel. There are only six restaurants in rugged Idaho City if you count the saloons and is 2,503 miles from the famed institution in Manhattan.

On the outskirts of town, off a dirt road, sits a Home Depot shed that's twelve feet by sixteen feet. The *Astoria* model was advertised with precut wood and is ready to assemble. It boasted a large 192-square-foot space and cost less than one night in a premium room at a fancy place in the *Big Apple*.

Being a shed, it had no electricity, bathroom facilities, or running water. Also being a shed, it doesn't require a county inspector to approve how it's put together, a big advantage for residents looking for ultracheap housing. But it's dry and doesn't leak and has a small electric generator, so it was good enough for Monique Neeley and her seven-year-old son, Ethan.

Deputy Gomez left the Meridian Police Department and joined the Boise County Sherriff's Office. This took him out of the schools, and he spent most of his time on patrol responding to 911 calls rather than investigating sexual predators. However, he continued to be active on his Facebook account, posting updates about the latest trends in teen sexting and online schemes targeting teens.

He dropped off a toy and a pair of donated athletic shoes for Ethan. He'd coordinated with the Boise Nike outlet store to get the shoes donated for needy families. The new sneakers felt like an early Christmas present to the growing boy who had been wearing tight year-old sneakers. Deputy Gomez felt gratified seeing Ethan's eyes light up. The smile of an innocent child even improved Monique's normally grouchy mood. That moment of joy made it worth all the effort.

But he couldn't stay long, and within minutes, Deputy Gomez was back in his patrol vehicle and waved goodbye. He headed south on State Highway 21 for his scheduled pickup of Abigail Gnojewski, a teenager who'd be his ride-along partner for the evening. Several students each year would accompany a deputy during their shift in a patrol vehicle as part of the department's community outreach program.

Two Hours Later

Boise is Idaho's largest city and state capital, which is located in the flat *Treasure Valley*, named for a treasure chest of resources and opportunities. Visitors often get confused by the fact that Boise is in Ada County, not in Boise County. Boise County is located north of the city and is sparsely populated. It's comprised of rugged mountain terrain and has lots of twisty county highways that can make a stomach turn.

"Can you pull over?" Abby asked, who felt nauseous from the fast driving on the mountain road.

"Sorry, we've got to get there. We're still another thirty minutes out," Deputy Gomez stated without looking at the seventeen-year-old. He was completely focused on the road. *She* was completely focused on trying not to retch.

"What should I do?" Abby yelled over the blaring siren on their way to a two-year-old's ATV accident.

"Open the window if you think you're going to puke," he replied in a matter-of-fact tone. They hit the next curve hard, with Deputy Gomez braking and then accelerating out of the turn.

That pushed Abby over the edge, and she lowered the window and braced against the door as her early dinner came back up and splattered onto Highway 55 and mostly avoided it coming back onto her long dark hair. It didn't bother Gomez; he'd seen much worse in the back of his patrol vehicle to complain.

Abby took a few moments to compose herself. "The child will have to be stabilized and may need CPR," she stated.

"I don't know the extent of the injuries," he told her.

"The victim's very young, so the procedures are different," she explained and ran through the training in her mind and then expressed it verbally. "The compressions will need to be administered with care, probably at half strength with just your thumbs."

"We'll have to see what condition the toddler is in. They called a flight-for-life helicopter," Deputy Gomez told her. He knew that Abby was an honor student, but her passionate knowledge of emergency medical care surprised him. She had received training, but this would be her first real-life emergency situation. Twenty-eight minutes later, they arrived.

The accident occurred near a trailhead that was several miles from the nearest town, and the child's father was instructed to drive to a parking lot where he was met by the Horseshoe Bend Fire Department. Despite Deputy Gomez's quick response to the 911 call, it took an hour to reach the scene because of the rural location.

A firefighter had performed CPR for *forty-five minutes* when they arrived. For Abby, the scene initially felt like it was out of a movie, with lights flashing and people scurrying about. But the *movie scene* feeling quickly faded as she absorbed the full impact of what she had witnessed.

This was not a drill.

It was dark outside, which made the flashing lights more prominent while also casting shadows on nearby people, vehicles, and trees. The air was still, cold, and crisp as she immediately felt winter's grip when she stepped out of the vehicle.

Then Abby tuned into the sound her boots made on the gravel as she approached. The *crunch* continued ominously with each step, as if she were crushing the life out of the child. It conjured images more associated with a horror movie than a rescue scene. It seemed louder than it should have, so she tried to walk gingerly to create less noise.

Several people shined their bright flashlights down toward the toddler while the firefighter tried to save his life. She wondered, *How can he perform CPR and keep the infant warm at the same time*? She noticed the distraught look on the firefighter's face. But his face showed more. True, he was *exhausted*, but his expression was unmistakable. It was the realization that he was losing the battle *for life*.

The *thump, thump* noise became louder. It brought the sound of hope, a helicopter to transport the young child to a nearby Boise hospital. It was about to land in a nearby field, and it was the child's only chance. She observed the copter's spotlight check the landing zone. Another firefighter was directing the pilot exactly where to touch down.

Abby noticed an SUV approach and come to a screeching stop. "My son!" a late-twentysomething woman shouted as she opened her vehicle door, too focused and distraught to close it. Abby barely heard her over the *thumping* from the helicopter.

The woman looked around the confusing scene, desperate to find her only child. Abby approached the distraught woman and led her toward the boy, but they couldn't get close because he was being lifted onto a stretcher for transport.

"That's my son!" she exclaimed and pleaded for good news. "How is he?"

"He's in critical condition and is being taken to Saint Alphonsus Medical Center," another firefighter told her. She nodded with understanding, which didn't provide any comfort.

"He's going to have the best people working on him," Abby told her with yearning, then added, "They're doing everything they can to save him."

They both turned and watched the firefighters approach the helicopter mere seconds after it touched the ground. Abby instinctively gave the mom a hug. She responded to the stranger's gesture and tightly held the teen.

But her grip loosened, and Abby then felt the woman's weight pressed against her. At first, Abby didn't understand what had happened, but then she saw that the woman's eyes were glazed over.

She fainted. Abby grabbed her and slowly placed her on the ground as gently as possible. She turned her body to lay the woman on her back. This would allow for better oxygen flow and level her heart rate. Abby took her coat off and placed it on the woman, who wasn't wearing one.

The teenager next looked around for something to help raise her legs to force blood flow to the brain. Instinctively, the teen rubbed the woman's hand to provide comfort. The firefighter who performed CPR noticed, along with Deputy Gomez, and joined Abby.

"I have a young son too," the firefighter told Abby, who nodded in empathy. He performed CPR on the woman's son as if he was his own. She studied his face for a moment and saw the distressed look in his eyes. He knew the chances for the toddler were slim. Abby wondered, *What do we tell the mom?* There wasn't time to ponder the question because she woke up.

"Alex," she faintly said.

The firefighter took over. "He's in the helicopter. They just left for the hospital," he told her and gestured up to the chopper heading south toward Boise.

"I need to go," she stammered and made a wobbly effort to sit up.

"We can have someone take you to the hospital," the firefighter instructed her, for he wasn't going to take the chance of letting her drive in that condition.

"Yes," she agreed and had no intention of arguing.

"Let's have you sit up for a few more minutes and see how you feel," Deputy Gomez suggested, and the firefighter nodded in agreement. The deputy's radio squawked, and he briefly walked away.

"Abby, we need to go. There's another call," Deputy Gomez stated.

She wanted to stay, but the deputy was gesturing for her to follow. Abby looked back at the woman with a hopeful expression, as if saying, *I'm rooting for your son.* She returned a smile and thanked her.

Deputy Gomez and Abby returned to the patrol vehicle. He gunned the engine, flipped on the lights and siren, and headed toward the next call of the evening, about thirty minutes away.

Abby blocked out the noise and contemplated what she'd observed. An innocent two-year-old's life hung in the balance. She wished she could have done more, and the situation weighed heavily on her.

But Abby realized she wasn't powerless or helpless. For a short moment, she could comfort a stranger on the worst day of her life. It had a lasting impact on the teenager, even though she probably wouldn't see the woman again.

It was only by chance that she was on this evening's ride along. An unplanned and random encounter she couldn't have predicted a few hours ago. And it wasn't a criminal investigation. Deputy Gomez was called to help in this life-and-death situation, and he considered it a routine 911 call.

She understood that whenever the police are called, it's because of a problem, and many times someone's in crisis, regardless of whether it ends with an arrest. His job was more than ticketing speeders or searching for stolen vehicles. Abby's evening started out unexpectedly, and the intensity level wasn't going to stop.

Thirty-Eight Minutes Later

"I've been to this house before," Deputy Gomez stated a few minutes before they arrived.

"You have?"

"Yes, this girl has been in a mental health facility before. She's had anger issues and a history of depression. She's a cutter and slit her wrists in a failed suicide attempt."

"Wow," Abby remarked and took in the situation.

"The dispatcher didn't say a whole lot more, so I don't know exactly what we'll be walking into. The first thing I'll need to do is calm everybody down," the deputy stated.

"Yeah, that makes sense. She could be depressed or bipolar."

"Possibly. I don't always see what led up to the situation," he replied.

"She could experience a manic episode, where she's extremely happy and then extremely sad. Self-harm is a concern when she hits that low," Abby stated and thought through everything presented at the training class she attended.

"She was pretty messed up the last time I saw her."

"The person can experience forceful emotions, like a short temper, or act out with risky behavior such as drugs."

"I don't know if she's on drugs, but last time, she had these empty and sad eyes," Deputy Gomez explained.

"That's common after the intense emotions. They're frequently followed by depression," she pointed out.

"That's got to be tough. How do you know all of this?" he asked.

"I've researched this subject a lot. It's complicated, and if the behavior is minor, it looks like normal teenage rebellion."

"As a deputy, I get involved after someone has gotten out of control, usually when a neighbor or a family member has called 911."

"Right. Unfortunately, there's no real cure. It can come from genetics or their environment," Abby commented.

"Most of the time when I get called into these situations, it's a result of raised tensions. Everyone's stress level is up, and people are out of control. But the way I see it, the root cause is their environment, like you said, usually because many people don't know how to be a parent."

"I guess there's not an instruction manual for that, right?" Abby jested.

"Well, it doesn't help when the mom's boyfriend is on meth and works only enough to feed his habit," Deputy Gomez replied in a serious tone.

"How do you know that?" Abby asked and challenged his assertion but was also curious about the answer.

"I've arrested him several times before, mostly low-level offenses," Deputy Gomez answered, as he stared at the road ahead and concentrated on his driving.

"Wow, that's really bad."

"Yup. I'm not sure if the mom is using too. This is officially a welfare check."

"What do you mean by that?"

"We don't know if someone committed a crime, but a deputy is sent to check things out and make sure everyone is okay. In this case, it's the welfare of the minor that I need to assess, especially since she could be suicidal."

"Shouldn't a counselor or social worker be called?"

"Sure, in the perfect world, but not at this time of night. Besides, there's not a budget for that. It defaults back to the sheriff's department."

"I hope she hasn't done anything too destructive."

"Yeah, me too. It could be life-threatening if any of them are on drugs. It's tough enough to be a good parent these days and almost impossible if one or both are on drugs. The kids always bear the brunt of the adults' mistakes and forget how it affects them."

"Yeah," Abby agreed and thought about what Deputy Gomez asserted, which was so obviously true. But then, why is it so hard for people to avoid drugs or alcohol abuse? She heard survivor stories from working with the *Safe in Harm's Way Foundation*. Many domestic violence situations involved addiction and had a detrimental impact on the children in the household.

"We don't know what we're walking into, so you stay behind me, and if it looks dangerous, I'm going to send you back to the vehicle. Do you understand?" he asked with authority.

"Yes."

Deputy Gomez and Abby approached the small two-story white house. It appeared run-down and needed upkeep, especially a fresh coat of paint. Abby noticed that one of the front windows was cracked and repaired with duct tape. Luckily, an outside light was left on. Deputy Gomez was normally cautious, and this incident wasn't an exception. Domestic disputes are prone to sudden escalation.

"Be careful, there might be ice," he cautioned and slowed down his pace as he approached the door. He also wanted to determine if any household members were outside.

Officer Gomez knocked on the door, and after a few seconds, a late thirtysomething woman opened the door. He peered inside and noticed a teen girl talking with a man. Both looked agitated, and the deputy recognized all three of them from the previous incident.

"You called the cops on me?" Stevie screeched when she turned her head to see who was at the door.

"That's right, they're gonna take you back to the loony bin!" Dustin threatened her with a menacing grin. He looked for any excuse to send her back to the mental health facility. He'd be happy with anything that got her out of the house.

"Don't call it a loony bin," Liz argued and walked back into the living room. "They're trying to help my daughter."

"She needs all the help she can get," he snapped back, his response dripping with sarcasm. "Maybe they can teach her to do what she's told, *for once!*" Dustin spit out with venom.

He and Liz had lived together for almost four years, but he never desired, nor would he win, any stepfather of the year award. He saw Stevie as a nuisance and a bratty, moody, and high-maintenance teenager. There was some truth to that, but he enjoyed bullying both Liz and Stevie. He needed to put them in their place and flex his superiority. Since he barely left the house, they were his convenient targets.

Liz only stuck around because she'd rather live with Dustin than be alone. She wouldn't admit that, of course, and constantly made excuses for his behavior. She saw a glimmer of hope whenever he was kind or complimentary, which was rare.

She wasn't scared of him, but even though the rental agreement for the house was in her name only, she knew it'd be difficult to get rid of him. It wasn't worth the hassle, so she simply maintained *the rut* as best as she could. Occasionally, she'd stick up for her daughter until she grew tired of arguing.

Deputy Gomez put his hands out and lowered his arms toward the floor in a gesture to calm them down. It only paused Liz and Dustin for a moment.

"Give him back his cigarettes, please, honey," Liz implored. She wanted the screaming to stop, and this time it was her daughter who was the instigator. Stevie knew exactly how to infuriate him, and it was way too easy to get Dustin spun up. Why couldn't she just leave well enough alone? Why did she have to stir the pot?

Liz's relationship with her daughter was tense and strained. Her patience for Stevie's antics had worn out a long time ago. The house was filled with anger and frustration. Stevie was frequently rebellious and seemed to always do the opposite of what she was asked. She'd find little ways to retaliate against the two of them, like hiding their beer. Or meth pipe. Or in this case, Dustin's cigarettes.

"You know that smoking is bad for you," Stevie teased. "I'm only trying to help you out."

"I'm done asking you where you hid them," Dustin warned.

"Fine, die of cancer, see if I care," Stevie hissed back.

"Tell him," Liz pleaded.

"Whatever. They're in the toaster oven."

"You're lucky I didn't use that to cook something," he exploded and took a threatening step toward her, then snarled, "You little b—"

"Okay, guys, that's enough," Deputy Gomez interrupted him and shifted his position directly in front of Dustin. He made eye contact and analyzed Dustin's movements. It didn't appear that Dustin was high, a relief to the deputy.

"But—" Dustin protested.

"No buts. I want everyone to take a deep breath. Go get your smokes back," he instructed Dustin and pointed to the kitchen.

"Okay," he grumbled and slowly walked in that direction.

"Let's all take a deep breath and see if you can work this out as a family," Deputy Gomez strongly suggested and then added, "we don't want anyone getting arrested tonight, do we?" He stared at Dustin, who seemed ready to hit the teen, and then focused back to Liz and Stevie, knowing any of them could physically assault each other.

"Maybe we call it a night, and everybody goes to bed. And in the morning, you all can try to work this out with cooler heads. What do you say?" Deputy Gomez proposed more as a directive than a question. After a few seconds, Stevie spoke up.

"I'm tired anyway, and I don't want to fight anymore," she expressed, and some of the tension left her body.

"That's fine with me," Liz answered. She too was drained from another night of bickering, where the argument went round and round, and nothing seemed to get resolved.

One of these days, Stevie would live in a household without strained relationships. But certainly, *that day* hadn't arrived. Everyone recognized the situation was simply a dispute and not a criminal offense. Liz looked at her live-in boyfriend, and Dustin knew Stevie wasn't going to be taken away tonight, so he nodded in reluctant agreement.

But before Deputy Gomez could ask the obvious next question, for Stevie knew it was coming, she told him, "I haven't harmed myself, and I'm not going to harm myself. I just want to *get some sleep*."

"Sleep? That's all you do around here is sleep and never pick up after yourself!" Liz snapped, for she spoke without thinking. She instantly remembered the argument from earlier when she'd asked Stevie to clean the frying pan she used to make herself lunch.

After rolling her eyes so hard that it was almost audible, Stevie had promised to clean the pan. As usual, she never got around to it. Liz was sick and tired of being everyone's maid, and she impulsively lashed out at her daughter. Her flash of anger surprised everyone, and the tension in the room instantly returned.

"Ugh, I guess I'm just a royal screwup. Is that what you want me to say? Okay, I admit it, I'm a loser! Are you satisfied?" Stevie seethed and then yelled, "I hate both of you and wish you'd leave me alone!"

She didn't wait for a response and ran up the stairs. A few seconds later, they all heard the door to her bedroom slam! Abby unconsciously took a step away, who tried to shrink into the background and take up as little space as possible.

Deputy Gomez immediately turned and projected an annoyed look at Liz, for that was the last thing she needed to say. Dustin smiled, pleased that this time, it wasn't him that got into it with Stevie.

"It's true. She's a slob and doesn't listen to her mother," Dustin added. He couldn't help but pile on.

"I don't care. We're trying to calm everybody down, not get her spun up again," the deputy corrected.

"But he's right," Liz protested and plopped herself down onto the old sofa. "She's too much trouble, and I can't handle her anymore," she cried.

Dealing with her defiant daughter had worn her down *and worn her out*. The deputy sensed a future standoff and wouldn't be surprised if Stevie soon became the county's newest runaway. All he could do was to ensure that didn't happen tonight.

Abby felt compelled to make sure the girl was okay, so she walked upstairs. When she reached the top, she told them, "I'm going to check in on Stevie." Deputy Gomez reacted with a small nod while Liz and Dustin were expressionless.

She gently knocked on her bedroom door. "Hi, my name is Abby. Are you okay?" Her question was met with silence, so she tried again, "Can I come in and talk to you for a minute?"

"*Whatever*," Stevie answered after a few seconds. The snotty attitude was so intense that Abby should have been armed with a box of tissues.

"Hi," Abby said as she entered the small bedroom. Stevie's response was a blank stare.

She noticed the girl's room was messy, with clothes thrown about with no order. She almost couldn't tell the color of the worn-out rug because, besides the clothes, the floor was filled with empty Amazon and Etsy boxes and dirty dishes left after eating several meals in her room. With Liz and Dustin around, Abby could see why Stevie would escape upstairs.

"How old are you?" Abby asked, looking to start a conversation.

"Fourteen," Stevie answered with a long sigh and sat on the bed tucked in the corner of the room. She clutched a pillow, and her tears formed streaks of mascara, which jetted downward from her eyes and reinforced the depressed look on her face. Her brown hair appeared matted, as if she had just woken up.

Stevie then asked in a snarky tone, "What are you, a junior cop or something?"

"No," Abby laughed loudly with a smile, surprised by the comment. She could only imagine the *looks* from her friends if they thought she was a junior deputy!

"Uh-huh," she coldly grunted.

"I'm in eleventh grade and with Deputy Gomez for a ride along, but just for the evening."

Abby went over to her, hesitated a moment, and when Stevie didn't protest, she sat down on the bed. She slowly and gently put her arm around her shoulder and told her, "I get it. I know what it's like."

"Yeah, sure," Stevie retorted with skepticism.

"I know you're going through a lot. Trying to grow up and high school is never easy. Trust me, I know," Abby told her with sincere caring. Stevie nodded her head and saw the older teen as genuine. She felt somewhat encouraged, so Abby continued, "Your mom and Dustin seem difficult to deal with."

"*Ya think?*" Stevie answered sarcastically.

Abby couldn't help but smile and made eye contact with the younger teenager, who stopped crying for the moment. "Yeah, *I do think that*!" Abby blurted out.

Stevie busted up laughing, and the awkward stress melted.

"It stinks, I know, and it seems like you're never going to get older. But someday, you won't have to deal with this," Abby returned in a more somber tone.

"That day can't come soon enough."

"Well, I'm only seventeen, and I actually grew up in a pretty disturbed household and sometimes lived with a different family."

"That must have sucked," Stevie commented.

"It did, so I understand what it's like to have a crappy homelife."

"I don't know what to do. But for sure, I don't want to go back to the *looney bin*, as Dustin called it."

"You can only take it one day at a time."

"Some arguments we get into are *so dumb*," Stevie complained.

"We all feel that way. It's very draining."

Stevie murmured, "Hmm," but was relieved to know she wasn't alone in her feelings.

"Today is a small piece of your life. There are so many things coming your way as you get older. You'll look back and realize that this moment is so insignificant," Abby attempted to convince the younger teen.

"Maybe. Most of the time, I feel like I'll be stuck here *forever*."

"I'm going to be a senior next year, and I'm already thinking about my life after high school. You're not that far behind me, so you only have a little way to go."

"I get it, but finishing high school seems *so* far away. I'm ready to take off now!"

"Deputy Gomez has told me some stories about runaway teens and couch surfing. Believe me, you don't want that life," Abby warned.

"Yeah, I know you're right. My friend Darcy, I think she's got it worse than me. She's stayed here a few times after running away, but Dustin kicks her out after a few days."

"Did she go back home?"

"No, not until she's run out of options. She won't tell me where she goes afterward or what happens there."

"I doubt it's anything good."

"Darcy stays until she's no longer welcome. Whenever she goes back home, it's worse than before, which is why she keeps running away," Stevie explained.

"That sounds like a nightmare situation for her. Do you want to talk about it with Officer Gomez?"

"No. Darcy will get in so much trouble if the cops get involved."

"Yeah, I hear you," Abby responded but also knew that when the cops don't get involved, nothing gets better. It's a tough thing to balance.

"I don't actually know any details. I try to be there for my friend. We've helped each other through our struggles."

"Some of my friends have parents that rag on them *all the time*. We support each other too. Those friends will get you through high school. You need them or you'll never survive," Abby replied.

"Yeah," Stevie agreed.

"Freshman and sophomore years can be pretty tough. You're not a kid anymore, but you're not an adult either."

"I can't wait to be your age. Does it get any better when you're a junior?"

"Well, not really," Abby answered and laughed at herself. "Everything is a big drama in high school, so no, that doesn't get better."

"I didn't think so," Stevie answered and also laughed. "*That* was wishful thinking."

"For sure. But the older you get, the more you can see beyond high school and living at home."

"It's definitely a daily battle for me," Stevie told her.

"Every one of my friends has problems too."

"Great," commented a dejected Stevie, who longed to be an adult and thought that if she was only a few years older, it would solve all her problems.

Sometimes teenagers are *so* naïve.

"I see a younger version of myself in you."

"Well then, I feel sorry for you!" Stevie razzed.

"I'm serious! We're not that different," Abby replied.

"But you seem so mature and put together."

"Me? Well, thanks, but I'm *far* from living a perfect life. What teen does, right?" Abby joked and bantered with Stevie. She lightly shoved the younger teen's shoulder and laughed again.

The younger teen reacted with amusement, and for the moment, she forgot about arguing with her mom and Dustin and proclaimed, "High school just sucks!"

"I know. Even the kids that look like they have the perfect life, I know they have problems. I think they just hide it better. High school is difficult for anyone."

"I thought you were here to make me feel better?" Stevie asked with a grin and nudged Abby back. Both understood that no one had a stress-free life.

"I guess my point is that you're not alone," Abby concluded.

"Yeah. I think it's a lot different from when my mom was in school, and I wish she'd be more relaxed with me."

"Didn't she attend high school in the last century or something?" Abby teased, and they both giggled. Then they heard a knock at the door.

"How's it going in here?" Deputy Gomez asked and entered the bedroom.

"I'm a little better," Stevie answered truthfully.

"Your mom and Dustin said they're going to bed and agreed to let everybody sleep on it. Are you good with that plan?" the deputy asked.

"Yeah, that's fine. I'm wiped out, anyway."

"Try to relax, and maybe you'll have a better day tomorrow," Deputy Gomez suggested.

"In this house? Now who's the one that needs to go to the looney bin?" Stevie teased with a snarky tone and flashed a genuine smile, showing to both the deputy and Abby that she was going to be okay for now.

"All right, I like that you're not taking yourself too seriously," he told her with a chuckle. When she nodded in understanding, he continued in a more serious tone, "They're struggling to figure out how to parent a teenager, so it's not easy for them. I'm not saying it's easy for you either, but maybe you can give each other a little bit of slack. What do you say?"

Stevie nodded again, yawned, and then asked, "Did you tell that to them?"

"Oh yeah, I absolutely stressed that point. They need to pick their battles, and everybody needs to stop *trying* to make each other crazy. I know you're walking on eggshells around here, and they promised to do better. They recognize they're half the problem. Sometimes parents are trapped in survival mode."

"Okay," Stevie acknowledged. It would be a major milestone if her mom and Dustin saw her as *only half* of the problem.

4:05 a.m.

"I got the impression that Stevie was more depressed than suicidal, at least for now," Abby declared.

"Yeah, but you never know when it'll escalate to the next level. She's already had a suicide attempt," Deputy Gomez reminded.

"True. Do you get many calls like that?" Abby asked.

"Often enough. I'm not a psychologist, but you see patterns after witnessing enough of these situations in the heat of an emotional blowup."

"You mean the depression or being bipolar?"

"That's part of it. People tend to focus on what the teen is doing and thinking, but I believe you have to look beyond that and understand the environment they live in. I almost always see it in a two-parent household."

"Really? Isn't having two parents better?" Abby asked, intrigued by where the officer was going with his observations.

"Most of the time, yes, *assuming* they're good parents. However, sometimes, there is a micromanaging parent in the household who wants to rule over the entire family. That parent normally has a method of control, be it sports, academics, chores, finances, or other things. Obviously, when parents expect achievement, that's a good thing, but it can go too far."

"Like if they demand the impossible?"

"Exactly, such as requiring perfect grades or pushing them for a sports scholarship. It becomes dangerous when you have unattainable expectations in a family that appears perfect."

"But is far from perfect," Abby added.

"The grass is always greener somewhere else. But if people perceive a teen lives in an ideal situation, they naively assume there aren't any problems. But every family goes through difficult times and has issues."

"I know about that," Abby admitted.

"Yeah, so, if someone needs help from their peers, they may not get empathy because their friends can't understand why they have anything to complain about. This dismissal of the teen's problems makes them feel alone. The kid doesn't think anyone is on their side or on their team, so to speak. I think loneliness is a huge factor," he stated.

Abby nodded her head in agreement, processing what the deputy told her. "Yeah, if you feel isolated, you lose hope, and when that happens..." She trailed off.

"That's when you might hurt yourself," Deputy Gomez finished the sentence. "Single parents are too busy surviving to be overcontrolling. Of course, being a single parent brings on a unique set of challenges, so I'm not saying that's better.

Ultimately, it comes down to someone having the parenting skills and not whether you have a spouse."

"Yes, that makes sense."

"That's just one scenario. There can be lots of other factors of teen suicide, such as cyberbullying, the pressure to fit in socially, or drug use."

"Usually, it is a feeling of inadequacy at the root of the emotions," Abby told him without revealing the details of her own experiences.

"I agree. You're a bright kid," he complimented.

"Thanks," Abby awkwardly responded, but pleased she received the praise and guessed that Deputy Gomez only made favorable remarks when he meant it.

"What did you think of your first ride along?" Deputy Gomez asked as he pulled into the Albertson's parking lot where they met at the beginning of his shift. They both noticed Abby's car parked by itself under a lamppost.

"I wasn't sure what to expect. There were some intense moments."

"Yup, that'll happen."

"My friends will never believe when I tell them about everything I've seen tonight. They'll think I'm exaggerating."

"*You* know it's real. It's not what's portrayed in the media, all the *defund-the-police* talk."

"It's a lot more complicated than I thought."

"Yup," Deputy Gomez replied and left it at that.

After a few moments, she murmured, "I keep thinking about Stevie."

"She's in a tough situation. Unfortunately, I've seen it many times."

"I understand her. She could hit rock bottom while all alone in her bedroom."

"She could, but at least for tonight, she's safe. You were able to calm her down and were a big help to her. For the mom at the accident too. That's a gift," Gomez complimented, thankful that Abby accompanied him that night.

Sometimes, working in a rural county forces you to rely on whoever is available. She responded better than some adults and acted beyond her years.

"Thanks," she said, and all the evening's activities flooded her mind. After a few moments of silence, she asked, "Your shift is almost over. What if you get another call right now? What happens?"

"Then we have to go."

***

For more information about Officer David Gomez, visit: https://www.facebook.com/search/top/?q=officer%20gomez and his YouTube channel at: https://www.youtube.com/channel/UCXkte-5lPIcRHLvvEtYOB2A

For more information about an organization exposing the links between all forms of sexual abuse and exploitation, visit The National Center on Sexual Exploitation at https://www.endsexualexploitation.org.

The National Center for Missing and Exploited Children is the nation's largest and most influential child protection organization. They lead the fight to protect children, creating vital resources for them and the people who keep them safe (https://www.missingkids.org).

Information for parents on how to talk to your kids about rejecting pornography can be found at Defend Young Minds at https://www.defendyoungminds.com

Road to Purity's mission is to reveal to society the physical and spiritual devastation of pornography and sexual addiction while leading men and women to the truth of authentic love and sexual purity. Their vision is to eliminate the desolation resulting from sexual sin and to reveal that there is another way. Information about help with pornography and sexual addiction can be found at https://www.roadtopurity.com.

Content Warning

The author's intention is to accurately portray the real wounds of abortion. It also contains discussions of grief and the pain experienced from a child lost to miscarriage and abortion. Some readers may find portions of the story to be intense or distressing. The purpose wasn't to cause the reader to relive a personal trauma, but rather, to reveal authentic voices through an insider's experience so that others may heal. The author hopes you join the decades-long transformational journey of Dr. Catherine Wheeler.

Dr. Catherine Wheeler: Chapter 2— *The Pebble in My Shoe*

Part 1: *The Line in the Sand*, August 1989

"You're three weeks out from your due date. Everything looks good for both Mom and baby," I joyfully tell her with a smile.

"I wish it was done," Stella Korek answers. "I'm tired of being pregnant."

"Oh, I understand." This is the first time I've seen Stella frustrated during her pregnancy, so I remind her, "It will go faster than expected. You've been through this before."

"I know, I know. My first two were like this, but I hope my little girl will be easier."

"Each birth is different, so you never know. What's important is both of you are healthy," I explain. Even though she probably remembers from her previous pregnancies, I retell her, "I'll see you once a week until little Elaine arrives to meet her momma."

This is the first time I'm serving as Stella's doctor during her pregnancy, as I was in medical school in Louisiana when she had her previous children. I'm in my second year of residency, and Stella and Elaine are new patients. Well, they're all new at this stage of my career.

"I'm so excited to see what she looks like," Stella perks up and beams.

I return with a smile of my own. "Me too," I quickly return the enthusiasm. "You're an expert now. Pretty soon, I'll be telling you to *push*."

"My second baby was faster than my first, so maybe this one will be even faster. Although twelve hours of contractions and another two hours to push him out doesn't sound fast!" Stella jokes. She's not nervous at all.

This is the best part of being an obstetrician. I love watching the baby grow inside the womb and help bring new life into the world. I'll never forget the first time I placed a newborn, less than a minute old, into his smiling and exhausted mother's arms. That moment was magical and made all the years of schooling and long hours at the hospital worth it. *That's* why I became a doctor.

I'm loving the residency program at the University of Utah Medical Center. The miracle of birth is amazing, and I'm privileged to care for both mother and child. It's the ultimate human act that only a woman can do. I hope to never tire of seeing a child take its first breath of air.

"You have experience and are prepared. You know what to expect, and I'll be here for you every step of the way," I reassure her.

"It'll go fine," Stella states confidently. She's had a normal pregnancy so far, and there isn't any indication that will change.

"I think so, but we'll monitor you and your baby for the next three weeks. Notify me if you have any concerns or symptoms, like bleeding or reduced baby movement. You can call me day or night if you have questions or worries," I instruct her.

"I will. You have a kid, right?" Stella asks.

"Two boys, a four and a two-and-a-half-year-old," I tell her.

"Two young ones, that's a handful," Stella replies and blows out a loud breath, for she knows the workload when you have two children in diapers. It helps that Stella is a fit and energetic twenty-nine-year-old.

"You should know. Pretty soon, you'll have three kids under six years old."

"Tyler starts the first-grade next month, so that'll provide a little break." Stella repositions herself to sit up straight on the examining table. She brushes back her long, straight black hair, and I notice the pregnancy glow in her face.

"How's your back feeling?" I ask, knowing that although she stays in good shape, this pregnancy has strained her back more than her previous ones. I've been monitoring the situation for several weeks.

"It hurts every day," she answers and reaches around to rub her lower back.

"Have you tried those stretching exercises we talked about?"

"Yes, but they don't help much," she laughs with a strained look on her face.

"Well, keep trying," I tell her with a good-natured attitude. "Any questions for me?"

"Nope, I know the drill. I guess I'll see you next week."

"Yes, you take care of yourself and that precious little girl," I say and stand up to leave the examination room.

One more patient before lunch.

I enter another room to see Brigette Young. I'm not looking forward to this discussion. Last week, I received a call from the radiologist performing the ultrasound. The technician observed something concerning. My office is in the same building, so I went to assess the situation.

Brigette was lying down on the examination table, and I studied the display on the ultrasound machine. The fetus was about one and a half inches long and should be developed enough to detect its limbs. It didn't take long to verify what the radiologist was worried about.

I delivered the news to the forty-year-old mother that her eleven-week-old fetus appeared to have amniotic band syndrome. This is a condition when fiber-like bands wrap around a portion of the baby's body and restrict the blood flow. These bands come from the membrane that surrounds the baby and amniotic fluid.

In this circumstance, I didn't see the baby's left leg moving, and it's about half the size of the right leg. The result is significantly stunted growth and is a serious and irreversible congenital deformity.

When I saw the picture on the ultrasound, my heart sank, and I tried to hide my emotions. But maybe my facial expression told the story because she started crying before I had a chance to utter a word. Brigette was heartbroken and winced as I described what was happening to her baby. She's now had a week to think about what she wants to do.

"Hi, Brigette, how are you?" I ask in a somber tone, but I already know the answer. How could she be anything other than distressed? If she goes to term, she'll have a burden for life. If she terminates, well, that's a hard decision too.

"Hello, Dr. Wheeler," she replies, avoiding the answer about how she's doing.

"We talked last week and reviewed what we believe is going on with your baby. I know it is a lot to process. Tell me what you're thinking at this point?"

"It's *all* I've thought about. I have five kids already, and at my age and with my school schedule, I don't think I can do it," she explains to me, referring to her large family and going back to school to get her degree in accounting. But she doesn't need to justify her choice to me.

Last week, I sent her home with the information that I thought she would need. As a doctor, I'm required to provide my patients not just the best health care, but also *informed consent*, so if there's a medical decision to be made, she has all the facts. I presented her with a table of options. It's not my decision, so I didn't leave anything out.

"Okay, so if I'm hearing you correctly, you want to terminate the pregnancy. Is that right?" I ask for absolute clarity, and there is a moment of awkward silence.

"Yes," she answers softly.

Abortion is legal, so I suppose that makes it an acceptable option. As a doctor, I've decided to perform abortions *only* when there is a severe genetic anomaly or severe birth defect. I can't fully explain or pinpoint why performing elective abortions bothers me. I'm simply not comfortable. Maybe it was being brought up as the daughter of a minister, child number nine of eleven. I'm not sure why, but that's my line in the sand.

"I understand. We can schedule a procedure at the end of the week," I tell her without emotion. Doctors are not here to make moral judgements.

"Does it take long?" she quietly asks.

"No. I will dilate your cervix, which we'll start a day beforehand. I'll check it again before the surgery begins, and once it's properly dilated, the tissue removal takes about five minutes." There's only one patient to focus on, so I keep it simple. There's no need for lots of details.

"Oh, okay," she comments, a little less gloomy.

"It's called a dilation and curettage, a D&C. It's still surgery, so there are risks."

"Sure, of course," Brigette answers.

"Let's review them."

"Okay," she responds, and I can see her mind whirring. She looks down at the floor a moment and then asks, "What are the issues?"

"The risk of a complication is low. Bleeding, infection, and incomplete removal of tissue are possible risks. The ultrasound machine will provide a detailed picture to help ensure I get everything out. Tearing the cervix during the procedure can affect future pregnancies, resulting in preterm birth or miscarriage."

"Wow, that's a lot!" she says, and I can see anxiety forming across her face.

"There are many things that can go wrong, but the chances are low. I know it sounds scary, but these are unlikely to occur," I inform her.

"I see."

"There are other rare problems, such as having a complication from anesthesia, but I've never seen that happen. It's possible the uterine wall could be perforated. We'll monitor you for heavy bleeding or other signs. If it's perforated, it may need to be repaired, but again, that's extremely rare," I confidently tell her.

"But you said this is a common procedure, right?"

"It is, and I've performed it many times. It's probably hard to hear all the ways the surgery can go wrong, but I want to be honest and fully disclose the possibilities so you can make a good decision for yourself," I tell her truthfully. Doctors perform D&Cs frequently for various reasons, although the risks are greater when ending a pregnancy. But it's not considered a *risky* surgery.

"I understand. Will I be put under a long time?"

"No, there'll be an anesthesiologist, two nurses, and the ultrasound technician who will watch my instruments on the screen to help guide me. We'll take care of you," I assure her.

Twenty-Six Minutes Later

"Dr. Wheeler."

I look up to see Dr. Esslinger, and she's holding a tray with her lunch. We're in the hospital cafeteria.

"Won't you join me?" I ask. She immediately sits down. Dr. Esslinger is a lovely woman about forty years old and was one of the first OB-GYN female doctors in Utah. She's also a professor, and I have a great deal of respect and fondness for her.

"How are you, Catherine?"

"I'm fine," I say without conviction, and she immediately picks up on it.

"Hmmm, really?" she asks with genuine interest.

"I just had a discussion with a patient who's pregnant with a severe birth anomaly," I tell her.

"Yes, that's difficult, but it happens sometimes," she says with an understanding tone. She's been my mentor since I started residency, and I know she'll provide logical and compassionate advice without me asking. I don't mind.

"I hate to see a woman put in that difficult situation," I reply and momentarily flash back to the look on Brigette's face. It's hard to shake the image of a scared, pregnant woman.

"What is she going to do?" Dr. Esslinger asks in a kind-hearted tone.

"D&C."

"Sometimes women face hard choices. Is she single?"

"Yes, she divorced several years ago."

"Life is harder for women than for men. Men leave a lot of the time, and women have no choice but to pick up the pieces," she says and then adds, "You know the difficulties of being a single mom."

I nod in understanding. Dr. Esslinger knows that my husband left me, and I'm raising two young children.

Luckily, I had family members to help care for the kids while I finished medical school at Tulane.

"Our job as doctors is to listen and do the right thing when the patient decides how to proceed," Dr. Esslinger continues.

"Yes, I agree. Society sometimes puts women in a box. They're not given a lot of choices for control over their lives," I tell her.

"Exactly. Women are forced to be tough sometimes. And we women should stick together, right?" she adds.

"Yes, especially us female doctors," I agree, referring to the fact that the hospital is mostly comprised of male doctors, many with religious convictions. My experience with religion was the constant focus on rules with rigid thinking, especially regarding females.

"Exactly. Women need the ability to provide for themselves. That's why we support their decisions. I care about them and want to help my patients navigate the hard choices they face without judgement," she continues in a tender but clinical manner.

I always appreciated Dr. Esslinger's way of supporting women in a variety of circumstances and medical decisions. But I'm still a little uneasy about performing an abortion, even on a child with an anomaly. Before medical school and residency, I honestly didn't think too deeply about the abortion issue. I care about women too, so that's why I'm helping my patient.

I'm not sure what I would've done if one of my children had a similar situation. It's a lifelong load to carry, and I wouldn't want that. What kind of life is that for the family? For the child?

"It's a tough choice, and I'm glad that I'm not the one making it," I tell her.

"It's not your job to think for them. The patient is educated to make an informed decision. You're trained to perform a surgery, and that's all there is to it. You take care of your patient," she reiterates.

"I will," I answer, knowing I'll do everything to provide Brigette the best health care.

"You're a fine doctor and have a heart for women. Now is when your patient needs compassion. You attend to the person in front of you and remember that it's a privilege to care for women."

Three Days Later

The patient is asleep. I hear the unmistakable sound of a heartbeat on the ultrasound machine. The screen displays the placenta and the baby's position. I see hand and leg movement. Everything looks as I expect.

I see the tissue clearly and focus on the task that needs to be done. It's not time for emotion; it's time to focus on my patient. I've predilated her cervix and usually don't need to further expand it. I check, and it's sufficiently dilated.

The cannula tube is attached to a vacuum suction machine. I slowly and with precision bring the cannula past the cervix and into her uterus. It's normal to see a gradual amount of bleeding. I need to be quick, efficient, and careful to minimize the bleeding. A pregnant uterus has an incredible amount of blood flow to sustain the fetus.

I watch the ultrasound to ensure the cannula doesn't perforate the uterine wall. I'm meticulous because the uterus is very soft, and I want to minimize any damage. Five minutes later, I'm finished. I recheck the ultrasound machine, and the technician tells me the uterine lining is thin. This confirms my work is complete.

The tissue is gone.

Part 2: *Humpty Dumpty*, Four Years Later, July 1993

"I'm not going to do it, so you'll have to find someone else," Dr. Fred Carlini tells me emphatically. Actually, it is more than that. He *is defiant*. My jaw involuntarily drops slightly. The lead nurse tells me he backed out, and I rush down the hall to find out what is going on.

"I don't understand. You're the assigned anesthesiologist for this procedure," I respond and feel my stomach tighten from stress. "The patient is ready to be wheeled into the operating room." The doctor scrunches his brow, and the jaw tightens on this late forty-something man whom I've always had a good relationship with, so I'm a little confused.

"Like I said, you'll need to find a different anesthesiologist. I don't take part in abortions," he bluntly affirms, and the words hang in the air. He's sitting in his chair staring at me, and I know my eyes plead for him to reconsider, but *his* gaze tells me the opposite. He isn't going to change his mind. I'm flustered *and* frustrated because I haven't had a last-minute substitution with another doctor before.

"Okay, I'll see if Dr. Gleeson can come in," I relent after a few seconds. I have no other choice but to delay surgery by forty-five minutes. I'm not going to argue with him about it. I can't figure out what's wrong with him. I've never sensed any attitude from him that he doesn't like or want to support women.

I ask the supervising nurse to find Dr. Gleeson, one of the other anesthesiologists on staff at our small hospital. I've been in private practice for over a year, and several doctors have offices in the same building, including myself. It's convenient, and I'm affiliated with the hospital and perform procedures here. But now I need to tell my patient about the delay. I dread the conversation; I hope there isn't a huge negative reaction.

"Carla, I'm so sorry, but we're not quite ready. We're waiting for one more team member," I inform her.

"Oh no, it's not canceled, is it?" she asks.

"No, you just relax and hopefully we'll get started in less than an hour," I say, trying to be positive, effectively telling her *it's no big deal.* She nods her head in understanding but is clearly unhappy.

But it's a big deal to me, making an anesthesiologist switch at the last minute. My patient, forty-six-year-old Carla Tahara, is pregnant with a Down syndrome child. As was customary with anyone at her age, I recommended an amniocentesis.

I typically gather a sample of the amniotic fluid from around the baby. We tested the chromosomes for genetic anomalies because the risk is higher for pregnant women over thirty-five years old. The results came in a week ago. Sadly, she's conceived a Down baby. Well, not for much longer because she's decided to end her pregnancy, and she's scheduled for surgery this morning.

During the office visit last week, I informed Carla about various local support groups and encouraged her to talk to them about what it's like having a child with Down syndrome. We discussed the symptoms, behaviors, and learning challenges; however, it was more from a medical perspective rather than a family dynamic. Later in the pregnancy, an ultrasound can be performed to check for specific Down syndrome anomalies. I've had other patients that chose to carry their child with Down syndrome, but that's not the case with Carla.

D&C is not possible since the fetus is halfway through the pregnancy and as big as a mango. Put candidly, the baby is too far developed; the head is too big, and its bones are too strong to be removed by a vacuum suction device. The uterus is nearly up to her belly button and is progressively getting larger. I'm trained to perform a second trimester abortion, a D&E procedure, and that's what I recommended. The D&E refers to dilation and evacuation.

Although it's a longer and more involved procedure than a D&C, I didn't see the point of going into the step-by-step process with Carla. I told her we simply remove the pregnancy tissue and the placenta. She didn't need to hear the gory details of what will happen to her baby.

We also discussed some aftereffects and risks. It's common to experience mild bleeding or spotting for the first two weeks and a cramp-like feeling, similar to a menstrual cycle. These contractions last several days, which indicates the uterus is shrinking and is getting back to its nonpregnant size.

I informed her about the risks of the D&E surgery, which is higher than a D&C. Both the baby and the uterus are bigger and thus require larger instruments to reach the top of the uterus, just below her belly button. The removal is more complex and takes longer. The cervix or uterus can get damaged during the procedure, which may lead to heavy bleeding.

I presented her options and rights and gave her a couple of days to think about it or come back for more questions. Lingering too long is risky with a growing baby. I told Carla that I'm experienced in the procedure, and a well-trained team will assist me. She chose to terminate, and here we are.

Luckily, Dr. Gleeson's available and is assigned to the surgery. We move my patient to the operating room. Dr. Gleeson arrives and sets up Carla's intravenous catheter. An oxygen mask is placed over Carla's mouth and nose, and I attach several pieces of equipment to her body to monitor her vitals throughout the surgery, such as her heart rate, blood pressure, and oxygen level.

Everything is in place, and Dr. Gleeson administers the anesthesia through the mask. I make idle chitchat with Carla as the anesthesia also starts through the intravenous drip.

She's soon out like a light. One nurse moves her into position while I scrub. The other nurse helps me with my gown and gloves; I'm ready.

The ultrasound technician will be present for the entire procedure and shows me the baby, which is about six inches long, and its heartbeat is strong and regular, churning out 150 beats per minute. Carla is showing, and the mother can usually feel the baby kick by now.

The child's brain is developing rapidly, and the baby has already learned how to suck and swallow. At this stage, the baby is developing its first needed survival skill: breathing. While in the womb, it breathes in amniotic fluid rather than air, and this *practice* helps develop the lungs. What I can't see is the pattern of swirls and creases on the baby's finger. This one-of-a-kind pattern will exist throughout the person's life. The fingerprints.

The time has come to focus and carry out the procedure. Emotion shuts off, and I concentrate on performing the D&E to ensure that complications and surprises are avoided.

I check with Dr. Gleeson, who tells me that Carla is properly anesthetized, which is the green light to begin. It's a small operating room, clean and sterile. The lights are bright, and the team is ready. Up until the woman goes into labor, the cervix is tightly closed to keep infections out and to maintain the baby inside the uterus. A closed cervix prevents a premature birth. Because it's constricted, the cervix needs to be dilated slowly.

To prepare my patient's cervix, I typically use an osmotic dilator called a laminaria the day before the surgery. I placed this in Carla's cervical canal, and it absorbs moisture and gradually expands. This is an important step because solely using mechanical dilation is riskier and may damage the cervix, increasing the likelihood of a future second trimester miscarriage and the risk of a preterm birth.

I next ask a nurse for a weighted speculum, which is a medical device, to pull back the back wall of the vagina.

I need to stabilize the cervix using an instrument called a tenaculum, and I inspect it. It needs to be dilated a little more. To do this, I insert a third tool, a metal dilator. I gradually use a series of larger dilators to stretch the cervix to the adequate dilation.

I pause for a moment each time to allow the tools to do their job. The ultrasound technician is watching and displays my instruments entering the uterine cavity. I check to ensure they're properly placed and aren't causing any damage. Everything looks good.

The fetus is housed in the uterus above the cervix. A sufficiently dilated cervix is required for the evacuation. That's an odd term, the E in D&E. Evacuation implies an *escape to safety*, yet that's the opposite of what's happening to the baby. But I block out *that* line of thinking. I refocus, and a few minutes later, Carla's ready. I'll be using a combination of suction and forceps, which are like clamps, to empty the uterus. In residency, they referred to this as *removing the pregnancy tissue*.

Now the *evacuation* part begins. First, the cannula is attached to the suction device, and I insert it into my patient's vagina and past the cervix. I suction out some of the amniotic fluid, which cushions the fetus while it floats within the amniotic sac. The fluid constantly circulates as the fetus inhales, swallows, and eventually urinates it out.

The fluid removal stabilizes the baby, so it doesn't move too much; otherwise, it is difficult to grasp with the instruments. This only takes a few minutes. When a woman is about to give birth and her *water breaks*, the amniotic sac is what's broken, and the fluid leaks out.

The fetus is too large and developed to suction it out entirely, so it must be removed in pieces with the sopher ovum forceps. This tool is typically over a foot long and is made of stainless steel and looks like a large set of pliers. It's this size because that's how far inside her body I need to go, long enough to reach near the top of the uterus. The nose of the clamp is rounded and has ridges, *like rows of teeth*, to provide a better grip and less slippage. At this stage of a pregnancy, the baby is frequently positioned such that the feet are closest to the cervix. This is the case with Carla's child.

With the baby in a breech position, feet first, its body parts will need to be removed, *piece by piece*. I place the clamp through the cervix and grab a foot. A leg is better, so I reposition the clamp. I notice the arms and legs flailing about, like it's trying to escape. Perhaps the baby knows what I'm doing and is attempting to *evacuate*. I involuntarily blink and push the nonmedical thoughts out of my head.

I notice its heartbeat speeds up to a rapid pace, which I expected. After another try, I successfully grasp its leg. I have a firm grip and pull. I can see that half of the leg is past the cervix. Essentially, I've started pulling the baby out of the uterus toward the birth canal. This is what I want.

With greater force and a slight twist of my wrist, I tug again and sense the resistance dissipate. The leg has been removed from its body. While still gripping the leg, I pull it completely out and carefully place it on the tray. There's blood dripping from the clamp. The nurse carefully uses a sponge to remove the leg. I replace the forceps inside the uterus.

After the second leg has been dismembered, I review the ultrasound, and the technician presents the body part closest to the cervix, so that's what I extract next. An arm proves a little more difficult to grip. I make another attempt, carefully watching the ultrasound as the instrument enters, to avoid puncturing the uterine wall.

Finally, I grasp one arm and slowly and deliberately increase the pressure on the fetus until I feel the arm detach from the torso. Again, I place the part on the tray. I repeat the process for the second arm. I barely notice the baby's heart has stopped.

The head is usually the most difficult part to *evacuate* and can roll around like a tennis ball. The skull is comprised of shifting plates of bone, softer and not completely developed compared to a newborn. But it's rigid enough.

It needs to be crushed.

At eighteen weeks, the head is the size of a plum. It's too big to make it past the cervix, so I widen the clamp as much as possible and grab the skull. I firmly apply pressure and strength to crush the skull, and I can feel a small vibration in my hand from the bone cracking like a walnut. It's inaudible to the medical team, so only *I know it's now obliterated.*

A white substance is leaking out of the cervix, confirming that it's the baby's brain. That's how I know the skull was sufficiently flattened and is in pieces. I'm almost done. I'll admit to you, I'm struggling to block out the true meaning of a baby's brain leaking out of the mother's body, but I successfully push any emotion out of my head.

The skull is still in my clamp, and I slowly twist it and remove the instrument and again place the body part on the tray.

The torso is next, and I concentrate on being quick, efficient, and careful because the blood flow continues to accelerate. I grasp it and again place the body part on the tray. I arrange it in the shape of a person. As expected, there's lots of blood on the clamp. There's also blood on my hands, and even though I am wearing surgical gloves, my fingers itch, and I feel the need to remove the glove.

But I don't; I go back to work.

I need to remove the placenta, which is healthy and well-attached. In the case where the baby has died in utero, the placenta would start to disintegrate, like a plant deprived of water. But Carla's placenta is performing exactly as I expected. Her baby was growing normally. Well, except for the Down syndrome part, that is.

Any remaining pieces and the placenta are suctioned out. I start at the top of the uterus and gradually rotate the device to remove anything. Next, I use a sharp curette and gently move the instrument down the uterine wall to feel for any remaining fragments. As the final part of the procedure, I reinsert the suction cannula to ensure the uterus is totally empty. The ultrasound displays the entire length of the uterus, and *everything is gone.*

I look at the tray and see the pieces. Intellectually, I know these are baby parts, but I won't allow myself to think deeper than this factual and medical observation. To ensure nothing is left in the uterus, the nurse arranges the body parts to resemble a human. It's like putting together the pieces of a puzzle.

I account for the head, two arms, two legs, the chest, back, and abdomen. It's all there. Anything left in the uterus could cause additional bleeding or an infection. I gaze down at the parts, and he looks like a miniature doll that's been taken apart.

But like Humpty Dumpty, neither myself, the nurses, all the king's horses and all the king's men will be able to put the baby back together again.

The nurse accounts for the sponges and instruments to ensure that nothing remains in the patient's body. The procedure is complete and successful.

Still focused, I now assess any risks or adverse effect on Carla. I was careful not to perforate the uterus or lacerate the cervix. If the cervix is lacerated, it could mean future pregnancies wouldn't be able to go to term. The muscle and connective tissue of the cervix are like a drawstring, and if it doesn't stay closed, a future baby can literally fall out of the uterus because the cervical opening is too large.

The most common complication is hemorrhaging, or excessive bleeding. Carla seems fine, but I'll monitor her situation and inform her of what to expect in the next week. We were in the operating room for a mere thirty minutes.

I step back to allow a nurse to clean the patient. My medical-only focus fades, and my stomach tightens as I observe the scene in front of me. The anesthesiologist is checking on Carla, who will probably wake up in about five minutes.

She'll transfer to a recovery room and about an hour later will be alert enough to be discharged from the hospital. A different nurse retrieves the instruments, cleans them, and places them in the sterilization machine. I can't keep my eyes off the baby parts, neatly arranged.

I keep my heart closed and push the emotion away. I'm slightly nauseous, and it's difficult to breathe. Maybe it's because of the mask I'm wearing. But if I'm being honest with you, it isn't the mask that's left me rattled. I know *what it is,* and I can't allow myself to think the *words*, let alone tell you about them.

I recall Dr. Carlini and his absolute refusal to be part of the abortion procedure. He was so *sure* of his decision. There was no doubt in his mind or the look on his face. There was only conviction and disdain in his voice. Although I was unhappy about a last-minute change with my medical team, deep down I admire the strong adherence to his principles.

I respected him previously, for he is a good doctor and seems like a genuinely nice person. I'm affiliated with this relatively small hospital, so we work with each other all the time. Everyone gets along, and there's a lot of mutual respect among us, including the staff. It's a great place to work, and the last thing I want to do is upset that harmony.

I can't shake the bad feeling that I've let a colleague down. To make matters worse, we had the conflict in front of the nurses. The only thing that would truly make it more embarrassing would be if his ardent refusal was on display in front of the patient. Luckily, he's a professional, and it wasn't within earshot of Carla or any other patients.

I reassess my position. I don't think he hates women and doesn't want to help them; he simply doesn't want to be part of an abortion. His reaction is forcing me to think deeper about performing the procedure. He likely didn't know about the baby's Down syndrome, but it wouldn't have made a difference. He was clearly very uncomfortable. He had an aversion to being part of the surgery team.

No, it was more than that. The look on his face, his body language, and tone of voice were unmistakable. There was no doubt in his mind or heart. The thought of helping me perform the abortion was *nauseating*. Is that how he feels about me as a doctor? My stomach is in a knot because I wonder if he's also repulsed by me as a *person*. I'll grant you this much; I guarantee Dr. Carlini has thought about the moral implications more than I have. I don't feel guilty that I haven't gone deep into the issue; I just haven't.

But maybe I should.

I don't want to ruin a pleasant workplace, and I honestly don't know how the other doctors feel about performing abortions. What about the nurses? They're in the operation room with a bird's eye view of the procedure. Removing limbs can't be easy to watch. I only did this because that's what the patient wanted.

I needed to turn off my empathy for the baby while I performed the abortion. It's like when I was in medical school, and we dissected a cadaver. Not long ago, that *body* was a living, breathing human, someone's family member, and I had to block out those thoughts during a classroom dissection.

I remove my gown and gloves and wash up when a horrible thought jumps into my head. Who are you kidding, Catherine? The cadaver's dead, but the baby wasn't. It was healthy, purely innocent, and *could* have been born. That's not a fair comparison.

Maybe this part of my practice isn't worth it. Perhaps I should step back from doing any future abortions. But the thoughts rattling around in my brain tell me it's *more* than just my desire for a harmonious workplace. It's *more* than not wanting to have a conflict with Dr. Carlini or anyone else. I know in my heart that it goes beyond that, but I'm not ready to *go there* with my thoughts and emotions.

I take a deep breath and watch the nurse take the body parts away. They are now considered medical waste and a hazardous material and will later be incinerated. It's at that moment that I decide never to do another abortion. Not a D&C. Not a D&E. There are plenty of clinics that I can refer my patients to. I won't tell them they *can't* have an abortion. But *I won't* be the doctor performing it. I've drawn another line in the sand.

395 Days Later, September 1994

My private practice is thriving, and I'm generally happy with how I've established myself in Utah. Being an OB-GYN is rewarding, except for the part about dealing with the insurance companies. I've remarried and have four kids now, and my husband and I are busy raising the family. Today's a typical Wednesday, but the events at work will set in motion a moment which will change my life.

"Something is going on with Taylor," my office assistant Charlene tells me before I enter the patient's room.

"Did she say what it is?"

"No, not exactly. Her mom is with her, and they both look as if they've been crying."

"Okay, thanks for the heads-up," I tell her. A teenage patient can be upset about a myriad of issues, so before I let my mind get too far ahead, I decide to find out what it is and enter the room.

Taylor and her mother Naomi are visibly distraught. The teen sits on the exam table while Naomi stands by the chair, too anxious to sit. Naomi's eyes are puffy and red, a stark color contrast to her ash white face, making her skin look ghost-like. But unlike ghosts that are meant to scare people, *she's* the one who looks scared.

I take a seat on the small round stool and roll toward them. Naomi sits in the chair. Her shoulder-length dark brown hair is drawn back in a long ponytail, and I immediately notice her right leg slightly bouncing up and down from stress and nervousness. The thirty-seven-year-old mother of three is out of her element.

Taylor, her oldest and only daughter, appears to be in no better condition. She's sixteen and has been my patient since thirteen. She's a pretty girl with long flowing hair to match her mother and is a starter on her school volleyball team. I've enjoyed watching her grow up. But her makeup and trendy designer clothes can't hide the facial expression that tells me she's under high duress and drama. She looks drained, emotionally and physically. Whatever it is, it's commanded her full attention.

"Good morning," I say to both of them, but they are in no mood for cheerful small talk.

"Dr. Wheeler, we have a situation," Naomi starts the conversation. Before she can continue, Taylor bursts out crying. Her voice is wailing and unclear, making it difficult to understand her.

I take a deep breath, and they follow my lead to pause the discussion. "Okay, let's talk about what's going on," I suggest.

"She's pregnant," Naomi blurts out, which sends Taylor into another fit of crying. Her nose is running, and I feel sorry for the teen. Her face is flushed, and her breathing is erratic. I stay quiet, giving her a few seconds to compose herself.

I hand her a tissue, and she quickly uses it, but requires another, so I give her the entire box. I wait for another few moments. Taylor blows her nose and wipes her eyes to reveal the face of someone fearful of the unknown. The best way to describe what I'm seeing is that she's *traumatized*. But first, I need to determine the facts.

"We'll need to run a test. When was your last period?"

"I'm a month late," she moans and makes a feeble attempt to hold back more tears.

"That doesn't necessarily mean you're pregnant. There are lots of things that cause a late menstruation," I calmly tell her. I'm about to go into the many reasons that affect a young woman's cycle, such as stress or intense athletic activity, when Naomi digs into her purse and pulls out three home pregnancy tests.

They all look the same.

They each have two lines.

She's pregnant.

The drugstore tests are pretty accurate, so I look at her and say, "I want to use our lab to be sure, but you have three with the same result, so it's probably correct. We'll do a urine test to confirm it. When you're pregnant, your cervix starts to soften, so I can check for that and the size of your uterus to determine how far along you are."

"Yes, you do your own test, but we know that she's... pregnant," Naomi states.

"Obviously, this was unexpected," I gently say to Taylor, and then I must ask her a question she's probably not expecting. "Was the sex consensual?"

Taylor silently nods, but Naomi gasps at my question. I then notice she also gestures her understanding. Everything would have gotten more complicated if she was raped. I've also had some patients assaulted while intoxicated.

"It was with my boyfriend," she clarifies. I haven't prescribed her birth control, and I was unaware that she was sexually active.

"I'm also going to check you for any STDs, like gonorrhea and chlamydia," I notify her in my most tender voice. No matter how soothing I try to communicate, I know this is adding salt to the wound. But these are necessary steps.

"What? This can't get any worse," Naomi cries out.

"Mom, I don't think I have *anything*," Taylor moans loudly, and her face flushes with embarrassment.

"*Thinking* isn't what you were doing," Naomi jabbed at her daughter, which doesn't help. The teen hadn't considered the potential consequences of her actions. I look at Taylor with tenderness and understanding. Naomi opens her mouth as if she was going to start talking again but decides against it.

"Do you mind waiting in the lobby for a few minutes while I check her out?" I state more as an instruction than a question.

Naomi stands up and mutters, "Sure." She opens the door and heads out.

"How are you doing with all of this?" I ask the teen.

"Not great. I don't know how this happened. I mean, *I know how it happened*, but I can't believe that it happened *to me*."

"Have you had other sexual partners?"

"No," Taylor answers and looks away, obviously not wanting to make eye contact.

"Were you using any form of protection?"

"*Sometimes* we used a condom," Taylor admits. As doctors, we're trained to hide expression, so I reflexively don't show any judgment.

"I understand."

"I guess it should have been every time," she laments, stating the obvious.

A conversation with my mentor, Dr. Esslinger, from residency comes to mind immediately. She informed me about new products that are long-acting, easy to use, and effective. Unwanted pregnancy would be an infrequent occurrence because these contraceptives, like IUDs and implants, have a high-efficacy rate. No patient responsibility is required, unlike taking a daily pill.

At the time, I connected the dots and assumed fewer abortions would be needed, hence the *rare* in the pro-choice, safe, legal, and rare mantra. Of course, you must use the contraception for it to work.

At her last appointment, I asked Taylor whether she was sexually active or thought she might be. She said she wasn't, but I reiterated things could happen between appointments and recommended not making any hasty decisions. I told her to come and see me if her circumstances changed. I have lots of literature on contraceptives, and condoms can be purchased just about anywhere.

But teens don't always make well-thought-out choices. That was last year, and I haven't seen her since, until today. I guess her plans changed, and I wish she would've talked to me about it. Teens frequently think the risks *they take* are low, and unwanted pregnancy and STDs only happen to *someone else.*

Unfortunately, our modern society encourages sex for immediate pleasure with the promise of absolutely no consequence. I'm not a prude, but if anyone mentions teaching abstinence education, you're looked at like a crazy person.

No one teaches the emotional impact of a sexual relationship. Most teens never think their heart will be broken. Or worse, regretting it and feeling used or devalued. It's not clear how Taylor feels about that part, but now is not the right time, so I refocus back on my patient.

"Okay, let's check you out," and I ask her to lie down on the table. She's already in an examination gown. I don't see any visible signs of an STD. The pelvic exam shows a softening cervix, and her uterine size is consistent with a six-to-seven-week pregnancy.

"What about the father?" I ask in a warm voice.

"Jason? He *freaked out* when I told him and wants nothing to do with me now," she exclaimed, and gets more agitated. "He broke up with me."

"That happens sometimes."

"I don't want to ruin his life too," she casually states.

"Is it okay if your mom rejoins us?" I ask, and Taylor nods. "Are you comfortable about sharing the results of your exam?"

Taylor approves, and a minute later, Naomi comes back into the room, and I repeat what I told Taylor. Naomi is relieved.

"The lab requires forty-eight hours for the STD tests. I didn't see any signs, so the risk is low, but we'll follow up when we get the results." There's no easy way around it. I can't yet confirm to Naomi that the STD worry is over. She wiggles her jaw, and her entire face becomes taut. She nods her head in acceptance, clearly communicating that she doesn't want to talk about it further.

"Taylor also needs a prenatal blood test, and we should get her scheduled for an ultrasound in the next few days," I suggest. With the likely scenario that Taylor is pregnant, we have a lot to talk about. But I never get a chance to get into any specifics.

"The other reason we're here is to get the termination scheduled," Naomi announces. She's no longer sidetracked by tests and the talk of STDs.

"You want an abortion?" I ask Taylor, and she cries again and nods her head. "It sounds like you've made up your mind."

"She has," Naomi answers for her daughter.

"I know it's a tough decision for you," I respond, but don't add anything because I'm not sure what else to say.

"Yeah," she answers, her stress still evident.

"Assuming your pregnancy test comes back positive, and based on everything we know, you're in the first trimester. That means a D&C to terminate the pregnancy. I have a brochure that provides some explanation. It's a common procedure that doesn't take long, but it is still surgery, which always has an element of risk," I explain and hand a pamphlet to both Taylor and her mom, and we review the preop procedures.

"So when can this be done?" Naomi asks. She doesn't want to look at brochures or have a discussion. She's focused on the outcome and adds, "I want my daughter to get her life back." Naomi clearly views the pregnancy as a heavy burden. Taylor stops crying and is maintaining control over her emotions.

"Probably within a week or so. I'm going to refer you to a clinic," I say and start to write down the names of two places they can contact.

"Can't you do it?" Taylor asks with surprise.

"I don't perform abortions anymore," I tell her with no intention of explaining *why*.

"Oh no, we don't want to go to *a clinic*. We don't know them," Naomi categorically rejects my referral. Neither one expected to go someplace else.

"I want you," Taylor says and starts to cry again. Her fear level jumps up a notch, which I distinctly see in her eyes. She recoils from the thought of going to a strange doctor in a strange clinic. It's a place that I'm sure she only wants to visit once.

"The clinic is well-known in the area," I counter; yet, it's a meager attempt.

"I can't stand the thought of taking my daughter to someplace like that. It would be too hard for her." Naomi has thought about their next steps. I'm guessing it's all she's been thinking about, and going to an abortion clinic was not part of the plan. I get it; she's advocating for her daughter's well-being.

"They do these procedures all the time."

"You have to be the one!" Naomi declares. She's a little forceful and sure of her request. "Please," she adds.

I get the feeling she is going to make her case.

"You know us, and we *trust you*. I don't want Taylor treated like a *number* at some strange clinic."

"You've been my doctor since the eighth grade," Taylor points out.

"Yes," Naomi agrees. "You should be the one who takes care of my daughter. You know her. She's a straight A student, and we need this procedure done right. She can't ruin her life at sixteen. Taylor needs to get back on track," she repeats. "It has to be you."

"I'm not going anywhere else," Taylor announces.

I'm feeling the pressure from both mother and daughter. Naomi continues raising her points, as if we're having a debate.

"She needs to study for the PSAT and is in several honors classes, even biology. You know she wants to be a doctor like you," Naomi reminds me, and I remember Taylor previously telling me about her aspirations. I retold her some memorable stories from medical school. I know she's a bright and ambitious girl, and we've always had a good doctor-patient relationship.

"I can't have my doctor be someone I don't know," Taylor implores.

"She may not finish high school on time. How can she attend college and medical school while raising a child?" Naomi asks, justifying her request.

"Perhaps you need some time to think about this," I deflect. Honestly, I want this uncomfortable discussion to end.

"No, we're on the same page on this," Naomi states, and Taylor also nods her head, assuring me that she and her mother are a united front.

Both Taylor and Naomi were among my first patients. Normally, I would hold my ground and refer them to the clinic, but this is different. I genuinely like Naomi and Taylor, and they are practically begging me. Although this is a purely elective abortion procedure, I decide to relent.

"Okay, we can get you scheduled for an early morning procedure on Tuesday or Wednesday of next week.

"Thank you," Naomi says, and I can feel the tension dissipate from the room. I feel temporarily relieved.

"Wait here. I'm going to look at my schedule."

While heading to the front desk, I remember Naomi's words about raising a child during medical school. It *is possible* to do. After all, *I did it.* I could've told them *my story.* Yes, it was a struggle at times, but I love my children, and it'd be hard to envision my life without them. I can't imagine my life without ever knowing them. Not only is that unfathomable, but it's also distressing to think of this world without my children in it. It's possible to pursue professional dreams as a young mother, and I could have explained how. I wouldn't tell her it's *easy,* but being pregnant isn't the end of your life.

I never planned to have kids or get married. But life has a way of happening while you're busy making other arrangements. You may know the old saying, "If you want to hear God laugh, tell Him your plans."

As a child, I didn't dream of growing up, getting married, and having a family. I even made a pact with one of my sisters that neither one of us would get married. We talked about all the adventures we would have. It was going to be an amazing life. Clearly, that pact fell apart. But I have an amazing life, just not in the way I imagined when I was younger.

When I found myself pregnant, I was already married. I was on birth control, but during my pharmacy class, I learned about the many risks, so I stopped taking the pill. The next thing I know, I'm pregnant. I never considered not having my son, but I remember feeling scared like Taylor. I was in my second year of medical school, wondering, *How was I going to do this*?

When I first found out, I still managed to make it to my microbiology lab on time. I was crying so hard that my best friend Leslie repeatedly asked, "What's wrong?" I was so upset that I couldn't answer her. "Is it cancer?" she asked.

"No, it's worse. I'm pregnant," I told her. I was very fearful and upset at that moment. I'd heard how awful pregnancy could be and that *modern women* should delay childbirth. Of course, they never told anyone that having children later in life involves more risks.

Without saying it expressly, it seemed they were pounding the message for women like me to avoid being saddled with a child. Focus on a career, they would tell me. You need a means to take care of yourself, so your career should be the priority. And there I was, a young pregnant woman who hadn't started her career.

A couple of days later, I had an epiphany. I surprised myself because I went from complete despair of how my life would change to *loving* this baby growing inside me. I felt this unwavering belief that motherhood is what I was created for. My life *was going to change*, I remember joyfully thinking. Even though the attitude and outlook turnaround happened quickly, I never looked back or felt hopeless. I never saw my pregnancy as a problem that needed to be solved. Could Taylor feel the same way? Could Naomi?

Being pregnant didn't ruin my life, and motherhood became a priority. It turned out to be a good thing! My friend Leslie was so positive. She kept saying, "It's going to be wonderful." She constantly told me about all the amazing things that I was going to *get to* experience. At fifteen weeks, I was feeling him move already. It was the most delightful thing. The gloom and impossibility of being pregnant were long gone.

My parents were so excited, and I received a lot of positive encouragement. I took a few months off from school after his birth. When I entered medical school, I originally wanted to be a hand surgeon, but after the birth of my first son, I decided during my third-year clinical rotation to become an OB-GYN. To make that a reality, I needed help, and my parents suggested that my younger sister move in to assist with taking care of the baby. It was difficult for my sister because she was alone with my son for long hours and days. My parents retired and moved to Louisiana to help.

Mom and Dad had eleven children, and they picked up their lives and move to another state *for me*. I was awestruck. I had my second son while in my fourth and last year of medical school. After graduation, I relocated to Utah for the residency program, and my parents moved to West Virginia to take care of my elderly grandfather.

We were both working, so I hired a nanny, but my relationship with my husband didn't improve, and he left during my second year of residency. So I understand what it's like not to have the baby's father involved with raising the children. I can see why Taylor is scared. I want to tell her that maybe you can't have everything, but you can have the important things in life.

But Taylor's closest family member, her mother, wants nothing to do with her daughter's pregnancy. I appreciate I was married and in my midtwenties, and she is only sixteen, and having an encouraging support system is vital to successfully raising a child if you're on your own.

But it's not my place to inject any judgments or give them my personal experiences and opinions. I had a support system to help me through medical school. She had a hard choice to make, and she made it. Naomi is on board with the termination. She doesn't see or doesn't want to see another way.

I've gone back on my promise to myself about performing any more abortions, especially an elective one like Taylor's. There wasn't a rape, and there's no genetic defect or anomaly. But I assured my patient that I'm going to take care of her, and that's what I'm going to do. I schedule Taylor for the procedure after the Labor Day holiday.

I've again moved the line in the sand.

Tuesday Morning

It is a gorgeous late summer day. The blue sky seems endless with no clouds in sight. The air is calm and slightly crisp as I walk out to my car. The pleasant weather puts me in a good mood. I've already made the arrangements with Dr. Gleeson, so there won't be any hiccups with the anesthesiologist. No last-minute changes. As the old *Holiday Inn* commercial used to say, "The best surprise is no surprise."

It's about 6:30 a.m., and the procedure is scheduled an hour later at the outpatient surgical center. Taylor and

Naomi arrive a minute later and check in with the nurse at the front desk. They're ushered into a private patient room a few minutes later and I give them a minute to get settled, and then I see how my patient's doing.

"Good morning. How are you feeling?" I ask Taylor.

"I'm okay," she responds with a nervous smile.

"Are you still wanting to proceed?" I ask. I'd be shocked if she backed out, but I always give the patient one last chance to change their mind.

"Yes, I just want it over with," Taylor answers, and her mother nods with approval.

"And how about you, Mom, are you doing okay?" I ask Naomi.

"Fine," she says with little emotion. They're not as distraught as last week and clearly accept their decision. Both mom and daughter were so fixated on getting Taylor's life back to normal and focused on her future. They saw no other answer than to abort the child. How can Taylor have the life she wants, and her mother has dreamed about, if she doesn't have the abortion? I still don't have any answers for them. But *that* discussion is over.

"Do you have questions?" I ask, and both Taylor and her mom shake their heads. I repeat what I said a week ago about the procedure and advise them on what to look for afterward. Dr. Gleeson visits with them to fully explain about going under anesthesia and the postoperative instructions.

Fifty-Three Minutes Later

It's been over a year since I performed my last abortion, although I've done several D&Cs for other reasons. I expect the procedure to be standard without any complications. The operating room is on the ground floor on the east side of the building, and I'm drawn to look outside again and see the cobalt sky and the Wasatch Mountain Range. The sun brightens up the space, and the windows are shaded and reflective from the outside so no one can see inside the room. It's a beautiful morning, but I clear my mind of the distraction and give Taylor my full and complete attention.

The patient is ready, and so am I. The procedure of suctioning out the pregnancy tissue will only take a few minutes. I sit on a small rolling stool. Slowly and deliberately, I bring the vacuum suction tube into the uterus.

And that's when *everything changes.*

Although there's an anesthesiologist, two nurses, an ultrasound technician, the patient, and myself, I suddenly feel the type of sadness associated with being alone while simultaneously sensing that the room is crowded. What is happening?

My skin feels overly sensitive, and the small hairs on my arm stiffen up. That's never happened before, and I notice them move as I exhale. It's at this moment when I figure out what's transpiring. The operating room has darkened. I look up and confirm the lights are still on, and the blinds are wide open.

There's *no logical* explanation.

Why is this room in the middle of a solar eclipse? Taylor is engulfed in a shadow. My heart literally skips a beat, and my throat is tight and scratchy. Do I hear diabolic whispers? My lungs feel like they're being squeezed by someone *or something.* The air is heavy, thick, and oppressive. For a moment, I forget how to breathe, and when I finally remember to exhale, it comes out too fast and then too slow.

I experience the malevolent dread of knowing that I'm being *watched.* My eyes involuntarily widen when it hits me. I know what's causing the darkness, and I formulate an image in my mind. The *darkness* approves of what I'm doing and reaches out to me as if it wants to shake my hand. I'm petrified, and I can't get *that image* out of my head. My right hand is holding the vacuum suction, and I subconsciously draw my left arm to my chest, as if I'm going to be burned by the fires of hell.

It's *unmistakable.*

The room is *filled with pure evil.*

I don't like horror movies, but a scene pops into my head. The unprotected teenage girl is babysitting in the 1979 classic movie *When a Stranger Calls*. The children have been put to bed upstairs several hours ago, and the babysitter is downstairs, watching television and eating popcorn. Suddenly, the phone rings: the caller tells her, "*Check the children.*"

The teen dismisses the call and goes back to watching television, not realizing the kids are upstairs, *murdered*. The anonymous crank caller dials back several times, and the babysitter eventually calls the police. Next, the scene focuses on the old rotary dial, and the simple everyday normal sound of a ringing phone raises the viewer's anxiety level.

The man calls the babysitter once again, and when she asks what the caller wants, he responds, "Your blood, all over me."

She's holding a fire poker for protection and is filled with fright. The police call back to inform her they traced the call, saying, "*The caller is inside the house!*"

That's the moment when the audience sees the teenager scared beyond belief. Except I'm not watching a movie. I'm the main character getting the phone call to *check the children*. That's what I am experiencing *right now*.

The murderer is coming from *inside the house*. The horror movie's dramatic music plays inside my head, and I can't make the sound stop. I'm in the middle of the movie scene, and this is *my* moment of *sheer terror* when I *know* there's evil present in this operating room.

I'm momentarily frozen. My eyes dart around the room, and the evil darkness is everywhere, filling the space, casting shadows in every corner like a thick coating of dark molasses. How do I escape? My stomach tightens, and I instantly feel ill. *What the hell* is going on?

I look at the medical team, expecting to see their fear too. But I don't. I see nothing. No emotion, just colleagues concentrating on the task at hand. They don't realize what's in the room with us. How can they be so oblivious?

The vacuum suction device is in place, but I haven't started. I'm still frozen, and I'm not quite sure what to do now. This thought slams into my head: *Stop right now!* I hesitate for another moment. Has time stood still? My colleagues haven't noticed my wavering. I now worry that they'll simultaneously look at me and shout, "Hurry up!"

They don't know what's happening. Am I losing my mind? No, my mind is sharp. But *I am losing it*. It's my heart that's filled with terror and anxiety.

But I can't stop. I'm in the middle of a surgery, so I keep my cool. If I delay, it increases the chances that my patient gets an infection. No surgeon stops halfway. But what if I stopped? I would have to tell my patient and her mom that *something happened*.

I can't do it. How am I going to explain this? I can't simply state that "fear gripped me because the devil was in the room, and doing the procedure is morally wrong." What kind of doctor says that to her patient? I resolve to finish so I don't have to come back another day to complete the job.

Six Minutes Later

It's done.

I wipe a bead of sweat from my brow. Although the room is at its normal temperature, I'm anything but comfortable. I remove the instruments from her body and nod to the nurses and Dr. Gleeson, who will monitor her progress to wake up. I can't get out of there fast enough, but I reduce my pace and slowly and purposefully leave the room to scrub out.

Naomi is in the waiting room, and I tell her that the procedure went well, with no complications, and reassure her that all the pregnancy tissue was removed. Taylor will soon transfer to the recovery room, and I switch back into doctor mode and shut off what I experienced in the operating room.

Eventually, Taylor is discharged, and Naomi takes her home. She'll probably be able to go back to school the next day. I return to my office, and I have a moment before my next patient. In that moment alone, I want to suppress the memory of what happened in the operating room. I'm unsettled and trying to process what just happened.

The experience has left me feeling like I'm Janet Leigh from a scene in Alfred Hitchcock's *Psycho.* I'm waiting for the devil to pull back the shower curtain to slice me into bits and *devour me.* I've never been more disturbed.

People overuse the phrase *shaken to the core*, but that's the best way I can describe it to you. I never saw the obvious conflict of my career, bringing life into the world, as a doctor promising to *do no harm* and try to save lives. Why didn't I find it at least *strange* that performing an abortion is the opposite? It's ending a life.

I will *never* perform another abortion.

On anyone.

At any stage of pregnancy.

For any reason.

Period.

I have never thought of a truer statement. I don't care what a patient says or how much she begs, it's not going to happen. At least by me.

I didn't see his face, but make no mistake, he was there. I was in the same room as Lucifer. My mind is running fast as I try to process my thoughts. It was real.

Why did that monster reveal himself to me in that moment? Maybe the devil was always present during an abortion. What if it was God's grace revealing the truth about abortion? I can't decide the *why* or the *how,* and I ultimately conclude *it doesn't matter*.

What *does* matter is that I'm a changed woman.

Forever.

There are no more lines in the sand.

There's no more sand.

I've blown up the sandbox.

Part 3: *Nine Jolts,* 17 Years Later, August 2010

A few years ago, I was recruited by the University of Utah to develop midlife women's health programs. I was part of an OB-GYN group of doctors and sold my portion of the practice. Working for the university was a fantastic career move, and I'm where I want to be professionally. The two sons from my first marriage are grown adults and have left the nest. I have two daughters with my second husband. The oldest will attend college in central Colorado, while the youngest is a senior in high school.

After dropping my older daughter off at school, we decide to spend a few days at our mountain cabin in Bear Lake, Utah. I decide to run on a local trail and was out for longer than my husband expected. As I'm making my way back, I see him speeding down the trail on an ATV.

I'm reminded of his obsession with expensive toys. He has an ATV, motorcycle, and a snowmobile. The ATV is his latest $10,000 purchase, which he never bothered to discuss with me before buying it. It's been the source of previous arguments.

He screeches to a halt and doesn't seem to notice or care that a cloud of dust covers everything on the trail, including me. *Of course,* he's not wearing a helmet. He has one, but it's collecting dust in the garage. He's not a stupid man, but you would think a lawyer would have a modicum of prudence when using such a machine.

I suppose sitting behind a desk all day is too safe, so he craves the adrenaline rush on his time off. He's not a timid rider, constantly pushing the limits of the ATV and his skills. I can't figure out why he's throwing caution out the window.

He takes risks, going deep into the backcountry. These trails are in remote areas, so if anything goes awry, or if he gets distracted for a second, something awful can happen. And before you think I'm being overprotective, know this. He'd also allowed our kids on the four-wheeler against my wishes, and they got out of control and rolled it!

Luckily, no one was hurt, but several of my patients have also rolled over their ATV, and one of them was left paralyzed. ATV accidents are common, so my concern isn't some irrational fear. He knows it was a safety concern of mine, but he dismissed it as silly. He does what he wants to do.

"Where's your helmet?" I ask, and I'm sure the look on my face must have shown disapproval.

He reacts by lashing out at me. Once again, we get into a huge argument. The fight degrades into opening old wounds, and we quickly go off on a tangent. We're not even arguing about the ATV anymore.

But that's what we do.

Fight.

Constantly.

I'll be honest with you, I've been unhappy in my marriage for a long time. About six years into the marriage, I seriously thought about ending it. I was ready to walk away, but a patient and friend convinced me to stay. She viewed marriage as a lifetime commitment, and you don't give up. You keep it together and put the family first, not the individual. The marriage vows were a bond made before God, and you don't break your promises, regardless of whether you've become unhappy. I followed her advice and continued the marriage and promised to never file for a divorce.

I went above and beyond the promise with the determination to create a happy home. I spent so much time and energy attempting to please him and elevated his needs above my own. Quite frankly, what *I wanted* was never part of the equation. My husband got his way on everything and always received priority in the marriage. I thought he'd be happy and satisfied. But I was mistaken.

I was *so wrong*. The morning after our fight, it jolted me when he announced his intention to leave me. Yes, we had a blowout argument, but we had plenty of those before. This one wasn't *all that* different, so his assertion to break up with me came as a surprise.

I'm realistic and acknowledge that we have problems. Real fundamental problems. I wasn't envisioning a mutual *I'm sorry,* and then we kiss and make up. But I didn't anticipate his declaration to give up on us.

I'm keeping my promise to our marriage, and I won't be the one to file for divorce. He's going to have to follow through. We'll see if it's a threat or a promise. He didn't say much after we came home, so I wasn't sure what was going to happen next. I couldn't think about it as I had to go to the airport.

Jolt 2: my father is in the hospital.

I visited with my parents for about a week and tended to Dad's needs, and my mom's too. It was a worrisome time. Initially, the doctors thought he had a heart attack, but it was just a scare.

My parents aged right in front of my eyes. Intellectually, we all know that our parents get old and are likely to die before their children. That's how it's supposed to happen, anyway. His health situation reinforced the fact that their time on this planet is limited. Luckily, his condition wasn't life-threatening, and it appeared he'd make a decent recovery. A few days after I return home, I'm hit with another jolt.

Our daughter that we dropped off at school in Colorado is upset about the news of our impending split. I'm shocked and annoyed that he immediately told the kids about moving out. Nothing was finalized and no plans were made. Why is he so hasty to separate? I decide to drive to Gunnison, Colorado, for the weekend.

This isn't how I wanted my daughter's first week of college to begin. She doesn't need the stress, and I don't know how to explain it to her. I don't have a lot of answers myself. She's seen us argue, and kids can sense when there's tension in the household, so she must know our marriage is far less than ideal.

I spend the weekend assuring her that everything will be *all right*, although I'm not sure what that means. What does *all right* look like for me? She sees right through my thin veil of confidence, which doesn't make either of us feel any better. I frankly don't know what will happen next, and I'm frustrated that the conversation with the kids happened so soon.

In my perfect world, we would've told them together, as I'm sure the communication from my husband was one-sided. I'm tired of being the *bad guy* in our relationship, and I don't want the kids to blame me for the marriage falling apart. I can easily imagine it playing out that way, which hurts and makes me angry.

I'm losing control, and it's frustrating because I don't know how to fix the relationship. I also have no clue about what might happen next. I leave Colorado feeling worse than when I arrived. We didn't resolve anything.

I must refocus because a few days later when I return home, I'm hit with jolt 4.

My husband is about to purchase a downtown condo. That's where he plans to live, and I wonder why is he doing this? Does he have someone on the side? Is he cheating on me like my first husband did?

He hands me a legal document to sign. It exempts the condo from our community property, so it won't be considered when our assets are divided in the event of a divorce. The funds used to buy the property were acquired during our marriage. I tell him I'm going to ask a lawyer about it, and *he has a fit*.

We're in the kitchen arguing, and he's infuriated and lashes out, calling me crazy and blaming me for the problems in the marriage. He's accusing me of being controlling and berating me, like a lawyer would badger a hostile witness. It's the epitome of an ugly argument.

He's working himself up in a frenzy like a caged cat, and the look on his face is passionate hatred. Or is it fear that he won't get what he wants? I've never seen him *this angry,* and nothing I say can calm him down; it has the opposite effect, and the tension in the room is so thick that I feel like I'm wearing concrete shoes. I walk away, but he follows me. He's insistent and won't let it go.

I try to counter his accusation of being controlling, and he simply tells me with all the certainty in the world, "You're wrong." He amps up to a level of rage that I've never seen. Can he keep his wrath in check, or is he going to take it out on me?

Now I'm frightened for my safety, and it prompts a distressing memory from my first marriage. I was in medical school studying, and I'd casually asked my first husband to lower the volume of the television so I could concentrate better. He took that as an insult and interpreted my request *as a demand.* The last thing he would tolerate was his wife telling him what to do. He instantly flies into a rage, scaring me and the children. Volatile and angry barely begin to describe my first husband.

I lock myself and the kids in the bedroom. My mother was also in the house, and she, too, locked herself in a room and called the police. They arrive soon, but not before he removed the television from the living room, threw it on the back porch, poured gasoline on it, and *lit it on fire.* Then he leaves.

I'll never forget the crazed look in his eyes. It's the same look that I now see in my second husband. I look around and see if I can physically escape, but I'm stuck. His mere gestures make me flinch, and I'm terrified he won't be able to control himself. I can't pacify him, so instead I appease him.

"Fine." I give in, grab a pen, and sign the document so he gets what he wants, *as usual.* There's no advantage or benefit to me. I don't get anything out of it, and it's a decision made in fear. He wins *again.*

I dread showing my lawyer what I signed, that is, when I hire one. I'm feeling manipulated and upset with myself that I caved in, but I'm forced to push those emotions to the side because a few days later, I'm hit with jolt 5.

Our friend Roger is killed in a motorcycle accident. He was another lawyer, and we'd known each other for years through my husband. The accident hit my husband hard, and I'm also upset. I go for a run to sort out things in my mind, and I fall, hurting my knee and landing on my face. The next day, we attend the solemn funeral together. I hobble in with my face black and blue from my injuries. It makes the funeral that much more painful because I feel as bad as I look.

The next week, I realize that Roger's death resets my perspective. Life is short. One day you're here, and another, *poof,* it's over. Life is precious. I know they're clichés, but that doesn't diminish their truthfulness. Petty problems become smaller when you look at the big picture.

A week later, Roger's death continues to occupy my mind. I'm attempting to process his passing. I'm sad and frustrated that his death happened so suddenly. He was my age. Accidents like his seem avoidable. They're tragic, and I have a hard time finding meaning from it.

That is, *until I do.*

Perhaps Roger's awful death isn't for nothing. It was unexpected, and my husband is grieving deeply. I see it on his face and hear it in his voice. Maybe he's also thinking about those clichés. He *is* impacted by Roger's death; there isn't a doubt. He must be taking stock of his life. In his marriage. Maybe this is the wake-up call we both need. Our marriage is worth saving! He's going to figure it out. He'll have a *change of heart*. I know it's true, and I convince myself he'll want to reconcile.

I imagine a romantic turnaround, where I hear a vehicle speeding down the street. He slams on the brakes, jumps out of the car, and rushes toward the house. He has flowers in one hand, champagne in the other, and a love-struck puppy dog grin pasted on his face. For dramatic purposes, he leaves the car in the middle of the street, but the neighbors don't mind. Instead, they smile and cheer the grand romantic gesture.

I can see it happening. I'll rush out to greet him and leap into his arms. It's better than a *Hallmark* movie ending. We'll kiss, and the chaos of the last month melts away. Our hearts will beat as one. The romance is on! The song *Reunited* by Peaches and Herb pops into my head. *Reunited and it feels so good!* The hard road of all these years will morph into happiness and bliss. It'll happen at sunset, and we'll pop open the champagne. It will spill everywhere, and neither of us will care.

Instead of coming over, he calls on the phone.

I hear his voice, and I'm filled with hope. He must be thinking the same thoughts. We're in sync, and he's about to profess his undying love for me. This is *the* movie scene I've been waiting for. The penultimate moment. Our friend didn't die for nothing.

Then he delivers jolt 6.

His voice is cool and unfeeling. He's giving me a courtesy call about his plan to pick up some furniture and personal belongings over the weekend. The Hollywood ending isn't happening.

Three Days Later

I'm going to visit my daughter in Colorado again, and I'm getting ready to leave. It's early morning, and my husband and a few of his family members show up at the door. They're here to take away half the furniture and all his stuff. They don't ask for my help, and I merely watch *our possessions* leave *our home*, one by one.

He won't make eye contact, but I hear him mutter, "I deserve to be happy." But that's what I've been trying to do all these years! Our marriage is disintegrating in front of me. I can't take it, so I head out to the garage, get in my car, and simply drive.

It's a quick trip to Colorado, and I'm back in a few days. When I return, the first thing I notice is that the house is *so* quiet. A different song pops loudly into my head, Sade singing, *So why did you make me cry, Why didn't you come get me one last time, You'll always know the reason why, We could've had the moon and the sky.*

Jolt 7: My husband of twenty years *has* left me.

This is the second time I've been abandoned by a husband, so maybe I'm the problem. Beating myself up is too tempting and easy. I'm good at that, effective at making myself feel like crap. For someone with enough brains to become a doctor and tenacious enough to get through medical school and residency with two kids, how come I wasn't smart enough to save this marriage? Why didn't my efforts bear fruit? My marriage has withered and died on the vine.

I don't want to stand in the middle of my living room, yearning for my husband and looking like an idiot. My mind screams with this guttural reaction, and I think, *My life is over*. Literally, and physically, like I'm going to fall down, shrivel up like a dead plant, and die. Someone will come in the house and find me face down on the floor, keeled over.

This is it.

It's ended.

All of it.

My life was built on a foundation of sand, and the tide has come in. It's getting washed back into the sea, and I don't know what to do. I've given *everything* to this marriage, and I'm left with a large empty hole. I want to scream *bloody murder*.

I think I'm going to throw up. My muscles hurt. My head pounds, and it feels like every artery is clogged with pain. I'm in both bodily and emotional agony. *How can I go on?* Someone, please tell me!

What do I do now? I'm not talking about hiring a lawyer or calculating how to split our assets and whether I can afford to stay in this house. Specifically, what should I do right now, *this second*? My mind is scrambling, getting nowhere, like I'm on a treadmill. I figuratively get off the treadmill and decide to do the outdoor version.

I need to run.

We live in a nice suburban neighborhood, and there are several running trails to choose from, so I pick one which weaves through several subdivisions and connects to other paths. I took up long-distance running several years ago. I enjoy the rhythmic pace and being outside.

Scenes from my marriage flash back. Throughout the years, our relationship was like a yo-yo, spinning around, going up and down, but not getting anywhere. We'd argue frequently, and the tension was unbearable at times, causing me to be an emotional wreck. I won't go into the specifics about all the stupid fights or about how many times it left me drained afterward. I replay these scenes in my mind *over and over again*. I make myself crazy sometimes. But I won't complain because we each have our own problems to work on.

We've been actively going to marriage counseling over the past *ten years*! As you already know, it hasn't worked. The counseling seemed to focus on *my* shortcomings. A year ago, he promised that if *I didn't fix my problems*, the marriage was over. Am I to blame for our relationship falling apart?

I worked really, really hard to keep it alive. It wasn't from lack of trying. Part of the reason was for our children and keeping the family together. I wanted to make the effort, not just for the kids, but for myself too. I still *love him*. We had twenty years together. That must mean something, shouldn't it? This can't be happening again. I don't want to do this to my kids *again*! *Why can't we just figure it out?*

We knew how to have a sexual relationship, but we never learned about how to handle the other parts of a marriage. Neither one of us possessed true conflict resolution skills, so the outcome would either result in an argument or plain silence along with tension, stress, and unhappiness.

My conflict resolution skill consisted of one thing: capitulation. A one-sided compromise isn't much of a solution. *I don't recommend it*. We both chronically demonstrated our expertise of not hearing the other person. Two broken people do not make a happy marriage.

After my first mile, it strikes me that maybe I've been running *from* something all these years. Maybe I need to run *to* something instead. I realize I have my own issues, but I'm surely not the sole cause of our marital difficulties.

I've been a *people pleaser* for so long. It sounds like a good thing rather than a flaw, but it's morphed into enabling the destructive habits of others. I have the *disease of nice*. I'm not suggesting that being nice is a bad behavior. Some would even call it virtuous.

I'll be honest with you and myself. My fear of being deserted has driven my behavior. The *niceness* is my way of controlling people so they don't leave. Being abandoned equates to being rejected. Ultimately, that's what my actions were trying to prevent, and I've failed miserably. I'm flabbergasted that the opposite has happened instead.

How could this marriage go down in flames after I put everyone else's needs above my own? I didn't let myself have *needs*. I didn't think about them, let alone ask that they be fulfilled. He can see that I'm miserable, but it doesn't matter. I cringe in physical pain when I concede I *don't matter to him*. That's a cold hard truth to face.

As I examine my past, I recognize the niceness disease clearly during my first marriage. I enabled my first husband to be unfaithful. I did anything and everything to keep him from leaving. And yet it wasn't enough. I wasn't *ever going to be enough*.

I was too nice and accommodating, which made me a target of his abuse. That was an unhealthy relationship, and it crashed and burned in the end. I wove a similar routine throughout my second marriage.

I loathe upsetting people and hate conflict so much that it was to my detriment. *Again*. We'd argue, and he'd tell me I'm wrong, *once again*. I'd clam up, and he'd continue doing his own thing. He'd get frustrated with my silence, accusing me of using it to control him. That wasn't my intention.

He would never let *me* ask for something. He'd shut it down, turn it around so I would be the troublemaker for bringing something up. Regardless of the subject, it was always blamed on me. So why should I bother speaking? Communicate my thoughts, desires, and feelings? *For what?* Why get into an argument when *nothing* is ever resolved? I didn't want to make him mad, so it was just easier to give in. Isn't that better?

Apparently not.

I've done a lot of personal exploring over the last decade getting to know myself better. Trying to look deeper, I discovered my desperation for inner peace. I'm *exhausted* from working so hard to *fix* myself or my marriage.

Are you going to suggest a good self-help book? Well, I've read them all. Do you want to recommend a book about how to have a successful marriage? Don't bother, I've gone through *every one of those*. Do you know a great therapist? We've been going to one for a decade. That's half the time we've been married!

I've taken up yoga and meditation, which is relaxing, but not long-lasting. Usually, I'm racking my brain to figure out *where* everything went wrong. *Why* everything went wrong. *How* everything went wrong. I'm worn out. And peace remains elusive.

I took up running after reading that, according to experienced marathoners; the mind shuts down around the nine-mile mark. You sort of *zone out*. That's as close to *peace* as I can get. But real soul-fulfilling peace is what I seek. I can't remember the last time I felt it.

I recognize a park I'm running through and know I've passed the five-mile mark, and my knee is bothering me. My mind wanders, and an old memory comes to me.

I was working on my PhD in nutrition and applied to medical school. I needed additional science credits, so I enrolled in a physiology class. One day, I was stung by fire ants, which are common in Louisiana. I wasn't swarmed by them, but it occurred enough times for me to feel lousy and exhausted. I stood up to get a glass of water and became dizzy, like my blood pressure was cratering.

Here's the thing. It was only a few weeks before that incident when I was in the classroom learning about allergies. I was experiencing classic symptoms of anaphylactic shock. I remember wanting to lie down on the couch and sleep it off.

But fire ant venom can be deadly. I wobbled my way back to the couch, stared at it for a second, but for some reason, I consciously *decided* to go to the hospital. I grabbed my purse and drove to the emergency room, but I'm not sure how I made it in one piece. My body simply performed the motions, and the next thing I know, I'm getting pumped full of epinephrine and antihistamines.

The doctor told me I was having a severe allergic reaction and was lucky to be treated early. My normal blood pressure is about 95/50, and the hospital clocked me in at thirty over an unmeasurable level. My cardiovascular system collapsed. I could've had serious complications such as kidney failure, heart arrhythmia, or death. Who knows what might have happened if I'd treated the symptoms with a *nap?*

I don't remember driving myself to the emergency room, let alone how I determined I needed medical attention, yet the action likely saved my life. What are the chances that comes together perfectly?

I pass the nine-mile mark, but my brain refuses to shut off. Thoughts flood in, and I can't stop the memories, no matter how hard I try.

I was in my last year of medical school, and my first son was about nine months old. I returned home after class, and my mom was babysitting. It's the afternoon, and I gave him a healthy snack, a piece of an orange. He made a noise, and I'll never forget the surprised look on his face. The orange was stuck; he's choking and turned blue. That orange was not coming out on its own.

So here's the thing, *again*. Only two weeks before the incident with the orange, I learned in class the emergency treatment for child CPR and choking. I knew exactly what to do. I pounded the child's back to dislodge the object. I clearly recall asking the professor what to do in case it fails. He's surprised by my question. Not the nature of the inquiry, but that I asked it since I rarely spoke in class. I sprang into action and pounded his back. The orange doesn't come out.

I next did an abdominal wall thrust. Given my son's age, I performed the movement while he's on his back. Think of it like the child's version of the Heimlich maneuver. That doesn't work, so I flipped him over onto his stomach and pounded his back. No orange.

I flipped him again and pushed his stomach. Nothing.

I flipped him over once again and pounded his back. This time, that orange came flying out of his mouth. If the lesson plan timing was different, my son might have died. I was trained only a few days before I needed it. Was it pure dumb luck? Tell me, what are the odds of that?

There must be more to those near-miss stories.

I remember one of our last marriage counseling sessions, when my husband and I were told by the therapist, "I've done everything I can for you. You've tried it all. The only thing left is pursuing your spirituality." At the time, I remember thinking, *We're really at the end of our rope!*

However, I gained some hope when we went to church together and accepted Jesus. We both recognized our need for Christ in our lives. I thought we were on the right track. But we didn't return to church, and the lackluster effort didn't bear any fruit. I suppose I shouldn't be surprised.

My legs feel tired, and I recognize the surroundings. I'm about a mile from home, which makes a twelve-mile loop, and my knee is killing me. *Home.* I get an eerie feeling when I think about *that word.* I return to a mostly empty house. My jaw scrunches, I tremble, and my stomach tightens. There's no way to deny it.

He's gone.

I go out to the porch and look outside. There's no one around. Nothing is happening, and it sinks in. *I'm alone.* I feel so helpless and hopeless. My life is a complete *train wreck.* I curl up on a chair and cry my eyes out. When I finish, I cry for a few hours more.

It's hard to describe my emotions accurately, and it's difficult to get the words just right to describe what's happening. I feel like a pot of water that's about to boil over. Inside me, something is about to reach its tipping point. And then it does.

I instantly think of my mother, who was a devoted Christian. When I think of her, I see the face of God. I remember a Bible verse, something about Jesus choosing you to go forth and bear fruit. Right then and there, I feel a gentle tug from God, drawing me in with love and gentleness, and I feel at ease.

My mother lived the devout Christian life. She talked the talk, but more importantly, *she walked the walk.* Knowing Jesus was the driving force behind her desire to serve others and be a good person. She wasn't a surface-level Christian. Her heart was on fire. I remember every morning while making breakfast, she'd recite to us children a verse from Psalm 118:24:

"This is the day which the LORD has made; we will rejoice and be glad." I hum the musical version of the Bible passage.

You don't bear fruit unless you have Jesus in your life. *That was it.* I've been searching everywhere, but it was right in front of me *the whole time*! I become overwhelmed with emotion, and I cry again.

I grew up the daughter of a minister. My mother epitomized what a caring, compassionate, and steadfast Christian should act like. She was *all in.* My parents were a great example of how to follow the light of Jesus. I was there. I witnessed it every day growing up. *But I missed it! I blew it.* How did I get offtrack?

As a kid, I attended church and did everything a minister's daughter should do. But when I left home to attend Colorado State University, I admit it, my relationship with Jesus and trying to be virtuous slipped away. I attended church frequently and mostly tried to do the right thing, but following Jesus wasn't a priority.

It took a year to fall away and become apathetic. During my second year at CSU, I decided to move in with my boyfriend. I relied on myself to determine my path of life. My parents lived in Denver at the time, and my father drove to campus to try to talk me out of it. But I wanted nothing to do with his advice.

No, *I knew better.* He left, discouraged and disappointed, but returned a minute later because he couldn't say goodbye without telling me he loved me.

That's like God's love. He's always loved me. He's been outside the door to my heart, waiting for me to invite him in. I look back at my life, and so many moments, I see God's guiding hand, like the near-death experiences. I simply didn't recognize His love at the time. But it's never too late. Anyone can change their heart, no matter what they've done. How did I not see this? All those years *wasted.*

The marriage counselor told me there's nothing left to try except spirituality. I should have tried that first. *Duh!* Without God in our marital relationship, is it any surprise it went awry?

I visualize my mom's face, and I cry out to God, *"I need you!"* I hear His soothing voice fill my heart with joy when He says, *"You are the redeemed and beloved child of God."*

He chose me!

It's jolt 8.

I hear His voice again. *The only way I'm going to survive is to follow Jesus.* That's my only hope. And not only survive my marriage ending, but the bigger picture—salvation. He speaks to me again. *I will never leave you, and I will take care of you. Always.*

I'm filled with a staggering amount of optimism and hope.

I see it clearly now, and I'm ready to give myself over to Him. I envision Jesus riding in on a white horse for me. To provide for me. *For me*! It's the pinnacle of beauty, and I start to relax.

It's such a stark contrast to what feminists have told me all along. You don't *need* a man. You should be the tough one. There's no time to relax and never allow yourself to be vulnerable. You be the provider.

My feminist attitude enabled my husband to shirk the responsibility of being the breadwinner. I hoped for him to be my knight in shining armor, but he declined to lead and care for the family. I suspect this is going to be a costly divorce for me. But *I will survive.*

Jesus invited me to be united as His beloved. It's an incredibly comforting moment. I know that now. I spent so much of my life rushing around and getting things done that I forgot to focus on what's *most* important.

My youngest daughter comes home and sees I've been crying and emotional. It's late in the evening now, and I must have been babbling because she returns a concerned look and decides to call my friend Peggy.

Peggy is a rock-solid Christian who's been encouraging me to attend church. I went on a few holidays like Christmas and Easter, but that's all. I wasn't serious. She arrives at my house and notices that most of the furniture is gone. I fill her in about my husband moving out. I'm still incredibly hurt by the disintegration of my marriage and pour my heart out, which is exactly what I need. She doesn't judge, try to problem-solve, or disparage my husband. Peggy simply listens.

She tells me that in this time of need, Jesus will be there for me. I smile, and Peggy returns a quizzical look. I tell her that God spoke and told me, "It's going to be very hard for a while, but you'll be okay."

I further explain that I had an epiphany and now know with clarity and certainty that Jesus is my rock, and my only choice is to follow his light. I pause for a moment and say, "I'm not the same woman I was this morning." She knows my declaration has *nothing* to do with my marital status.

"I can see it in your eyes, Catherine."

"You can?"

"Yes, I know it's been a painful day, maybe the worst day of your life, but it could also be the best day of your life."

"You're right, my life won't be the same."

"Following Jesus, it's a lifelong journey, and you've taken a big step today. But as you know, every long expedition starts with a few small steps. Just keep moving your feet, and you'll get there," Peggy encourages. "I'll be here. You can lean on me and God."

Peggy understands the power of Christ and rejoices. Her smile is infectious, and I join her. It's an intense and reassuring moment that I'll never forget. I'm changed deep inside because I've received a great gift.

I'm filled with not only grace but also with *peace*.

Now, *I'm all in.*
And I realize, *I'm meant for more.*

The Next Day

I wake up early, but I'm fully rested. I remember everything from yesterday, and for a second, I wonder if the fear, pain, and heartache will come rushing back and take over. It doesn't. I let out a deep breath, and I'm cautiously optimistic.

As the day goes on, I feel stronger, even though I'm still sad that my marriage is ending. I won't be facing it alone. That's the difference. I won't fall apart because I don't have to overcome any obstacles by myself.

I have hope for the days ahead. I'm many things: a mother, daughter, sister, friend, and doctor. But first and foremost, I'm a child of God. It's refreshing and invigorating, and I can't help but smile. I *should* smile and laugh aloud to no one in particular. I notice a hint of joy in my amusement. The grin is still pasted across my face.

I *know* that my life has changed forever, and this is day 1. I'm like a caterpillar that's transformed into a big, beautiful butterfly. There's no going back. And let me tell you, I know this deep in my heart, all throughout my gut and permeating my brain. His will and His word will be in my heart and on my lips.

Three Months later, November 2010

My mom sent me a framed picture of the "Footprints in the Sand" poem by Mary Stevenson. The poem tells the story of someone walking along the beach with the Lord. Difficult scenes of the person's life flash back, and there's only one set of footprints in the sand. The person thinks it's because the Lord abandoned her when He was needed most. The ending of the poem goes like this: "*The times when you have seen only one set of footprints, is when I carried you.*"

God has been carrying me all along, nudging me toward the person who I am today. It thrilled my parents that I've turned to God since my lowest moment, and I haven't looked back.

My knee is still not in great shape, so Peggy and I go on walks, and it's nonstop talking. Peggy has been great these last few months and so supportive during my turmoil. I don't want a divorce, and despite all our arguments and conflicts, I'm willing to work it out. I want to communicate better, and I keep thinking God will bring us back together. There's still time for redemption, but my husband needs to be a willing participant.

Peggy asked me what I was looking for in a husband when I married him twenty years ago. I didn't have a cognizant answer for her. I'm not a stupid person, but I felt stupid at that moment. Perhaps my problem was not knowing what I wanted from the relationship, or what a healthy relationship looked like.

Our discussions explored my disease of nice. Being nice is great. Nice people are wonderful, but being nice differs from gentle, caring, and loving. For so long, I felt responsible for making other people happy. I used to focus on not upsetting my husband and avoiding an argument. This resulted in enabling bad habits, which set us up for the eventual failure. I see that now.

I wasn't in a good place, so how could I have attracted a healthy person? He wanted somebody who's going to always be nice and *put up with anything*. Blugh! No wonder, the marriage is headed toward divorce. I've learned about myself, and now I can work on changing this behavior. Giving up running enabled me to concentrate more on God and find healing. I will let God make the changes that I couldn't do on my own, and realizing this opportunity is exhilarating.

Talking with Peggy has sparked me to ponder some questions that I never previously considered. Most of our time isn't talking about my marriage but strengthening the most important relationship of all, with Jesus Christ.

Peggy's been prodding me along for about a decade to embrace Christianity, but it went nowhere. After my moment on the porch, our friendship changed and has gone deeper. We've had many long discussions about God, various scripture passages, and the meaning of life. We've grown closer, and I've learned so much. I'm grateful for my friend.

God put this discipleship in place for me. He's been patiently waiting for me to come around. He could have given up on me, but He didn't. I'm floored. He's leading me to a purpose with a future. The future starts now with my renewed baptism.

I was first baptized when I was a teenager. At that time and into adulthood, I saw my faith mandating an effort to do good and avoid sin. My mindset today is more profound and multilayered. I'm seeking to strengthen my relationship with Jesus. I would lay down my life for Him. As you probably know, that's exactly what He did for all of us.

Most of my adult life, I've held huge false notions about Christianity. I can boil it down to one misperception. Previously, I thought devoted Christians were constrained by a bunch of rules. I assumed following Christ was all about what you were required to give up. I was completely misled and had it backward. *I'm gaining everything*! It's a newfound freedom. I'm a sponge, and my soul thirsts for Christ.

Instead of running from God, I'm actively pursuing Him. This is the most exciting time of my life.

I'm baptized at Peggy's church, confirming my love for Jesus this time as an adult, in front of the congregation of about two hundred people. I've recommitted myself to Jesus Christ as my Lord and Savior. After the ceremony, I feel alive and rejuvenated. I'm grinning from ear to ear with happiness, and for the first time in a long while, I look forward to the road ahead. It's going to be bumpy with a lot of potholes, but my heart knows it's the *right* path. No one said life would be easy. I'm walking back to my seat, and my eyes become wide as saucers.

It's jolt 9. You're not going to believe who's there.

In the fourth row, I see Taylor, my last abortion patient. After the service, I walk outside, and I see her chatting to the pastor. She moves along to let someone else talk to him, and our eyes meet, and I walk toward her.

"Dr. Wheeler, how are you?"

"I'm doing well," I answer.

"That was a beautiful baptism ceremony," Taylor comments.

"Thanks."

"This is my husband Robert and my three children: Bobby, Tony, and Peter," she introduces. Taylor's now in her early thirties and looks older, which obviously makes sense since I'm talking to a fully grown woman. My first impression is that they look like a happy and content family. I recall the last time I saw her was for an annual checkup shortly after high school graduation. After that, I don't know what happened to her. She explains to her husband that she was my former patient.

"It's great to meet all of you," I answer. The three young boys appear to be about six, four, and two years old.

"I haven't seen you at this church before," I observe.

"We live in Ogden now. Robert's parents live locally, and we are visiting them afterward."

"That works out conveniently," I respond. Taylor was Mormon when she was a patient, so there must be a story about how she came to this church. I notice her youngest son is becoming impatient. "I bet those boys are keeping you busy."

"Oh yes. I quit my job as a pharmacy technician after my youngest was born. I love being a stay-at-home mom."

"They're at a precious age, but wait until they're teenagers," I joke, and both she and Robert laugh.

"It was nice to meet you," Robert states, and now all three kids look like they're ready to leave. I take the hint.

"Take care, Taylor," I tell her, and we go to our respective cars.

Afterward, I return home.

I've started a program with *Celebrate Recovery*, which is a Christ-centered twelve-step program for people struggling with hurt, hang-ups, and habits. Bad habits! Sometimes I think they created it with me in mind, but it's more than working through self-improvements. They emphasize regular prayer and proactively deepening my union with Christ. I want to go to the next level. I'm chasing Jesus, and He's letting me catch Him.

Part of the process is to address long-term pains and suffering. Seeing Taylor again has me profoundly thinking, *once again*, this time about the pain from my experience with losing unborn babies. I had two miscarriages.

Nobody talks about the real and long-lasting grief after a miscarriage. Usually, people respond with comments such as "Everything happens for a reason" or "That's too bad, you can try again" or "Don't worry, you're young and can always have another." They act like the lost pregnancies *didn't count*! Sometimes it's better for well-meaning people to not say anything at all. My lost babies were unique human beings.

During my first marriage, these miscarriages cut me deeply. I was in a dark place, and not just because of the loss. As I said, my first husband was abusive, and I know he was having an affair, and there I was getting pregnant! This happened during my first year of residency. My workload was huge, and the stress of my marital relationship was a factor in causing the miscarriages; I'm convinced of it.

I noticed bleeding and went in for an ultrasound, and everything looked okay. There was a strong and steady heartbeat. My confidence surged that the baby would make it. But the bleeding continued, and I went in for another ultrasound. The room was filled with silence. I thought something was wrong with the machine, but the chill in the room verified my worst fear. My baby's heartbeat was gone.

I was dumbfounded as to what happened. There used to be a strong and normal heartbeat. How could it have simply stopped? That didn't make any sense. I felt shell-shocked because I could see the baby on the machine. It was there. But it wasn't moving, and the sonar submarine-sounding beat was missing. If I wasn't familiar with the machine myself, I wouldn't have believed it. I couldn't get out of there fast enough.

I became sick to my stomach knowing that I was carrying around a dead baby. I felt like a failure and questioned myself as a woman. My husband wasn't any help and seemed indifferent about the miscarriage, which only fed my guilt of failure.

I had to have a D&C to remove the baby, and I refused general anesthesia. Why, you wonder? Because I was busy and had to get back to work. It's so obvious now, I was avoiding the grief process. Instead, I carried it like an extra twenty pounds of weight all these years, one of several sufferings that I didn't let go. I can now see how it dragged me down.

When I was pregnant, I was so excited, but after the miscarriage, I never thought through the loss. I felt numb for months and went through the motions of the day. I didn't know who to blame, so I blamed myself and buried the pain. At the time, I didn't view those lost babies as human beings.

As a doctor, I know I didn't do anything irresponsible to cause the miscarriages, like smoking or drinking. But logic didn't help me feel any better. I didn't deal with the grief. I never allowed myself to go through that process and let it all out.

All I felt was sorrow. That's all I had to offer my baby, the *sadness*. It never occurred to me that I needed to heal. Why would I think it would magically happen? But I did and believed if I didn't think about it, the pain would go away. I got out a shovel and *buried that pain*, but pain like that finds another way to manifest itself.

I finally have permission, so I'm going to grieve for them now.

I sit on the couch and the house is quiet, and I invite God in. I'm having a good cry; you know the kind that wells up and soon becomes uncontrollable. But this time, I don't try to control it. I hand it over to God and give Him my burden, and guess what? He took it. My always-gracious God will carry the load.

It took a while, but I eventually understand what God wants me to know: "Those babies are in heaven." I gasp, not in fright, but in exultation. For the first time, I *fully* understand why human life is so important, so valuable. I never considered them as complete humans from the very moment of conception, *with a soul*. They were innocent, and God brought them to heaven to be with Him. I yearn for Christ even more.

We've lost them from our physical world, our temporary living space. But they're not lost to God. My sadness transforms into joy. My babies are okay. I correct myself, they're better than okay—they're in heaven.

And that brings me peace.

One Year later, 2011

I'm embracing God and truly celebrating my healing and recovery journey. I've asked God to forgive me for performing abortions. It caused harm and isn't what God wanted for his children when I bought the lie that I was helping women.

God planted the seeds to stir in my heart the intrinsic value of the unborn. It's taken time, but I'm clearly going down that path. He's been slowly bringing into the light what I did in the darkness. He is showing me the lies of the modern secular world. Children and family are sacred. It's so simple, and I'm struggling to understand why it's such a hard concept for half the population to recognize.

It wasn't the political talking points or morality arguments that touched my heart. Science didn't convince me, such as the number of weeks an unborn baby is viable outside the womb. It wasn't about who made the stronger case in a debate. It's *much simpler* than that. What permeated my heart was knowing the innate *humanity* of the unborn.

I could argue that I didn't do *that* many abortions. It wasn't hundreds, like some other doctors. I *only* performed about a dozen. Maybe you think I'm not as bad as some others. Maybe you even think that it's easy for God to forgive me, right? Maybe He grades on a curve, and I'm not *that bad* of a person. I stopped doing them, remember? But we both know that's a lie. It's merely a deflection. That's not how God works. That's a modern culture's empty argument, pointing to someone else's worse behavior.

The babies I aborted possessed human souls. The babies *I killed* are in heaven. There, I said it; I killed them. I know it sounds harsh, but I won't sugarcoat it. I take full ownership.

There's more.

I never thought about those babies as individuals or how they felt about being aborted. For a moment, I'm fearful about what they might say. I pray to God for more forgiveness, more mercy, more healing, and more grace. That's when God reveals the answer, and let me tell you with all honesty, it isn't what I expected.

"The babies love you *and* forgive you."

I'm blown away. I'm the one who harmed them, and they *love me*? I sit quietly, trying to comprehend the concept. Finally, I understand why they love me. They're in heaven. There's no hate in heaven. There's no pain in heaven. They don't despise the people on earth. Those in heaven don't want vengeance. Heaven is where our faith is replaced with sight and understanding. Where peace is everlasting. Heaven is filled with love.

I'm reading the Old Testament in Isaiah 42, where the servant (Jesus) will come to establish justice on the earth but will not break a weak reed or quench smoldering flames. Jesus recognized people are fallible and frequently stray from His path and think they know better and end up choosing sin. Jesus wasn't put on this earth to *crush people*. He came to *save people*. His death on the cross was to redeem *our sins*.

The gentle hand of God has tenderly guided me along, and He's been *so* patient with me. He waited until I was finally ready. His hand is holding mine. You may think that's the end of my healing journey, but there's more.

A lot more.

God loved me so much, and I was able to love back. He forgave so much, which allowed me to pour my love to Jesus, unreserved. The ugliness of sin isn't on display, but instead it's the beauty of the restoration. In order to save me, he revealed my sins in a gentle manner.

So many people falsely believe that Christianity wants to control people through shaming them. They've got it backward. God wants to free us from shame through His mercy. God wants me to walk in His light. So that's what I'm going to do.

***

The messy divorce was finalized two and a half years after my husband left. Even into 2014, I was convinced we'd reconcile and held that conviction until the paperwork was completed. I knew it was truly over when I had to *pay him money*. However, God gave me hope in a difficult situation because I saw His goodness and greatness. I simply turned my life over to God, knowing that He would give me direction.

My job at the university was funded as part of a larger project sponsored by a wealthy donor. But the money dried up, and I sought a career move. I went to work at a gynecology clinic. But that was short-lived. Back in my thirties, I developed a heart arrhythmia, where my heart rate was irregular, sometimes too fast or too slow. It became progressively worse, and I pushed through it to keep working until the day I couldn't.

My condition worsened during long work hours or when I was on call. I looked for a job that didn't have those requirements, but could not find one. After many discussions with my cardiologist, I had to stop working.

My mom had a stroke in 2015. She and Dad were retired and living with my sister Helen in Phoenix, Arizona. Helen was the primary caregiver and lovingly cared for my parents for about a year. Mom now needed more. I had the time, so I sold my house in Utah and moved to Arizona. It seemed like my life was a bunch of dominos falling, one disaster after another.

But God knew what He was doing. Once again, His hand is on the steering wheel, guiding me to what I was supposed to do next. My dad was also getting sick, so now it was my turn to absorb some of the responsibility from Helen and help take care of my parents. It was a home hospice situation, and being a doctor, I could manage their medication. Mom's health progressively declined and required constant attention. During the last two weeks of her life, I was at the house almost 24/7.

My parents accepted Mom's limited remaining future, and I did too, but not at first. As a doctor, I wanted to make them better, rid them of their diseases, and I felt helpless when there wasn't any medication or surgery that would cure what ailed them. Mom was doomed to die. I take that back, *doomed* was not their attitude or presence of mind. Mom didn't wish to die, but we all accepted that it was soon ending.

In fact, they were grateful for the life they experienced, and Mom was looking forward to meeting Jesus. Her attitude of *dying with grace* impacted me. I was sad knowing her last day on earth was coming soon. But the sadness was *for me*, not for her.

But I soon realized that this was a golden *opportunity* to spend more time with them. We didn't have a deep discussion about the meaning of life because we didn't need to. Words would clutter our ears. What *was needed* was to be together.

Daily, I sat with them in a quiet, loving presence. It was a chance to reflect and revel in the effortless exchange of love.

The medication eased their pain, yet they never complained, blamed, or pitied themselves. My mom was the anchor and glue of the family, always joyful and a servant of God. Her joy was never ending, no matter what the situation, including her life coming to an end. It was inspiring.

One of my last memories of being with my mom was simply sitting in silence next to her on the bed as she rested her head on my shoulder. She was weak and didn't feel like talking. Simply being together was enough. I was there for her, and I can't think of a more *beautiful quiet moment* between mother and daughter.

Mom didn't struggle with her situation, and both parents were at peace, so my fear quickly dissolved. We got to say our goodbyes. Wow, what *a gift* it was for all of us! It wasn't scary, and in fact, it was beautiful to be with them. My mother soon after died during a glorious sunrise. I thought that was fitting.

As ready as she was and as much time as we spent together in her last few months of life, it was hard to process. It was just *so final*. I got into a routine, spending time with my mom on a daily basis, and then suddenly, it was over.

Looking back, I'm grateful that her passing was peaceful and serene, a truly natural way to die. I was so appreciative for the experience. Even though my dad was older than my mom, he lived a few more years.

***

In January 2017, God's hand once again guided me in a new direction, and I stepped into it. My oldest daughter was starting nursing school in Spokane, Washington, and the details of this new part of her life were not coming together, including a place to live. She needed my emotional support and asked if I would come to Spokane to help. I agreed and moved 1,329 miles due north.

PART 4: *PATH OF LIFE*, APRIL 2017

After the church service ends, I drive to my friend's house for a Sunday brunch. I've become active in the local Christian church, and that's where I met my new friend, Rose Cappola. She's a superb cook, so I am looking forward to eating whatever she's made for brunch.

"These eggs are great," I tell her and take another bite.

"It's an old family tradition. I butter some sourdough bread and grill it, cut a circular hole in the center of the bread, and fry the egg in it. Some people call it *bird in a nest*."

"I call it eggs *Rose Cappola,* and the piece of bread is great for dipping," I add.

She's also prepared pancakes along with fresh fruit. Mmm, good stuff.

My Christian faith journey continues, and Rose leads a Bible study group. She's forty-eight years old and lives in a small, older house. Her husband is out of town for a few days, and it was a perfect opportunity to have some girl time. At our last group session, she shared her abortion history as a young woman and how she benefited from abortion recovery services.

"That was powerful, what you talked about at our last Bible study session," I tell her with genuine admiration. "That took some courage."

"It took several years before I became comfortable talking about it. I finally let go of the shame and guilt after a volunteer helped me work through the forgiveness process. The turning point was when I named my baby and had a memorial. We do that based on Psalm 139, which describes being created in the mother's womb."

"That's a beautiful tribute to the child," I tell her.

"Other women were there for a baby memorial as part of their healing journey. I know the truth and how wrong my actions were, but Jesus is all about mercy and forgiveness," she explains.

"Yes. That's so true, He's the great redeemer," I add, knowing my journey to seek forgiveness.

"I condemned myself for many years, but the only way my heart rests is when I'm in His presence. I didn't allow myself to move forward until I followed Christ," Rose continues.

"How did you hear about the abortion recovery facilitators?" I inquire.

"I originally started out as a volunteer teaching a childbirth class, helping young mothers at the pregnancy center. After I opened up about my past, they recommended I attend the recovery group, so it turned out they helped me!" she explains and then adds, "I wasn't aware how desperately I needed my heart repaired."

"Most of us try to deal with the pain on our own, which frequently doesn't work or makes it worse," I respond. "We don't realize how we need to work through those issues *with* God. When my second marriage ended, I turned to Him for strength. He didn't deny me and did the heavy lifting. It was only then that my life finally made sense."

"Well, you know my marriage was a fiasco at times. We've talked about it before, but I've only recently come to realize how my abortion affected it," Rose admits.

"How so?" I ask, intrigued, since most people have an abortion to *preserve* a relationship or because they think they can't afford to have a baby.

"I was twenty and nowhere near prepared for parenthood when I became pregnant. And my boyfriend wasn't ready either. I was convinced he'd break up with me, and being a single mom was the last thing I wanted."

"What happened?"

"Rick and I continued dating and got married about two years later. I remember thinking at the time that I was justified having the abortion *to save* our relationship," Rose described her mindset calmly and continued, "I kept creating all these great reasons why having the abortion helped me. I was scared and thought at the time it was the best decision."

"You made a hard choice," I comment, recalling my old line of reasoning so many years ago. I marveled at how my way of thinking has changed since then. I assume Rose has shared her story before and was comfortable talking about a difficult time in her life, which I found amazing.

"Yes, that's how I saw it, as a tough choice," she replies and nods her head.

"Were you hoping for marriage all along?"

"Yes, and when we got engaged, it seemed like it worked out for the best. It was the answer I was looking for," Rose explains.

"*Seemed* like it worked out? It wasn't what you hoped for?" I ask.

"I was excited about the engagement and planning the wedding, but after having the abortion, our relationship was never the same, even after we were married. We have two wonderful kids together, but there was this lingering guilt that I tried to suppress for so long. I never dealt with those feelings, and I know it caused problems in our marriage," Rose acknowledges.

"You never got over the trauma," I observe.

"Right, that's an accurate way to describe it. We should've had a great marriage from the start. There were some good times, but so many things weren't working, always a little off, and I could never figure out why," Rose comments and pauses to eat some of the brunch.

"Do you think the abortion was at the root of your relationship problems?" I bluntly ask and wonder if I was getting too personal.

Rose awkwardly smiles but responds anyway, "Absolutely. It took years to figure it out, to see its full impact. I don't know what my life would be like if I'd kept the child, but you're right, it was always an unresolved issue, like a dark cloud over our marriage," she explains and tears up momentarily.

I understand the sentiment, make eye contact, and offer a warm, small smile. It's hard for anyone to open up, even if it's not the first time, so I appreciate her letting me into her world.

"I've learned, and sometimes the hard way, denying a problem exists doesn't make it go away. Sometimes, it festers and gets worse. I also fought with my husband for no apparent reason," I tell her. As someone who was once an authority on self-criticism, I add, "I always assumed there was something wrong with me."

"Me too. I had this nagging feeling that I was holding back in our marriage, trying to build a wall so I wouldn't get hurt. The marriage became worse after we had kids," Rose tells me.

"You didn't forget about the abortion after you had children," I conclude.

"I thought about *it more*. I often wondered how could I possibly be a good parent *if I killed my child in the womb*? How could I choose this one and not the other one? Why would God *ever give me another child?*" Rose reveals and again tears up.

I'm affected too. My windpipe seems to close, and I have a difficult time breathing. How do I answer her question? We both pause and try to compose ourselves.

"I understand why you'd think that," is all I can come up with.

"I've heard other women struggle with the same question," Rose admits and adds, "it's more common than people think."

"All that self-doubt and believing you don't deserve another chance at motherhood will grind a hole in your soul," I softly remark.

"I think it did. Sometimes, I expected my child to get some horrible disease *to punish me*. Then I felt worse, scared that my child would suffer *because of me*," Rose explains in a wavering voice.

Her emotions are raw and on full display. I understand her sentiment, for I've been there myself, but that doesn't provide any solace. "You beat yourself up pretty bad."

"It was a special skill I developed," she says with a bit of humor as someone who is no longer anchored to the pain, and the mood lifts. She takes a bite of food, and I follow her lead. There are a few moments of silence until she starts again.

"It was difficult to embrace motherhood with this internal struggle of mine," Rose adds, once again serious. "I'd do anything for my kids, a sacrificial love that parents have, so I had this inner conflict, loving my child that was born and beating myself up for aborting a different child."

"I know that must have been hard. You have a great relationship with your adult children. You obviously did a lot of things *right*," I point out and bolster her confidence a little.

"Yes, I'm being a negative, Nelly. There were many glorious moments raising my kids."

"You can feel good about that, and your marriage is intact," I convince her, and she returns an appreciative smile. No matter how much healing you've received, an encouraging word from a friend goes a long way.

"You're right! There are so many ordinary moments that don't seem special at the time, yet when I look back on them, they're *magical experiences* I'll never forget."

"The unspoken joy of parenthood. It's not always the big moments that capture your heart," I beam with exuberance, remembering my own special memories with my kids.

"It took a lot of hard work and prayer, but I'm so happy Rick and I sought healing *together*. Once Jesus entered our marriage, it forever changed it for the better," Rose says and pauses a moment, and her facial expression indicates she's not finished talking. "There are deep levels of healing, and Jesus will help continue that process and take you to the next level."

"Yes, you were lucky."

"I know some couples that couldn't recover from their abortion loss," Rose admits.

"When you go to God to heal your marriage, the relationship can strengthen and be even better," I say. I hoped that would have happened in my marriage, and I'm convinced that if we had brought God in, we'd still be together today.

Rose speaks, and I refocus on her words. "God made our marriage beautiful," she states and pauses for a moment. We both eat some more food in silence, and after a few minutes, Rose wants to continue the conversation.

"Speaking of motherhood, *can you imagine* what it was like to be Jesus's mom? To be asked by the angel Gabriel to carry the Son of God?" Rose asks, and I can tell by the way she asked the question, that she's thought about it before.

So have I.

"If I could go back in time and meet someone other than Jesus, it would be Mary," I affirm to her.

"What an honor it would be to meet the first Christians. I'd love to know what Jesus was like as a baby," Rose exclaims.

"What were his first words?" I ask, picking up the pace of our conversation.

"That blows my mind, witnessing those precious moments that all moms in the world treasure. Knowing Jesus as a baby, wow, it's difficult to fathom."

"Exactly. That would be so cool to chat with her, mom to mom, and compare child-rearing experiences. I wonder what her voice sounds like. What a gift that would be," I exclaim and beam from simply *the thought* of having that conversation.

"I bet we'd have a lot in common," Rose states.

"Yes. As a child, he was vulnerable like any other kid, especially during that time in history," I add and notice Rose clam up. She gets up from the kitchen table to refill her cup of coffee. When she returns, I see her wipe a tear.

"What is it?" I gently ask and reach out my hand to grasp hers.

"Our conversation about Mary. I was so far from being a mother like her," she says and wells up further.

"No one can compare herself to Mary."

"*I know*. But I aborted my child. Even after I had kids, if anyone talked about abortion, whether as a political issue or knowing somebody who had one, I would instantly feel shame and not say a word. I'd try to change the subject or get busy doing something else. I was terrified that someone would find out about mine."

"You didn't want to be judged?"

"It was more than that. I wanted to forget it ever happened. Looking back, I can see how empty I was inside. I had bouts of depression. After giving birth to both kids, I remember fits of uncontrollable crying. I convinced myself it was postpartum depression," she adds.

"I met many patients who had abortions, and none were *proud*. Even those women who were pro-choice. They're defensive, and most don't realize it. I can see it because I've done it myself, trying to rationalize it away so they can view their actions as acceptable," I explain.

"And that's a problem with the abortion activists, being loud and proud about it. It diverts from the reality that women need to heal, regardless of your political leanings," Rose asserts, who absolutely had the personal experience to back up her claim. "I've talked to many women in post-abortion recovery, and no one ever warned them about the physical and emotional reaction."

"Many times, a woman feels pressured into having the abortion."

"So much for the *choice*," Rose asserts.

"Right. She may be pushed into the decision and told it's nothing to worry about."

"We instinctively know it's *something*. When the grief and loss are ignored, the trauma is buried, and no one talks about *that*," I reply.

"Society tells us to *move on*," Rose explains and is visibly frustrated.

"It's the medical associations too. I've read studies that specifically conclude that women don't suffer emotionally after their abortion, and it didn't fit reality or make any sense. There were serious flaws."

"Oh, I never heard about those."

"They study a small number of participants for a limited amount of time. A very narrow approach. Many women initially view their abortion as *dodging a bullet*, but they don't ask them about it five or ten years later."

"They don't follow up," Rose adds.

"Right. Time isn't invested in the participant. People will be more honest and provide details when they feel safe and comfortable with their doctor. Building that relationship takes a while and over a longer period. A patient's perspective may change."

"That was the case for me," Rose says and adds, "I was in such a rush to have the abortion. There wasn't time for reflection."

"The medical profession is in total denial about abortion and the impact on people, spreading the lie that women don't regret their abortion. And all I could think about is, *Who are these researchers*? It's trauma to your soul," I point out emphatically, a little fired up.

"That's why so many women need to talk to someone. They're told *it's no big deal*, but it is, and when they have regret or confusion, they think something's wrong with them," Rose adds and continues, "the culture tells us not to feel bad about it."

"They're trying to destigmatize abortion and make it seem like a normal medical procedure where grief isn't an issue. It's not a tonsillectomy. I believe they see only the data in a particularly biased manner. They don't recognize the obvious: women aren't prepared for the emotional aftermath."

"So many of us in the group talked about how they were reluctant to initially tell people about the distress it was causing."

"Because they incorrectly assumed they were the only ones."

"Right. Meeting other women with similar experiences was very helpful. Ultimately, you don't fully recover without bringing Christ into the equation," Rose maintains.

"It's so logical and makes sense to have Christ help you through the process, yet so many are in denial about their suppressed pain. I should know. I was like that in the past," I reveal.

"They're scared, which I understand. I finally faced the ungrieved loss, self-hatred, shame, and guilt. Each woman has her own unique experience. Some react soon afterward. But with me, it took years to fully work through all those feelings. I couldn't forgive myself until I fully accepted God's love and mercy. They need to trust God. That's the only way," Rose states with authority, and she pauses.

I sense that she's finished with reliving her story. So I muster the courage to tell her mine. "Can I confide in you about something?"

"You had an abortion?" she asks, mouth agape.

"No, but I performed them," I admit. I confessed to being an abortion doctor for the first time. I proceed to expose my past to Rose, including the horrifying experience from the last time I performed an abortion. "It's as if I came *this close* to touching the devil," I recount and hold up my hand with my thumb and index finger a half an inch apart.

"Sheesh, I never thought about whether Satan was in the room during the abortion," Rose reacts.

"It was a terrifying moment, but I'm glad I saw it. It was a turning point in my life."

Rose is silent for a full minute as she fully absorbs my story, and she shudders. I can almost see the gears in her brain moving. Her reflection is profound.

"I've been in many group settings, and we've talked about how our abortions influenced our lives. The guilt we've felt and everything we just talked about. But we never thought about how it impacted the doctor who performed the abortion," Rose tells me in a serious and compelling manner.

I can see it in her face, her taut jaw and laser focus on me. I want to divert my eyes but realize her intention isn't to confront me. Her expression is concern *for me.* The next words out of her mouth surprise me, forcing me to think about something I didn't even know I should address.

"It must have affected you too. You couldn't have gone through it unscathed. Catherine, maybe you should volunteer your time at a pregnancy resource center. It might help with your healing journey."

Six Months Later, October 2017

I love chocolate. Rose knows this too and points out that a local nonprofit, *Path of Life,* is having an open house, featuring a dessert bar. Not just any dessert bar, but a flowing fountain of dark chocolate and strawberries. That's all I needed to hear.

I want to give back to the community, and this organization is looking for volunteers. Rose encouraged me to contact them months ago, but I didn't bother. The lure of chocolate was the final incentive I needed. Rose was already a volunteer there and previously attended group recovery discussions.

They need help and I need chocolate, so off I go.

I meet Sheri Olsen, the executive director, and we casually chat about the organization and what they were looking for as a medical volunteer. Seeing that many of their clients are pregnant women, my OB-GYN background is a good fit. I thought they might want me to start right away, but Sheri wants to talk further so we can get to know one another. Three days later, we get together for coffee.

"Hi, Catherine, thanks for meeting me," Sheri greets me as I enter the coffee shop. I get myself a latte, and we sit at a table in the corner.

"Sure. I enjoyed the chocolate-themed open house," I tell her, recalling what a treat it was to enjoy the desserts. Sheri is a petite woman with brown hair speckled with gray.

"We had a good turnout. I'm glad you came. So let's get into it. Why do you want to volunteer at the *Path of Life*?" Sheri begins with a no-nonsense approach.

"I've lived in Spokane since January of this year. My daughter is attending nursing school, and I moved here to help her. I was an OB-GYN for about twenty-four years, and I want to spend my time giving back to the community. Rose Cappola recommended I talk to you."

"Yes, Rose is lovely."

"She's the leader of our Bible study group," I inform her.

"Gotcha. We're a tight-knit group, and I like to get to know our volunteers. Everyone is required to attend training to learn about our philosophy. Some volunteers work with clients, while some help in other ways. Much of what we do is confidential and, as a doctor, you'd be used to that."

"Definitely. My practice was in the Salt Lake City area, and I took care of patients from every age and background.

I saw many new patients at the start of their pregnancy. Sometimes it was unexpected."

"Right. We offer pregnancy testing, which is the most common service we provide, but we also offer emotional support, STD testing, and post-abortion recovery. We have educational resources for sexual health and relational wholeness. It's a compassionate approach that adheres to biblical standards," Sheri elaborates and hands me some of the organization's brochures.

"I like the Christ-centered model. I'm completely following Jesus now, and that's part of the appeal of working with you."

"Were you previously a fallen-away Christian?"

"I guess you could say that. God was always speaking to me, but I wasn't listening all those years. I returned to my faith at fifty, after my second marriage ended. That was about six years ago," I explain.

"We're around the same age. Here is our statement of faith. All the volunteers must be aligned with these principles," Sheri says and hands me a two-page document.

I review it, and it's quickly clear that the organization adheres to biblical Christian teachings, which is great. They also offer services for those with unwanted same-sex attraction.

"I'll take this home and reread it, but I agree with what's in there."

"That's wonderful. On the medical side, many clients request an ultrasound, which is free too."

"That's good," I state.

"When it comes to abortion, we don't perform them or refer clients to another organization, such as Planned Parenthood. We believe God has special plans and purposes for both mother and baby," Sheri continues, and I nod with understanding.

"I completely agree, but I should disclose something to you," I state, and Sheri leans in as she doesn't want to miss a word.

"Early in my practice, I did a few abortions, but I later stopped."

"Was that when you came back to the church?"

"No, the last abortion I performed was in 1994, but it wasn't until fifteen years later when my second marriage ended did I fully commit to Christ," I tell her and provide the context of my last abortion procedure with Taylor. I add, "I was never comfortable doing them. I bought the secular view that I was helping women. I mostly limited them to severe anomalies and genetic defects, like Down syndrome, for example."

I notice Sheri shift her posture. *Almost* imperceptibly, I see her nose crinkle, and with a calm and even tone, she says, "I have a seventeen-year-old daughter, Haleigh, with Down syndrome."

I was not expecting her to say *that*. I don't know how to respond and have difficulty extracting my proverbial foot out of my mouth. All I can manage to say is, "I didn't mean..." My voice trails off, and honestly, I don't know *what I mean*.

"It's okay," Sheri responds without any anger, which is somewhat surprising as I'm sure she must have interpreted my comment as grotesque. Her facial expression is kind and relaxed. She's not going to attack me, but I'm not going to be let off the hook that easily because she follows up with, "Can I share my background?"

"Yes, please," I quickly answer, grateful for the deflection.

"I had an abortion when I was fifteen," Sheri states in a composed manner. "This was the late 1970s, after it became legal."

"Oh," I mutter and gesture for her to continue.

"I had another one at sixteen. And a third abortion at eighteen. I thought I was making the *right* decision but didn't have a clue how it would impact me years down the road."

"That must have been a tumultuous period of your life," I blurt out the first thought that popped into my head, stating the obvious. There must be an interesting story about how she went from having three abortions to running a crisis pregnancy center. Sheri doesn't miss a beat.

"I was in a lot of lousy relationships that ended badly. I always was the first one to blame myself."

"But it's more complex than that, right?" I ask.

"Oh, it is. I now see how the abortions messed up my relationships, which were awful to begin with, so I guess, in a way, I'm lucky we didn't stay together. I had a habit of falling for the wrong guy, including a husband. I still can't believe I stayed in that marriage for nine years. What on earth was I thinking?" she jokes, and it breaks some of the tension.

"I've had my share of bad marriages," I admit, smile, and laugh with her. She pauses a moment, and I see her thoughtful expression return.

"He was abusive, and I let it continue because I believed I deserved to be treated badly. Over time, I made the connection that it traced back to the shame from aborting my babies," Sheri confesses and takes a break to sip her coffee.

I briefly tell her about my two bad marriages, and we both endured similar experiences. We are alike in several ways.

"Like you, later in adulthood, I found God and turned my life around," Sheri explains. "Only through God could I begin my abortion healing and recovery journey."

"That must have been difficult."

"It was, but it was part of God's plan because it was critical to my development as a person. It's allowed me to help others who come to the *Path of Life*. I freely share my history, and our clients know I've been in the exact same position they are. Sometimes, we connect pretty quickly."

"Your healing has probably helped you become more compassionate with your clients," I observe.

"No doubt," she concurs.

"There isn't a clean getaway for the person who had the abortion, is there?" I ask a question which I already know its answer.

"Not at all. Back then, I thought I was lifting a weight off my shoulders, choosing the only option to an impossible situation. Every woman's experience is unique, and emotions range from relief to anger to sadness and guilt. Sometimes all at once."

"Most people don't realize how complex and long-lasting the emotional side of abortion is. No one prepares the women for that. I've had several patients with prior abortions, and the aftereffects are usually more intense than expected."

"I agree. Abortion clinics simply want to crank out procedures, and there's no support afterward. Many of our clients don't know what to expect other than their pregnancy was ending. A place like the *Path of Life* provides support and an opportunity for the client to open their heart."

"Do they respond to that?"

"Most times, and even though we're faith-based, we don't force religion on anyone. That never works, anyway. I tell clients that my faith in Jesus helped me come to terms with those choices. As that got stronger, my pain subsided. Ultimately, we say it's up to them, but we'll provide medical services or baby clothes, regardless."

"That makes sense," I reply and nod my head.

"There's a point to my story, which made finding Chuck so special. God was waiting to send him into my life."

"Chuck?"

"That's the part I'm getting to. We dated for three years before we married. I was in my early thirties," Sheri explains and immediately smiles. I marvel at the woman in front of me, who is truly happy.

"God's timing is always best, isn't it?"

"I agree," Sheri states, becomes quiet, and her face drops.

"What is it?"

"For the longest time, I thought I'd never get pregnant. This time, I wanted to have a child. I conceived but had a miscarriage. I thought it was God's punishment. I couldn't stop the fear, doubt, and self-blame from resurfacing."

"That's understandable," I reply.

"Abortion loss and grief share similarities, but abortion is more traumatic due to its intentional nature. I prayed and grieved to come to terms with my miscarriage and the loss of my baby. I put it in God's hands," she explains.

"Right, and that's when you had Haleigh?"

"No, our first child was born perfectly healthy. But a few years later, I had another miscarriage."

"I know what that's like," I offer, and my face involuntarily tightens. "I also had two miscarriages and didn't mourn for those babies until many years later."

"So you understand," Sheri utters and nods her head. It's a unique connection, a bonding moment that occurs between women who've experienced a similar loss.

"There's the lingering thoughts of *what might have been*," I tell her, one of the few people with whom I've discussed my miscarriage pain. I trust Sheri completely, and I surprise myself with how quickly I've let down my typical boundaries.

"I was pregnant with a baby I wanted to keep, and I loved my child in the womb. I couldn't wait to meet the baby and was reading books about what to expect during a pregnancy and tips for an easier childbirth," Sheri adds.

"I know what you mean. As an expectant mother, I couldn't wait to meet my baby. I kept wondering if I was the reason the baby died. What did I do wrong?" I explain.

"That makes the loss so much harder. I couldn't look at my body because it betrayed me."

"As a doctor, I knew babies are pretty resilient, but that knowledge didn't help me emotionally."

"I never thought about how doctors react to their own miscarriage," Sheri says and pauses in thought.

"There's such a range of emotions."

"I felt like I let my husband down and everyone else I told about the pregnancy. I started projecting that emotion outward, jealous of other pregnant women. The last thing I wanted to hear from friends and family was a baby announcement, so I couldn't be happy for other people," Sheri declares with an *oomph*, obviously transported back in time to those primal emotions.

"The face of unresolved grief isn't pretty. You can't force yourself to *simply get over it*," I declare.

"That's impossible. Then I saw this new book by Rachael Nicole Miller called *Silent Stories*. There are so many other women who've had similar experiences. It's beautifully written and gave me some insight."

"One out of four pregnancies end in a miscarriage for a variety of reasons, yet it's a hidden grief that people don't talk about," I state.

"No, they don't. But then my miracle occurred."

"Haleigh?"

"*Yes*, but it didn't start that way."

"How so?" I ask, absorbed in Sheri's story. My coffee's getting cold, but I don't care.

"It was the year 2000, and I went in for my twenty-week ultrasound, and they informed us that our baby showed abnormalities. I once again filled up with negative thoughts. *Now it's payback time*. I allowed myself to be happy and suddenly felt that I no longer deserved it."

"It's so easy to beat ourselves up, isn't it?"

"Yes, it was a tough time. We went back a few days later for another ultrasound and were offered an amniocentesis test. I'd just turned forty," Sheri continues.

"There's an increase in risk at that age, for sure, although most give birth to healthy babies," I say in doctor mode.

"Exactly, and there was a chance she might not survive the amnio test, so we declined it. We didn't know for sure whether Haleigh had Down syndrome, but the chances were high. Later, we had a 3D ultrasound at the thirty-two-week mark."

"What did it show?"

"She had excess fluid on one side of her brain. The doctor told us to consider a late-term abortion, which is available in the state of Washington. They gave me a book that painted the worst-case scenarios, pointing out the many burdens. It was making the case that a child with Down syndrome didn't have any value," Sheri explains, and her mouth and lips appear crunched. Even all these years later, the frustration is apparent. "For the next five weeks, they kept asking if I wanted to have the abortion. They were pushing it."

"Because they didn't see that her life mattered," I conclude.

"Right, even being so close to my due date, well past the point of viability outside the womb. They didn't see me as *a woman with child*," Sheri grumbles.

"They denied the obvious. You were carrying a person inside. Like Dr. Seuss says, *a person's a person, no matter how small.*"

"So true. I had to trust in God. And Chuck's reaction was amazing. He told me we were going to learn so many things from this child. He was spot on about that!" Sheri boasts, and I can almost see her mind fill with memories, her emotions swinging away from irritation.

I'm fully focused on Sheri's experience, which is driving home the point that kids with genetic anomalies are vibrant people. They offer something beautiful that many so-called *normal* people overlook. We live in a world where people are easily discarded. I wanted to hear more. I zoom back to link with Sheri's eyes.

"Chuck was all in. We were going to parent as a team."

"Like you're supposed to," I throw in.

"Yes, and at our last appointment, they did another ultrasound, and the pictures were so vivid I could see her hair floating. In the next moment, the specialist brought up the abortion option *again*. Chuck reminded the doctor that we'd previously said no *multiple times*. I'll never forget the look on his face, daring them to convince us otherwise."

"How did they respond?" I ask.

"Silence," Sheri quips and continues, "after she was born, they doubted Haleigh would be able to nurse, but guess what, she latched on and has been defying the *so-called* experts ever since," Sheri exclaims this time with proud defiance, the uncomplicated joy of motherhood gushing out of her pores.

It's impressive.

"I can tell that she's brought a lot to your family."

"For sure. Just like any kid, she's had her ups and down, thrills and frustrations."

"What's she like?" I ask, wanting to hear about Haleigh the person, not simply the child she decided to keep.

"She's great and has her own unique personality. I remember one time she was sitting right next to her older sister who told Haleigh, *you're in my bubble*. Haleigh was about four years old and interpreted that literally. She puts her hand out, points with her index finger, and pokes her sister's shoulder and says, *pop*!"

"That's awesome," I erupt with delight, amazed that she could share a humorous memory in the middle of this serious discussion.

"Right, it was so funny. I laughed for days," Sheri recalls, and a wide grin covers her beaming face. "There are many humorous moments like that."

"I bet."

"It's her generous heart that really impresses people. Her capacity for love is endless."

"So many people discount the impact an individual can have on other people. That's a huge contribution to society," I profess.

"That's a good point, I never thought of it that way. People focus on the IQ level, even though she's smarter than *everyone* expected. Guess her favorite school subjects."

"Art and history?" I predict.

"Algebra and Latin!" squeals the proud mama bear.

"Wow, that's so cool," I exclaim. "I didn't know anyone learned Latin anymore."

"She loves it. She's also very creative and thrives on social interaction. Sometimes I can't get her to hush," Sheri teases, and her happiness is infectious.

"I can see that your daughter brings *so much joy* to your life."

"She has and does. Don't get me wrong, my oldest daughter receives just as much attention, so she's not left out in any way."

"How do they get along?" I wonder, knowing about sibling rivalries.

"Haleigh adores her older sister."

"Both of your children are blessings, not a burden." The more I learned about Haleigh, the more I'm convinced of this.

"Yes. I regret my abortions, and I'm unapologetically pro-life, which brings me back to the *Path of Life*."

"Oh yeah, that's what we were supposed to talk about," I joke and Sheri nods.

"We're not a political organization. If a client brings up the legality or pro-abortion talking points, we simply won't engage at that level. We circle back to biblical standards. Our volunteer's number one priority is to be compassionate, not to have a debate. We seek to determine which of our services will benefit the client."

"It's all free, right?"

"Yes, our typical client is someone with an unexpected pregnancy, so they're usually confused, scared, and stressed. We aim to eliminate obstacles to alternative options for women instead of convincing them what to do. We also offer childbirth classes, diapers, clothes, car seats, etc. Knowing that support is available after the child is born is vital to a young woman, so that mountain looks less daunting to climb. What makes us successful is showing love and dignity to everyone."

I'm taking in everything that Sheri has told me. I see the passion *and* compassion in her eyes. With her background, it's easy to envision her effortlessly building relationships with the young women who walk through the door. I didn't realize that crisis pregnancy centers provide so many services. I finish off the last of my cold coffee, and I'm astonished that pro-abortion advocates think it's a simple decision and you never give it another thought afterward. That's clearly the exception and not the rule.

"I'm sorry if I upset you about doing an abortion on a Down syndrome child."

"You didn't upset me," she remarks with kindness. I get the feeling this isn't the first time she's had this conversation.

"Talking to you, it hammered home the connection that taking a life isn't right, regardless of whether there is something genetically *wrong with the baby*. There isn't anything *wrong* with Haleigh," I tell her, but I'm uncomfortable with how it came out. Sheri picks up on it.

"I didn't intend to make you feel awkward," she offers.

"I deserved it," I counter with seriousness. She returns an easygoing smile. She's not holding anything against me. I'm grateful to her for allowing me to temporarily drop the guilt.

"So, about volunteering?"

"Yes, I'm interested," I reply.

"You'll need to complete the standard training. But more important than that, Catherine, I think you would benefit from talking to an abortion recovery volunteer."

"I've considered it for a year, but the timing is right, and I believe it's the next part of my journey."

"It wouldn't be appropriate in a group setting because they're usually blaming the abortion doctor."

"I never thought about that."

"People try to lay blame in all directions," Sheri explains.

"A one-on-one setup would be best for everyone. I'm not saying you should keep your past a secret, but sometimes those group sessions can get intense, so that's not the best place to talk about your experiences."

Haleigh Olsen, age twenty-one, reprinted with permission.

Four Months Later

I'm standing outside with my abortion recovery facilitator, Debbie King. At first, the discussions were a little overwhelming, but over time, I was relieved to share my past. The journey includes an important step: to recognize the lives of the abortion victims that I personally ended. It didn't matter if I did a lot of *good* as a doctor; what I did was bad, and it may sound strange, but the *shame* I felt for performing abortions led me to receive God's healing, and *that was beautiful.*

Path of Life has an annual memorial for the babies. The Salvation Army has a building nearby, and they allow us to place flowers on the chain-link fence on their property. It's a solemn moment, and Debbie and I seem to communicate nonverbally, as if she's giving me a hug. I want to comfort her too because like many volunteers, Debbie also chose abortion forty-three years ago.

I worked weekly with Debbie using the *Forgiven and Set Free* workbook by Linda Cochrane, which is a post-abortion bible study. It's not written for doctors, but the forgiveness process is the same.

"This is another piece of the healing process," Debbie tells me.

"Yes, it's the acknowledgement that the journey is real, and the babies aren't forgotten," I reply softly.

"Their lives mattered."

"They were meant to be on earth. Their ordinary lives could have had an extraordinary impact on others, but we'll never know. It's those small moments that mean so much."

"The ripple effect," Debbie adds.

"More like a tidal wave. Being aborted trivialized their lives."

"Unfortunately, so many women and men haven't taken the opportunity to heal. I wish I could help all of them. God wants us to reconcile with Him, our community, and ourselves."

"I think everyone inherently knows that taking a human life is wrong, especially Christians," I declare.

"And yet, half the people who have an abortion view themselves as Christians."

"Most churches are silent about abortion, wasting the opportunity to use the pulpit to promote a culture of life."

"Deep down, they know it's wrong, and Christians may experience a harsher level of guilt, blaming themselves because they should have known better," I add.

"I think that's true," Debbie responds and nods her head. "That's what *the enemy* wants, encouraging the woman to go through with the abortion and then turn around and beat yourself up with guilt for not protecting your baby."

"That's how the devil works, wanting us to hate ourselves and relish in our sins."

"Many people try to ignore the guilt, but don't realize that they're also suppressing the happiness in their life," Debbie admits to me, and I know she's including herself.

I immediately think about my friend Rose. I think that's exactly what happened to her. It's sad that Rose and many others lived through the torment, but I'm happy that she's found her way back to God.

"The women need to understand that they aren't alone," I reply, pause, and take a deep breath, then add, "yes, the guilt and grief is a burden, but when you expose yourself, put it out there and hand it over to God, the weight on your shoulder will be lifted."

"It's not easy, especially if time has passed. It's difficult to open an old scar that's partially healed," Debbie says. She's volunteered as a facilitator for many years and truly understands what it takes to walk the road to redemption.

"Oh, I understand, time *doesn't* heal all wounds," I say with the authority of someone who's taken a long time to travel that bumpy and pothole-laced road.

"It boils down to receiving compassion," Debbie expounds, something she's probably said thousands of times, but I don't mind being reminded of the compassion *I've received.*

"Just like the title of the book, they need to be set free of the bonds of guilt, falsely believing that they're defined by their abortion decision and that their action is unforgivable."

"It starts with believing that you're worthy of receiving healing and grace," she continues. Debbie always seems to know the right words to say.

"Sometimes that's a huge obstacle. It seems so obvious, yet sometimes we don't allow ourselves to accept it. It all goes back to the guilt and thinking that we deserve to feel bad," I remark.

"That's why the workbook is great and usually takes two to three months to complete, chipping away at your internal resistance and building you up with the love of Jesus."

"I like how each of the book's concepts were tied to scripture. That was a big help for me," I say with genuine appreciation for Debbie's love and support these last few months.

"It starts with hope and ends with freedom, and Jesus is there to walk with you the entire journey," Debbie concludes, and that succinctly sums up my experiences these past few months.

"Exactly, the spiritual healing is vital, a necessary step toward wholeness," I finalize.

Suddenly, I hear a car come to an abrupt stop. I watch it pull over, and I'm concerned that an angry pro-abortion supporter will try to stop and hassle us. It's a young man about thirty, and his face is stern and stiff. I immediately expect the worst-case scenario. He is walking directly toward me, and I wonder if I should be concerned for my safety. Debbie steps a foot closer so we can protect each other if need be.

"Are these roses for aborted babies?" he asks, and I'm convinced we're going to have a confrontation.

I still don't like conflict, but I'm not going to lie to him, nor am I going to stop, so I gather enough conviction to calmly answer him, "Yes, that's right." I'm not expecting what happens next.

The young man stares at me, and there's an awkward silence as I figure out how he's going to respond. He puts his hands in his pockets and starts to shuffle and twist his hips. *He's* trying to muster *enough courage* to react to me. His voice cracks as he asks, "Can I help?"

"What?" I ask with surprise and realize his taut face isn't from anger. I see anguish. "Sure, okay," I continue and hand him a rose.

He takes the flower and holds it and then looks at me. He's distraught, and I can tell that he's trying to decide how much he wants to divulge to me, a complete stranger. "It's for my aborted baby," he tells me, but I'm not quick enough to comment, so he continues, "six years ago, I got my girlfriend pregnant. I wanted her to have the baby."

Now I get it.

"I'm so sorry. The pain can last a long time," I offer him.

"I wanted to support her and asked her dad for permission to marry her, but she wanted nothing to do with me or the baby," he explains.

"You didn't have a say," I reply, something he knows all too well.

"She was determined to have the abortion," he states. "She said it *had* to be that way."

The father of the baby is often overlooked in the abortion debate and recovery outreach. He often has zero part in the decision. Of course, sometimes he's pressuring the woman to get rid of *the problem*, his responsibility. But what about the other times where he wants to be a father? The feminists don't have an answer for that.

"It's all of society. Our culture says that the father doesn't matter. That's in line with their attitude that the baby doesn't matter either, so I guess I shouldn't be surprised," Debbie pipes in.

The man nods with despondent understanding. "I'm Darren, by the way," he says and puts out his hand.

"I'm Catherine," I return and see the grief on his face, and he's desperately trying to hold back his tears. It's difficult for him to talk about it, but it seems like he hasn't had anyone willing to listen.

So I will.

"I hated her for the longest time, but I've made peace with it. I've forgiven her," he tells me, and his eyes dart away.

"It's a hard road that takes years to come to terms with," I present to him, but my words seem inadequate. Mere words never seem enough to heal the broken heart.

"I know," he acknowledges and lets out a loud sigh and brushes back his wavy brown hair. "We were having a boy, and even after all these years, I still think about him."

"Go ahead, place the rose in the fence," I encourage him.

He pauses and then links the flower stem in the fence. Darren turns to look at me, and tears are welling up in his eyes. He's trying hard not to lose it.

"Stupid me, I even bought a kid's size baseball glove. I imagined taking a baby picture in a little *Mariners* uniform next to the glove. But I never had the chance to play catch *with my son. I miss him,*" he says, and the floodgate of tears opens. Soon, I'm crying too, feeling helpless and unable to comfort a stranger about the innocent blood spilled. I do the only thing I can.

"Will you help me put up the rest of the roses?" I ask.

"Yes," he says inaudibly and nods his head.

***

I head back to Sheri's office, and we say some prayers, including Psalm 16:11, which inspired the organization's name, "You make known to me the Path of Life; You will fill me with joy in Your presence, with eternal pleasures at Your right hand."

The name of the organization, it's brilliant because as a baby grows inside a woman's uterus, it's exactly that, a path of life. I fully see the humanity of the unborn, and I'm amazed at my journey and grateful to get to know the other volunteers and be around so many caring and pro-life people. I paid heavy dues to get here, while Jesus paid the *ulti-*

mate price. It took a long time, and my life is in a good place now. However, I get the feeling my trekking isn't over.

I tell her about the man who stopped to help put roses in the fence. She wipes a tear from her eye. "I was never much of a crier until I grieved my own losses. It was something I had to be taught. That was beautiful," she comments.

"It was. I felt God's presence with us. I've never seen that young man before," I tell her.

"They're the ones no one talks about. What happens to men like that?"

"They probably suffer in silence, and we meet them and are oblivious. We've had some take part in the recovery services, but not many. I wish more would attend," Sheri states and lets out a deep breath. "You've opened yourself up in the months since we first met," she tells me.

"Really?"

"Absolutely, you're much less reserved. You're a great volunteer."

"I no longer think I'm going to get beat up if people know my past," I admit my greatest fear about volunteering at *Path of Life*.

"We've all felt that way at some point."

"I was always worried that someone would view me as an uncaring person. I've learned to let go. My abortionist past doesn't dominate my life," I explain.

"That's real progress. There will still be good days and bad days," Sheri warns.

"Oh, I understand. Since being involved in this ministry, my view of crisis pregnancy centers has changed completely."

"What were you thinking previously?" Sheri asks, a little perplexed.

"I thought organizations like this lied to young women and pressured them to have the baby. The whole *forced birth* argument that pro-abortion people make, accusing us of guilting women with a hardline approach, telling them they'll go to hell, things like that. It all started in my residency program."

"What did they teach you?"

"They treat abortion as another medical procedure. It's merely a clump of cells. Most medical professional associations are pro-abortion and demonize pregnancy centers. They don't know, or more likely don't care, that most abortion providers don't offer help or encouragement. They start with the attitude that the young women *need* an abortion," I explain, suddenly agitated.

"What about medical school?" Sheri inquires.

"In school and training for OB-GYN doctors and nurses, they talk about caring for two patients. But when they get to the topic of abortion, *suddenly* there's only one patient. They changed the Hippocratic oath to conveniently forget about patient 2."

"There are so many other options to abortion, such as single or married parenting, adoption or getting assistance until the mother is able to do it," Sheri states.

"Especially if she is still in high school."

"Right. We guide our clients through the various options, like many other pregnancy centers around the country. Organizations like ours are typically portrayed incorrectly," Sheri explains. "The pro-abortion industry wants to scare away our potential clients, so they flat-out lie."

"What the PRCs do for women is beautiful. I think abortion clinics are more interested in the money. The profit margin is high, with insurance companies covering the procedure, and the government subsidizing places like Planned Parenthood."

"They want the volume and treat it like a business transaction. Our goal is to build a long-term relationship. They trust our professionalism, and we follow the laws and utilize experts, such as yourself, to help develop our medical policies and procedures."

"It's turned out to be the opposite of what I expected. I like how everything you do comes back to biblical truth teachings, but not in a forceful manner," I explain.

"We don't hit people over the head with the Bible," Sheri jests and adds, "only the individual can decide to let Jesus into their lives."

"I like the gentle approach that you and the staff use."

"Thanks. When they come in, many clients believe their life is doomed. It's that one moment of restored hope that can *change everything.*"

"Yes, if they believe good things are coming, or at least good things are possible, abortion isn't viewed as their only choice," I add.

"Each person has a unique background and perspective, so the first challenge is figuring out what that is for the individual. Most of the time, it usually traces back to a broken relationship."

"They may have engaged in sex for the age-old reason, trading sex for love," I point out.

"That usually doesn't work and sets them up for disappointment," Sheri says. "For us, the first hour with a new client is so important, finding out who they are, and what are her fears. We also seek to understand her hopes, dreams, and her practical needs."

"By being a good listener."

"Absolutely. If we don't start building trust the first time we meet a new client, we usually don't see her again. The trust is created when they see that we truly care about them. Ultimately, we can't offer hope or help until we get to know her."

"Even if they choose abortion, you still treat them with respect and offer encouragement," I say with the knowledge of seeing firsthand how they interact with their clients.

"Exactly. We're always willing to listen. We never want a client to feel alone. I think people are surprised to hear that."

"I know. I never would have guessed it."

"So if you had this negative view, why did you want to volunteer with us?"

"You had chocolate," I joke and laugh at myself, "I'm only half kidding!"

"Seriously, why did you come here?"

"Once again, I think God opened the door and told me to walk through it. It was His plan."

***

To find out more about Path of Life, visit: https://www.pathoflifespokane.org/

To find more about abortion recovery services, go to https://supportafterabortion.com/

Innocent Blood

She said it had to be
Shouldn't matter much to me
It's my body and my choice
She took away my voice
My heart was ripped in two
Over the child I never knew
Only God can heal me now
I miss my unborn child
I cry myself to sleep
For the child I never knew
What could of should have been
Is taken from me
With every passing hour
My stomach turns sour
For the child that never was
There are no words

Written by Andrew and Adrienne LaRue, used with permission. To listen to the entire song, go to: https://soundcloud.com/andrew-larue1

***

Portion of the Hippocratic oath prior to 1964: I will not give a lethal drug to anyone if I am asked, nor will I advise such a plan; similarly, I will not give a woman a pessary to cause an abortion.

Later changed:

Most especially must I tread with care in matters of life and death. If it is given me to save a life, all thanks. But it may also be within my power to take a life; this awesome responsibility must be faced with great humbleness and awareness of my own frailty. Above all, I must not play at God.

Revised by Dr. Louis Lasagne, dean of Tufts University, 1964

***

My daughter finished nursing school, and she decided to move out of Spokane. I hear Colorado calling me back. My son lives in a small rural town along with his wife and children. It's the perfect excuse to relocate, and I do in June 2019. Shortly after moving, my dad dies at the age of ninety-eight years old.

Part 5: *Speak the Truth*, September 2020

I settle in the same town as my son and his family in the Colorado mountains; yet, I'm only an hour from Denver and the surrounding metro. God's persistently nudging me to speak the truth about abortion. It's election season, and Proposition 115 is on Colorado's ballot.

Abortion is allowed up to the moment of a live birth, and prop 115 would restrict such abortions after twenty-two weeks. Exceptions are made for certain rare circumstances that threaten the mother's life. I research the issue and decide to contact the sponsor.

After a few email exchanges, I meet the woman who champions the proposition. After we make our introductions at a restaurant, I tell her my story, and Giuliana Day explains how and why she sponsored prop 115, and her passion to protect the unborn is evident.

"Many draw the line with abortion when a baby is viable outside the womb. Surely people can see how wrong it is to abort after twenty-two weeks," I reason.

"Not in Colorado," she pronounces.

"I know. The heartbeat is detected at six weeks, fetal pain can be felt at fifteen weeks, and viability outside the womb at twenty-two weeks, but why do we have so many lines?" I wonder aloud.

"We shouldn't. The value starts at conception and doesn't incrementally go up after reaching a man-made milestone. It's amazingly difficult to convince some people that human beings are made in the image of God and have rights from the moment of human existence," Giuliana states confidently, yet I easily sense her remorse because so many people are passionate about death.

"It seems so obvious, the value of human life, yet pro-choice people would be more upset if we were aborting cute puppies," I quip, remembering how blind I was about the babies I aborted. Being confronted with the lies I believed about abortion has been one *jolt* after another as they've been exposed to me. I love animals, especially dogs, but I understand people are at the top of the hierarchy. We're above animals, but so many people *choose not* to see the humanity of the unborn.

"It's true, and very sad. The abortion lobby is outspending us, blasting a media campaign with arguments that don't make any sense, such as abortion is health care. They act like pregnancy is a disease."

"And don't forget about *get your hands off my body*. They don't apply that logic and keep their hands off the baby's body," I submit.

"The most vulnerable don't have any rights." Giuliana nods, and I can see the look of frustration on her face.

"Even if you don't believe in God or the Bible, when you devalue life, you're essentially opening the door for other situations where life isn't deemed worthy to continue," I add. "It's a slippery slope we've already started."

"That's true. They never want to address the core issue. What *exactly* does an abortion end?" Giuliana emphatically states, and she is a woman who already knows the truth. The petite forty-something woman softly speaks with *conviction*. I can tell we're going to be friends. We take a break in the conversation and order our lunch.

"Let's get back to talking about you. It's an amazing story," she tells me.

"Thanks. I had no idea late-term abortions were performed at all. Colorado has some of the most *anything goes* laws regarding abortion."

"Politically, Colorado has turned hard left in the last decade."

"That's for sure. I've done some research about late-term procedures and how they're performed. It's risky and much more complicated because the baby is so large. I'm so glad that you have the fortitude to speak the truth."

"Yes, and my approach is to communicate the truth in a kind manner."

"I agree. The other side is always so angry," I say.

"You don't win people over by yelling at them."

"Exactly. People need to know the whole truth."

"That's truly being pro-woman, but that could be uncomfortable," Giuliana says, and it's exactly what I'm thinking too.

"Nobody changes their mind without some discomfort, but that's when they'll think deeper about it," I point out with my own *conviction* because I *know* that feeling.

"That's how the conversion starts, and you try to win hearts and minds, but mostly hearts. I know many people who were once pro-choice," she says.

"Me too. The other side doesn't have any stories about somebody who was pro-life for thirty years and then switches to be pro-abortion. The conversion doesn't get undone," I observe.

"That's so true," Giuliana confirms, and soon enough our food arrives. After a few minutes, she starts up the conversation. "The abortion drug usage is growing quickly. As a doctor, what's your take on it?" she asks.

"I've done a ton of research, and it's four times as risky as a first trimester abortion surgery. I've heard of women going to the emergency room with significant hemorrhaging. About 15 percent of women who choose a chemical abortion experience a profound hemorrhage."

"That's high. The abortion industry is pushing this as an easy alternative, which is having unintended consequences. People aren't being told the risks, and many women are surprised by what it does to their body," she states.

"The medical organizations, which in reality are abortion advocates, are frankly lying. I'm so upset with the American College of OB-GYNs and the American Medical Association. I don't trust them anymore. They're partnering with the abortion lobby and try to suppress any contrary evidence," I say with a fire in my voice. The *so-called* medical authority's activism really burns me up.

"And those are the gold *standard* in the medical community."

"Doctors rely on biased publications linked to the abortion lobby. They don't present opposing points of view, even in the editorial section."

"Don't forget, the drug companies aren't much better," she reminds me. "They advertise it's safe and convenient, but these companies are in it for the money."

"Which is why they're at many universities, handing them out like candy. They deceive women into believing it's no different from taking something for a headache. It's a powerful drug that forces the body to birth the baby, and some women have reported their shock from seeing a fully formed baby dropping into the toilet."

"Can you imagine the horror of seeing that?" I ask but didn't verbalize the obvious next question. *What do you do if your baby is floating in the toilet?*

"And many times, it happens when they're alone," Giuliana adds.

I'm imagining the distress the experience would cause, and suddenly I'm not hungry anymore.

"I think many people *want* to be oblivious," she tells me.

"Yes, and they *catch* this worldview without thinking," I say with sadness because I know so many are purposefully deceived. I conclude with, "We need to prepare our youth to think through the issue, seek the thorough truth, and follow the evidence where it leads."

"But that's not what is happening in schools today. The abortion lobby has a lot of influence in many school systems," she tells me, and I sense she knows the fight against abortion may be an uphill battle. We both take a breath and a break.

We're silent for a few minutes, and I know God's nudging me again. "Is there anything I can do to help?" I inquire.

"Yes. We're having a benefit coming up soon, and we need a keynote speaker. Would you be willing to give a talk?"

***

I've joined the Colson Fellowship program and attended several classes and events. I'm learning to boldly stand for the truth and deeply absorbing the Christian worldview and critical thinking skills. I wish people would acknowledge abortion's harm and focus on the baby. I strive to encourage people to learn the truth, not intimidate them with forceful tactics.

Disappointment doesn't begin to explain my feeling about how most Christian churches are silent about abortion. Honestly, their ineffectiveness is part of the problem. The church should be a welcoming and supportive place while simultaneously standing up for what's true and right.

The pulpit must address the value and dignity of human life in relation to the gospel's themes of forgiveness, healing, and new life. I was so glad to meet Joni Shepherd, who founded Hope and Grace Global, which provides specific training for church leaders and congregations called *Get Equipped.*

An abortion provider shouldn't be the first place a woman with an unplanned pregnancy thinks of visiting. Churches have a tremendous opportunity to explain God's teaching of sexuality and marriage and how behavior outside that can have damaging consequences. We're still trying to undo the mess from the sexual revolution and *free love.*

Abortion would never have become normalized without first accepting sex outside of marriage.

Calling out the injustice of abortion must come from the pulpit because, as Martin Luther King once said, "It may be true that the law cannot change the heart, but it can restrain the heartless." However, laws set a baseline for morality, but not all laws align with God's laws and thus lead to injustice.

Joni and I become fast friends, and I'll join her efforts to get the word out to Christian churches to heal wounds, be compassionate, and actively support Moms and Dads that choose life. That's why I'm so impressed with Joni's message of helping women without the shame.

I desire to reach those with little knowledge who've been misled by abortion industry slogans. Perhaps a person hasn't given it much thought, let alone had a meaningful conversation. Maybe they think it has nothing to do with them. They could be trying to conceal the effects of an abortion, whether it's theirs or someone else's.

It's also possible that they haven't sought forgiveness. The worst case is that the person simply doesn't care. I want to figure out how to talk to people and connect. We're all responsible to speak up and stand for life.

It's strange to look back at my blindness. When I think about performing the D&Es, I'm reminded of the guts hanging out of an animal that's been run over.

Roadkill.

Or a mouse stuck in a trap. Is that what the audience will conjure up in their mind when I speak to them?

Last week, for the first time, I've had mice in my house. They were caught on a sticky trap, still alive and suffering. I have an affinity for animals, which is probably why I became a vegetarian, and the last thing I want to see is one suffering. When I see a hamburger, I think of a cow quietly eating grass in a pasture.

I want my son to come over and do something with the mouse, but he's out of town. He told me to "put it in a paper bag and hit its head with something."

I get a shovel, not to hit the mouse, but to scoop it up and get it out of the house. I can't kill an innocent creature, and I'm standing there holding this shovel, not wanting to go near it and staring at the mouse. It looks worried and scared, and a thought popped into my head, *You did that to babies. You turned them into roadkill.* Wow! After all these years and my long redemption journey, I'm still haunted by what I did.

Every time I'm driving, I notice roadkill and hear that voice in my head, *You did this to babies,* not in a condemning way, but with the conviction of absolute truth. I'm reminded of Amos 6:1, *Woe to the complacent ones.* God expects his followers not only to do what's right but also to *stand up* for what's right.

It's becoming clear that God wants me to talk about this because those are the doors that keep opening. I'm literally saying "*yes,* God." I don't perform abortions anymore, but I get it; this is the direction He's sending me. He wants me to tell my story actively, particularly about His redemption. That's the plan for me, so I'm *all in.*

October 2020

I'm speaking at the fundraiser today, and I'll admit, I'm nervous and frightened. Public speaking isn't something I enjoy, and I'll never remember everything I want to say, so I'll read from a script. I'll be talking for about fifteen minutes in front of over fifty people. It's at a restaurant, so at least the audience will have something to do besides look at me.

My story starts with performing the abortions. Will I bore them stiff? Or worse, will the audience be repelled and look at me as if I'm a monster?

Giuliana introduces me. She gives me a hug, smiles, and says in her Peruvian accent, "You'll do great."

I tell God, *I can't do this unless you want me to and provide me with the strength.* I start my presentation by reciting a part of Proverbs 31, "*Speak up for those who cannot speak for themselves,*" and I'm now the voice of the voiceless. I feel God's presence, and a sense of calm comes over me, as the prayer helps me over my fear of speaking to a bunch of strangers.

God wants it, so I do it.

***

"I'm so proud of you," Giuliana tells me after I'm finished and continues, "that was powerful!"

"Do you think so?" I ask.

"Yes, I saw several people tearing up. Your personal experience, story of redemption and forgiveness was very impactful and moving, exactly what I was hoping for," she expresses, and I have a feeling this won't be the last time Giuliana will ask me to speak at an event.

I'm mingling with the audience, and a woman approaches me. "Thank you for sharing your story. It's hard to admit what you did was wrong and have a change of heart. I'm Millie Malone," a thin middle-aged woman tells me.

"Thank you," I reply, and I see her cheeks involuntarily twitch, and she looks at me and then her eyes dart away as if deep in thought. Clearly, she wants to say something, so I open the door.

"Tell me about you," I suggest. She waits a few long seconds before answering.

"My father was a rapist," she bluntly announces, and I'm taken aback. For a moment, I don't know how to respond. Her words were said not in an accusatory tone, but more informative, as if she'd said, *my father sells insurance.*

"Your mom was...," I say, but unclear whether I want to describe her conception out loud.

"My mom was raped. The family wanted her to have an abortion. I'm here, so obviously she didn't," Millie says, and it's evident she doesn't harbor bitterness.

"She chose life," I beam and marvel at the woman in front of me. She wouldn't be here if her mother decided to end a living reminder of her rapist.

"Yes, my mother couldn't do it, have an abortion. For the longest time, I didn't know *why* I was born. I always felt as if I let my mom down for not doing something *important* with my life. I struggled with that for years."

"But you eventually found *it?*" I guess.

"Yes, through the grace of God, I found my way here and tell people about how I was conceived and that a child shouldn't be condemned to death because of the sins of the father," Millie testifies. "I'm living proof of that."

"Anyone raped needs help and support after a traumatic experience. Abortion only piles on more trauma," I reply and admit to myself that I haven't thought much about rape victims.

"I'm a licensed counselor, and I've worked with many victims of sexual assault, and you're right. Aborting the pregnancy *doesn't help* the woman heal from her trauma," Millie tells me as someone with an expertise in the area. What she says seems so logical.

"Your career has an enormous impact on people. You're doing a lot of good."

"Thanks. Some women are repulsed by the idea of having a rapist's baby. It's difficult and can be retraumatizing, but I've also had clients experience healing by having their baby," Millie informs me. She wants to continue, and I slightly nod, encouraging her, "Some rape victims become depressed and suicidal. If she's pregnant, it can be therapeutic if they find their *purpose* in caring for their baby."

"Maybe that was God's redemption plan, turning something evil into something positive," I suggest, and there's no doubt about her desire to help people.

"I think so, but it's a touchy subject. Even many pro-life people agree with an exception for rape or incest situations."

"I know. But that's where you come in as a professional counselor."

"It's difficult. No one is saying that it is. I'm living proof that good things can come from bad beginnings," she explains.

"A person's value isn't diminished based on how you were conceived. Anyone who meets you must know it," I tell her.

"Yes, and thank you," she says, but doesn't seem comfortable with my compliment.

"You're in such a unique position, given your background and professional training."

"You are too. That's why you're here," Millie reminds me.

"Like I said in my talk, I wasn't always pro-life. God persisted with me, gently opening my eyes at the right time."

"There wasn't a sudden turn around or epiphany?"

"A lot of moments, nudging me in that direction. So many don't know the truth, but it's motivated me to keep going. I think if God revealed to me His plan all at once, I would have messed it up!" I joke and laugh, but in reality, I'm completely serious.

***

According to the Colorado News Collaborative's FollowtheMoneyCO project, proponents spent $505,488 to end late-term abortions, compared to the opponents who spent nearly $9 million to defeat the proposition. Opponents included Planned Parenthood of the Rocky Mountains, Washington D.C.-based North Fund, Planned Parenthood

Action Fund, Cobalt Advocates, formerly known as NARAL Pro-Choice Colorado, and Planned Parenthood Federation of America.

On November 3, 2020, the Colorado voters easily defeated Proposition 115.

June 2021

I'm enjoying the mountain living and continue to speak about the value of life, and I've joined the research team of the American Association of Pro-Life OBGYN's. I'm also consciously aware that the mice haven't returned. It's time for my monthly Costco run, so I head down Interstate 70 toward suburbia. By the time I get down the hill, it's almost lunchtime. I usually have a bag of almonds for lunch, but my stomach tells me I need to eat an actual meal. I reluctantly give in and exit the freeway to find a Panera Bread restaurant.

It's a little crowded, and I order a Mediterranean veggie sandwich with a side of tomato soup. I find an unoccupied table and sit down. A few minutes later, I'm enjoying my food, and that's when I key into the conversation at the table next to me. Three women in their twenties are having lunch and talking about the new Texas Heartbeat law.

"I'm so glad I live in Colorado instead of Texas," cites a blond woman with purple tips. I'll refer to her as Charlotte.

"Because of the new law?" asks a tall woman with long, straight, dark hair tied in a ponytail, who I'll name as Tracy.

"Yes, they're a bunch of old white men trying to control a woman's body," Charlotte snaps.

"It's a heartbeat, so that means something," counters Martha, another tall woman with curly shoulder-length brown, hair. She looks like a Martha, a simple and practical name.

"It's only an electrical impulse," Charlotte replies and continues, "Texas is so restrictive."

"What's the law in Colorado?" inquires Tracy.

"You can have an abortion at *any time*," Charlotte answers, and a small smile appears on her face.

"Up until the moment of birth," Martha clarifies.

"Well, it gives the woman a choice. She doesn't have to decide right away," Charlotte adds.

"Yes, but someone can get an abortion on her due date. That's about three to four months *after* the baby is viable outside the womb," Martha counters, and Charlotte scowls.

As President John Adams said, *facts are stubborn things*.

"That's not the point. A woman should be able to do whatever she wants with her body," Charlotte answers, her voice rising.

I can't believe this is happening. I merely came here for lunch, and I'm listening to an abortion debate. What am I supposed to do? I'm not prepared to tell them what I know. When Charlotte finishes her sentence, I silently start to pray, asking God to please change their minds. I recognize why I was so hungry; God put me in this restaurant for a reason.

"I guess that makes sense," Tracy mutters.

"That's right. How can you be against women's health care rights?" Charlotte challenges and stares at Martha.

"I'm not, but..." She trails off, but clearly doesn't have a meaningful rebuttal.

"I don't know about you, but I don't like the government telling me what to do with my body," Charlotte says.

I'm unsure what to do. This is a private conversation, but I hear each word clearly, and my stomach tightens. I'm forced to decide. *Do I say something or not?* As you know, I don't like conflict, but I can't prevent myself from hearing them talk, and my stress level goes up with each passing word.

"It's a moral issue," Martha insists.

"No, it's a reproductive rights issue. It's about a woman having control over her life," Charlotte insists.

"But God teaches us that life has value." Martha finds enough courage to object to Charlotte's assertion.

"The fetus isn't born. No one is saying you can't have a baby. But no one should force me to have one," Charlotte states, clearly agitated at her friend and finishes up with, "Besides, what's God have to do with it?"

And there you have it, the root of the abortion logic. Cancel God. That's when it hits me. Jesus didn't avoid confrontation, so neither should I, and the next thing I know, I find myself sitting in the open chair with the three ladies.

"I'm sorry, I didn't mean to overhear you talking, but I'm right next to you, and I wanted you to know that I'm a doctor who performed abortions," I inform them.

"Cool," Charlotte quickly replies and nods her head in approval.

"The baby at six weeks has a formed heart that's beating and pumping blood, so yes, it is a real heartbeat," I reply, and Charlotte's small smile drops as fast as a guy wearing cement shoes is pushed off a boat by the mafia.

"But you did the abortions, right?" Tracy asks.

"Yes, I thought I was helping teens and women with the hard choices they had to make," I explain calmly and look mostly at Tracy and continue, "but I came to realize that the unborn baby, or the clump of cells that the abortion industry uses as a description, is a tiny human being, with an equal value to those outside of a womb."

"*We all* started out as an unborn baby," Martha points out, and that seems to resonate with Tracy. Charlotte is unfazed.

"But what about a woman's rights?" Charlotte challenges.

"I'm all for supporting women. The unborn baby in your body has a unique DNA and all the body parts to become a person. Does he or she have rights?"

"Not until it's born," Charlotte contends.

"You're choosing convenience over life and dismissing an important point. For every baby aborted, we'll never know who that person might have loved or what friendships were never created. Each person is a unique individual, whether the contributions are great or small."

I let that sink in a moment.

"Do any of you have kids?" I inquire and see Charlotte recoil as if I've suggested she tattoo *ugly* on their forehead.

There's an opening, so I take it.

"I have four kids," I tell them. "I loved them while they were in my womb. It's something only a mother can understand. I never planned to have children, and my firstborn was an unexpected pregnancy during medical school."

"Obviously, it didn't stop you from becoming a doctor," Martha points out.

"Right. I struggled at times, but it was manageable. Maybe you'll experience motherhood one day."

"I definitely want kids eventually," Martha interjected.

"The female body is optimal for pregnancy from late teens through midtwenties," I let them know.

"That doesn't make sense. People have babies older than that. My aunt had a child when she was forty-five years old," Charlotte tells us.

"Of course *you can*. I'm merely saying the risk of complication rises gradually in your twenties and then rapidly increases after age thirty-five. Society convinces women to get married later, or not at all, and the trend is having kids later in life," I reply.

"Yeah, that's why women should be able to have abortions because of the pregnancy risk," Charlotte quickly steps in and smugly assumes she made a point.

"It's tragic if a woman dies because of a pregnancy, but it's extremely uncommon. For instance, in 2020, it was 24 deaths per 100,000 live births, according to the CDC. It's so uncommon that the average woman rarely needs to worry about it."

"But what about serious birth defects where they are going to die, anyway? What's the point of that?" Charlotte contends.

"That happened with my nephew's child, and their baby went into perinatal hospice, which I'd never heard of because it's so rare."

"Hospice for babies?" Tracy asks.

"Exactly. It is an opportunity to care for the child with dignity and love. It's a precious *gift of time* that's so meaningful for everyone," I inform them and add, "they have the chance to bond with the child and create significant memories, even if it's not very long."

"Wow, that's so sad," Tracy voices.

"It can be, but it also can be beautiful and compassionate and ultimately may help with the grieving process. Many people *absolutely cherish* the limited time with their child," I counter, and I notice Tracy purse her lips and soak in what I've told her.

"Hmm, I guess I never thought of it that way," Tracy says, and I surmise she's rethinking that maybe a child is a treasure instead of a weight to carry.

"What about the other side of the coin?" Charlotte says and then asks, "What are the numbers for dying from an abortion?"

"The data compilation for abortion complications and deaths in the United States is sketchy because many large states don't track abortions, and none of the states keep accurate records. It's all voluntary and inconsistent. But in countries like Finland, there are registries for pregnancy, birth, abortion, and death as part of their health care system, so the data is more accurate."

"I suppose it boils down to whether the woman is ready to have a child, doesn't it?" Tracy asks with sincere concern.

"You shouldn't have to bring an unwanted child into this world," Charlotte adds.

"There are alternatives," I counter.

"Like adoption," Martha declares.

"Absolutely. Also, a family member can help a young mom while she gets her life together. I'm not telling you that all children are wanted by their birth mother, or an unexpected pregnancy is easy. It's not."

"That's why we should have access to an abortion," Charlotte reasons.

"Isn't the child worth it? Why is the answer *to kill the innocent child*?" I ask softly and make direct eye contact with Charlotte.

She doesn't have an answer.

Nobody else responds.

"You're making women poor," Charlotte contends.

"Kids are expensive throughout their childhood. What if people used the same logic about their expensive two-year-old or teenager?" I ask, and again the question hangs in the air without a response.

"Yeah, but..." Charlotte speaks but then backs off because there isn't a solid argument against the statement.

"People with difficult lives, the ones who've persevered through hard challenges, are usually the most beautiful people, you know?" I throw it out there.

"Those are inspirational stories, like my cousin who had his leg blown off in Afghanistan. He battled his disability and depression for years," Martha pipes up, looks at Tracy and adds, "but his determination is awesome. You know my cousin Jackson."

Tracy nods in recognition, pauses, and finally says, "But I wouldn't want to purposefully make someone have a hard life."

"I don't either, but we're talking about human life. If NASA found a simple bacteria cell on another planet, the headlines would proclaim they've discovered an alien life form. Shouldn't that also be true about our own species?" I ask, and I'm pleasantly surprised they haven't told me to go back to my table.

"It's not the same," Charlotte insists, but I can see that she hasn't truly thought deeply and critically about it.

I shake my head and gently smile. I'm amazed that I've remained calm, and the words seem to come to me at the right time. "As a society, we should support women and children, providing better maternity care, not shouting how proud we are about ending life," I continue.

"I'm not saying it's a great idea to have an abortion," Charlotte says, backtracking a bit but then asserts, "I'm saying that people should have the right to decide for themselves. I may not have one, but I'm not going to outlaw it for someone else."

"Again, it's *not your body* we're talking about," I point out.

"I don't see it that way. Besides, it's totally safe, and we don't want to go back in time," Charlotte contends.

"The abortion industry wants you to think it's as safe as taking a Tylenol. When you get into the second trimester, the risks go up exponentially," I inform them. I then explain about risks of future preterm birth, infertility, and the mental health issues, specifically depression and suicide. The women listen and seem surprised at the details, but they don't argue or ask questions, so I decide to keep going.

"In 2006, I was president of the Utah Medical Association, and a bill was presented to the legislature to require anesthesia for abortions because of fetal pain," I redirect the conversation and notice I have their attention, especially Tracy who looks horrified, but they need to hear the truth, so I continue, "I was to testify on behalf of the UMA, and I remember a sick feeling came over me because I never considered that the baby might feel pain during the abortion. Newer studies show fetal pain may occur as early as fifteen weeks. In a second trimester abortion, you're literally ripping the body apart, *piece by piece*."

"Eww," Tracy gasps.

"There's very sophisticated 4D ultrasound technology which has enhanced the ability to use a baby's facial expression to assess fetal pain," I add.

"I don't want to think about that," Martha declares, and the mood at the table is going downhill.

"I won't get graphic, but the more developed the baby is, the more difficult the procedure. When the baby reaches the third trimester, the procedure for the second trimester cannot be done."

"I don't get it. That doesn't make sense," Tracy comments.

"The baby is simply too big, so to abort the child, the baby has to be *dead first*."

"What?" Tracy asks.

"They won't induce labor until the baby is killed, otherwise half would be born alive. The entire *purpose* is to end a life. What's worse is when the baby is birthed alive, and some states allow the doctors and nurses to do *nothing*, meaning the newborn suffers and eventually dies."

"That's horrible," Martha cringes.

"Absolutely, so the only way is to stop the baby's heart by injecting a toxic dosage of a drug, usually digoxin. Once the baby dies, they induce labor, so the woman has a stillborn," I explain.

"But they have to make sure the drug doesn't go into the mother, right?" Martha wonders.

"Correct. But it's not as simple as it sounds."

"Why not?" Tracy asks.

"Digoxin has been around a while and is used to treat heart conditions. It's given to the baby as an overdose, and it's injected directly into the baby or amniotic fluid. The heart doesn't stop immediately because it takes time for the poison to work, anywhere from four to twenty-four hours."

"Twenty-four hours is a long time," Tracy complains.

"Yes, normal side effects of this drug are abdominal pain, nausea, and retching, so they're probably more severe in an overdose situation. Many patients have reported that the baby becomes extremely active, kicking like crazy, obviously struggling and suffering."

"That sounds awful," Martha adds.

"It's like they're trying to escape, but they can't, and eventually there's no movement."

"Okay, that's gross," Charlotte concludes.

"I agree. Remember, their goal isn't to birth the child alive," I say and let the truth settle in.

"The abortion industry doesn't want people to know the complete picture," I inform them. "The question you should ask yourself is a simple one. Are you ending life or not? *You are what you celebrate,* so why would someone be proud of death?" I ask, and I can't believe how easily the words are rolling off my tongue.

"I don't know, but it feels like the government shouldn't have a say in my health care," Charlotte contends, grasping at straws to bolster her argument.

"It's not health care for the baby," Martha adds, and I'm pleased that she has figured it out.

I've got one last thing to say, so I jump in.

"I haven't met many women who found happiness by ending their pregnancy. Many carried guilt because they believed the lie that sex *is just sex,* and it's fun. As opposed to it's a beautiful thing God designed for bringing people together and bonding them for life and raising up the next generation." After saying that, we're all quiet for the moment.

In the silence at our table, I marvel at how God put me in the right place at the right time to have a meaningful conversation with these young women. It was unusual for me to stop for lunch. I don't know if I changed any hearts, but I definitely saw Charlotte waver on her pro-abortion stance and appear a little uncomfortable. Maybe I got her thinking, softening her heart and questioning the lies she's been told.

Like a *pebble in her shoe*, I saw her discomfort. Perhaps it will spark her desire to learn the truth. It's a lot to process, and the three women look tired, so I end it.

"Look, I'm going back to my table. I'm sorry that I interrupted your lunch," I add kindly, but in reality, *I'm not sorry*.

I stand up and leave them with a final thought, "When people think of Colorado, images of hiking, skiing, rafting, and the mountains should come to mind."

"Yes," Tracy agrees.

"Instead, we're known for supporting a *culture of death*. Now that you know the truth, what are you going to do?"

***

After the defeat of Colorado's Proposition 115, Giuliana Day formed the nonprofit, Life Decisions, to help individuals who are struggling with unplanned or a challenging pregnancy and pregnancy-related issues by connecting families, single parents, and individuals with a list of hundreds of free or low-cost resources through the Life Decisions Resource app.

A unique cell phone application that also provides information and resources about the abortion pill reversal, a pregnancy helpline, and hotlines for human trafficking and domestic violence.

Catherine and Giuliana became friends and, along with another doctor, travel across Colorado telling the truth about abortion through statewide presentations. For more information about Life Decisions, go to: https://www.lifedecisions.me/

***

Two major studies were done that found over 50 percent of abortions are performed on women who identify with the Christian faith. This is because the church is rarely the safest place to go in such a crisis. People tend to be reactive or silent in these matters rather than proactive and redemptive.

Most pastors are uncomfortable with the subject and haven't been trained to speak clearly about the topic and its moral implications. The result is silence in the church that ends up perpetuating abortion. The newest generation makes the same fatal choices because there is no redeeming testimony from the previous generations. What most pastors and congregations do not realize is that overcoming these obstacles is not that difficult if approached humbly from the choice to become part of the solution rather than remaining part of the problem.

Hope and Grace Global (HGG) was founded in 2016 with a mission to equip the local church to become a safe haven that PROACTIVELY champions biblical sexuality and life and REDEMPTIVELY heals those wounded by sexual sin or abortion so that the church may become

- empowered by truth,
- healed by grace,
- champions for life,
- a safe haven.

HGG promotes healing by grace through Bible studies for overcoming sexual sin and abortion trauma and loss. You can become a champion for all life through the biblical truth regarding God's design for our bodies, sex, and life, preventing unwed pregnancy, walking alongside those with past sexual or abortion trauma, and empowering those in untimely pregnancies to choose life. The natural outcome is that the church becomes a safe haven where people in crisis can freely come to receive grace and practical help without condemnation.

Joni Shepherd founded Hope and Grace Global after leading abortion healing Bible studies for nearly thirty years and experiencing much resistance in asking pastors to talk about the subject in redemptive ways. Joni lost her first child to the deception of abortion after being judged and abandoned by her church during her first pregnancy. She sought help from an organization which she thought would help her "plan for parenthood."

They were much kinder than her church but offered only one terrible solution, though it felt like her only choice. Her abortion left her feeling as though it didn't matter what she did now. With her second pregnancy, she felt it was best to skip the church and go directly to the abortion clinic. Her life spiraled from there until she found an abortion healing Bible study seven years later.

Hope and Grace Academy, a division of HGG, teaches the church how to overcome this cultural and ecclesial disaster by educating the body, commissioning Hope and Grace Advocates and Ambassadors, and certifying SafeChurches through their SafeChurch™ Project. Hope and Grace Global's Vision is *"Truth in Love, Hope in Grace – The Local Church Certified Safe."*

Below are links to information about the SafeChurch™ Project and Hope and Grace Academy's courses.

https://hopeandgraceglobal.org/partnership/safechurch-project/

https://hopeandgraceglobal.org/partnership/safechurch-project/get-equipped/

https://hopeandgraceglobal.org/be-the-solution/

***

Resources to learn the truth about abortion:

The Charlotte Lozier Institute advises and leads the pro-life movement with groundbreaking scientific, statistical, and medical research. They leverage this research to educate policymakers, the media, and the public on the value of life from fertilization to natural death. For more information, visit: https://lozierinstitute.org/about/

Additional information from well-known authors:

1. *The Case for Life: Equipping Christians to Engage the Culture* by Scott Klusendorf, https://prolifetraining.com/about-speaker/scott-klusendorf/
2. *Tactics, 10th Anniversary Edition: A Game Plan for Discussing Your Christian Convictions* by Gregory Koukl
3. *Contenders: A Church-Wide Strategy to Unmask Abortion, Defeat Its Advocates, Empower Christians, and Change the World* by Marc Newman

CLEMENT: CHAPTER 3— *TERROR OF DEMONS*

The Archangel Michael Defeating Satan, Guido Reni, 1635

INTRODUCTION: AUTHOR'S NOTE

This chapter and the compelling story about spiritual warfare should appeal to people of all faiths, and even to those who may be agnostic or atheist. Some characters that appear in the story are Catholic priests, and several prayers are recited. Catholic principles, sacraments, and procedures are mentioned throughout the chapter, and Christians of all denominations will recognize similarities. It is not necessary to understand the Catholic faith to read the chapter. However, some context and background may be helpful to the reader and is provided below.

Included in the chapter are several references to saints and the Virgin Mary, also called the Blessed Mother. Catholic doctrine absolutely rejects the worship of anyone but God and rejects all worship of statues, whether of Christ or the saints.

The Church allows praying to the saints in order to ask for their intercession with the one true God. The Church also allows one to make statues to remind a person of Christ or the saint. We ask the saints to pray for us because they dedicated themselves to God and serve as beautiful examples of how we too should fulfill our baptism through service to Christ and His Church.

The Catholic Church has always taught that a Christian can worship only God, Father, Son and Holy Spirit. No creature, no matter how good or beautiful—no angel, no saint, not even the Virgin Mary—deserves worship. The saints are alive in heaven because of the life they have received through their faith in Christ Jesus.

Many wonder why demons are afraid of the Virgin Mary. Her humility was so radical that it crushes the "proud head" of Satan and is the surest defense against him and his attacks. Famed exorcist Fr. Gabriel Amorth summed the explanation he received from a demon during an exorcism. The demon told him, "She makes me angry because she is the humblest of all creatures, and because I am the proudest; because she is the purest of all creatures, and I am not; because, of all creatures, she is the most obedient to God, and I am a rebel!" (source: www.aletia.org).

Mary is the Mother of God and is the link between our broken humanity and the boundless divinity present in the triune God. Honoring Mary glorifies and obeys God more than if we do not venerate her. Honoring Mary brings us closer to Jesus. Because the Church is the body of Christ, and Mary is Christ's mother, she is also the mother of the Church. This means that in addition to having a special relationship with Jesus, Mary also has a special relationship with the church. She belongs to the church, and the church belongs to her (sources: https://www.catholic.com and https://www.uscatholic.org and https://www.aleteia.org).

The "Hail Mary" prayer is our greatest prayer to Mary, who is the Mother of the Church and a spiritual mother to each of us. The first part of the Hail Mary is taken from the Gospel. It incorporates the words of the Angel Gabriel at the Annunciation ("Hail Mary, full of grace, the Lord is with you" [Lk 1:28]) and the words of Elizabeth to Mary at the Visitation ("Blessed are you among women and blessed is the fruit of your womb" [Lk 1:42]).

The angel's greeting to Mary can be translated "rejoice," indicating that the promised Messiah, Mary's Son, is coming to save His people. The words of Elizabeth to Mary are a benediction, echoing God's favor to the Blessed Virgin in choosing her to be the Mother of His Son.

The second part of the prayer ("Holy Mary, Mother of God, pray for us sinners now and at the hour of our death. Amen") is the Church's reflection on Mary's intercessory role as the Mother of God for all of us as members of the Church. It reflects the Church's teaching on her preeminent place in the communion of saints in interceding for God's people (source: https://marian.org/). Mary is full of grace because the Lord is with her. By asking her to pray for us, we acknowledge that we are poor sinners.

Adoration is also mentioned in the chapter and is a sign of devotion to and worship of Jesus Christ, who is present in the consecrated host (communion.) It is typically a quiet prayer time offered in local churches. By the consecration of the bread and wine, there takes place a change of the whole substance of the bread into the substance of the body of Christ our Lord and of the whole substance of the wine into the substance of his blood. This means that while the appearance of bread and wine remains, the substance is changed (through the power of God) completely to the body and blood of Christ.

Throughout the chapter, much about angels, demons, virtues, vices, and the seven deadly sins are discussed, as well as certain cleansing, protection, and deliverance prayers are revealed in the story. The author has provided a reference guide at the end of the chapter.

"The devil's finest trick is to persuade you that he does not exist."
—Charles Baudelaire

PART 1: *THE ACCOMPLICE*, JUNE 2018

"Are demons real?"

"Yes, of course," he answered, surprised by the question and then added, "for example, the serpent in the Garden of Eden—"

"*I know about that*," Kennedy Flowers cut him off. "I'm asking about the rest of *them*."

Fr. Jeremy Whitburn paused a moment before answering. The young priest didn't recognize the voice from the other side of the old wooden confessional booth but could distinguish some of the man's features through the fabric screen. "Let's back up a minute. What's going on?"

"You're my last resort. I can't get rid of these headaches," Ken explained and whispered close to the confessional screen. "I think I have a demon inside."

"Why do you say that?" the young priest inquired.

"I get this intense pain for a few minutes, but it lingers and it's difficult to concentrate, especially at work."

"Migraines?"

"No, I don't think it's that," Ken said with conviction.

"Do you need to see a doctor? Could it be stress?" the priest asked.

"I'm always stressed, and I always have been," Ken scoffed with impatience, not looking directly at the priest. "That's *not it*."

"Maybe it's remorse. Do you have something to confess? Isn't that why you're here?" Fr. Whitburn redirected the conversation.

"Yes, maybe if I confess, it'll go away," Ken reasoned, cleared his throat, and moved his shirt collar around even though it wasn't tight around his neck.

"Let's start with that," Fr. Whitburn suggested.

"Father, it's so noisy in here, and I need your help," Ken begged and started to cough.

"Go on."

"I, I should tell you," Ken stammered and coughed again and had a difficult time speaking.

Fr. Whitburn was familiar with reluctance in the confessional booth. It can be awkward for people to open up. He waited a solid thirty seconds, hoping the man would speak and ask for forgiveness. It seemed as if he was trying to talk, but no words came forth.

"I know it might be difficult. Tell me what's on your mind," he encouraged, intending the open-ended question to prompt a discussion.

"I'm not sure I'm ready."

"All right, let's start with a prayer. Hail Mary full of grace."

"No, *not to her*," Ken interrupted in a louder tone and noisily sucked in air, which startled the priest.

Fr. Whitburn immediately wondered if the man on the other side of the old thin wall was having a panic attack or hyperventilating.

"I want you to get rid of *them*!" Ken pleaded in a loud whisper and cleared his throat.

Clearly, this man was hesitant to provide details. Perhaps there was embarrassment and a hesitancy to admit his sins. Or maybe he was going to come up with excuses for his behavior, as in *the devil made me do it*, as the priest sometimes heard. Since he didn't know the man, he was only guessing. But *something* felt different, and the young priest recognized the man's tone of voice.

Desperation.

"I can recite a deliverance prayer," he offered.

"Yes, that's what I need," the man quickly agreed.

Fr. Whitburn found what he needed in his confessional books. "This is a cleansing prayer."

"Thank you, Father," Ken approved, his voice cracked and cleared his throat once again.

"Heavenly Father, in the Name of Jesus Christ our Lord and Savior, by the power of the Holy Spirit, we pray that the cleansing power of the precious blood of Your Son come upon us right now," Fr. Whitburn delivered in a calm voice. In the back of his mind, he realized that he'd never read this particular prayer. He noticed the man on the other side of the screen start to fidget in his seat.

"Purify us and wash us clean with the blood of Jesus from the top of our heads down to the very soles of our feet. Let this blood penetrate the very marrow of our bones to cleanse us from any entanglement from whatever evil spirits we have encountered during our intercession."

"*Ahh,*" Ken interrupted him with a guttural sound and appeared to be writhing in pain.

"Anoint us with the gifts of the Holy Spirit and refresh our body, soul, and spirit, and may the sign of Your holy cross drive away all evil spirits from us," the priest said and heard Ken violently cough again. He decided to quickly finish.

"In the Name of the Father and of the Son and of the Holy Spirit, amen," Fr. Whitburn concluded.

"*Non me ne andrò.*"

"What?"

"I will not leave," he bellowed, this time in an unrecognizable voice. It was then that Ken's face contorted.

"What?" the priest asked again.

The left side of Ken's face went flabby, and his mouth opened wide. His teeth looked black, and his tongue appeared engorged.

Fr. Whitburn tried to focus on what was happening on the other side of the screen in the dimly lit century-old church. He tried to understand what was happening in front of him. *Can I believe my eyes*?

The young priest purposefully blinked as the image in front of him continued to appear deformed. He could hear Ken deeply inhale, and the man's breath was hot and putrid. Fr. Whitburn was stunned and unsure of his next move. He redirected his thoughts back to the prayer book, but that concentration was short-lived.

"Arrgh," Ken grunted and shook his neck from side to side.

Fr. Whitburn couldn't see Ken's neck muscles pulsing, but instead sensed it happening. His own heart rate increased, and he began to sweat.

Whatever controlled Ken saw an opening to confuse the young priest. Ken pressed his face up against the confessional screen window and made his face appear more distorted. Fr. Whitburn observed his deformed mouth open even wider.

He can't possibly stretch it any further.

And then he did and passed the point of what was physically plausible.

The young priest gasped at the sight in front of him.

Ken's mouth stretched over six inches in diameter, and suddenly their eyes locked for a moment. The dimly lit space shadowed the inside of Ken's mouth, making it appear like a bottomless pit.

The flustered priest's heart raced faster, and he felt cold and hot at the same time. It was then that Ken involuntarily kicked the confessional's dark walnut wood. The echo in the room lasted longer than expected. Fr. Whitburn almost asked if Ken was okay but held back. The question was ludicrous.

Fr. Whitburn regained his wits and focused on the prayer book and nervously recited, "Come, Holy Spirit, renew us, fill us anew with Your power, love and joy. Strengthen us where we have felt weak and clothe us with Your light. Fill us with life. And Lord Jesus, please send your holy angels to minister to us and our families."

Fr. Whitburn looked up from reading the book and observed Ken coughing uncontrollably. He couldn't tell whether Ken's face and mouth were back to normal, and he was about to look for another deliverance prayer when Ken suddenly became calm. The man looked at the priest directly, and his face no longer appeared misshapen.

"I'm sorry, Father. I feel sick," Ken told him with an unsteady voice and immediately jumped out of the confessional chair, opened the door, and bolted past a parishioner waiting her turn to talk to the priest and almost knocked her over. Before Fr. Whitburn had a chance to react, Ken was gone.

Twelve Days Later

Father Whitburn pulled into the small strip mall parking lot, which was home to Monarch Street Coffee House. Ken apologized for leaving the confessional and proposed meeting elsewhere two days earlier. Ever since he briefly met with Ken, Fr. Whitburn could think of little else. It'd all happened so fast, and he was wondering what *he actually saw.*

Well, he knew what he witnessed; he wasn't in denial, but then again, maybe he misinterpreted. Doubt crept in. *Maybe* Ken was a mentally disturbed person, and it's *possible* he observed a serious bout of mania.

But the young priest couldn't quite let it go. The way Ken reacted to the deliverance prayer and the twisted look on his face. Yes, the lighting *wasn't the brightest* in the confessional room, and the screen *might have* warped his view. But then again, no parishioner had previously appeared so distorted.

In the seminary, he learned about angels and demons. The professors talked about exorcisms at a high level, but there wasn't any formal training. He prayed about it, and his gut told him he observed more than a mental illness lapse. However, since he didn't know who the man was, he eventually forgot about the incident. But it all came flooding back when he received a call from Ken, who suggested they get together.

Fr. Whitburn entered the shop and saw Ken at a table in the corner. "I'm sorry, Father," Ken offered with sincerity as the priest sat in the chair across from him. "I'm not sure what happened, and thanks for meeting me on neutral ground."

"You're right, it was a strange moment," Father Whitburn agreed with an awkward smile and thought about Ken's odd choice of words, meeting at a *neutral* location.

"I don't know what else to do, or who to turn to. But I don't think I can go back there. It was too intense," Ken admitted in a loud whisper.

"Why did you come to the church?"

"I can't remember everything that happened or what I told you, but I needed a priest," he said in a calm and measured tone.

Fr. Whitburn was unsure what to expect and started to relax as Ken appeared to be in total control. He hoped that would continue. "Let me just come right out and say it. Lots of people think they're under demonic influence, but in reality, it's more likely to be a mental health issue."

"Maybe, but I don't think I'm *crazy*," Ken said crassly, instantly perturbed and rubbed his temple and brushed back his jet-black hair.

"I didn't say *that*," Fr. Whitburn backtracked and added, "it could be stress or a traumatic event," the priest suggested even though he saw *something* manifest, and Ken spoke an unfamiliar language. However, he purposefully wanted to remain skeptical.

Despite being under thirty and a priest for only three years, he wasn't willing to back down. St. Benedict's pastor became seriously ill six weeks ago, and he'd been extremely busy, but not overwhelmed, trying to lead the parish before the bishop assigned a more seasoned replacement.

He intended to learn as much as he could while temporarily in charge. One of the first skills he practiced was to combine mental fortitude and humility, and his lanky body communicated it well.

Fr. Whitburn sat in silence and watched Ken lean back in the chair and fold his arms, his muscular tone on display in the tight T-shirt with the wording KF Construction. The priest watched Ken decide on how to react.

His posture oozed; *you've insulted me.*

It's been a long while since Ken *let it go*, but that's exactly what happened.

"Okay, Father. It's something more. I don't always feel like myself."

"Can you provide some background or context? Have you been to a therapist or psychiatrist?"

"*For years*, and nothing got better. I'm tired of the head shrinker's pills, which made me feel worse. I've seen medical doctors about the headaches, had a CT scan, and there's no tumor or anything like that. No one can give me an explanation."

"Hmm," Fr. Whitburn responded and clicked his tongue in thought.

"I have *awful nightmares*. I'm at my wit's end, so I came to you."

"What makes you think it is something supernatural?" the priest asked.

"Honestly, I don't know for sure. In my gut, I know *I'm not alone*. I'm terrified of church. It took every ounce of courage to walk into that confessional room, and then, well, I'm not sure what happened," Ken explained.

"You exhibited strange behavior, but I don't want to jump to any conclusions."

"I understand. You need to be careful. Recently, I started thinking more about God and dug out an old crucifix from my childhood. I haven't looked at it in a decade, and it scared me to pick it up, and when I saw the image of Christ on the cross, it blinded me for a moment. I panicked and quickly put it back in the box."

"Hmm," Fr. Whitburn replied.

Ken said in a low tone, "*I had* to cover it, and that's when I became convinced that a doctor couldn't solve my problems."

"Maybe," Fr. Whitburn replied and trailed off, processing the potential sources that influenced Ken's reaction to a crucifix.

"That's why I want to know. *Are demons real*?" Ken whispered.

"*Yes*, but let's talk a minute about what you know about demons. Or angels, for that matter."

"Not much other than what I've seen in movies."

"Hollywood gets it wrong most of the time."

"That doesn't surprise me, but they *do* exist, right?"

"Yes, in the beginning, God created the angels," Fr. Whitburn explained. "They were instantly infused with all the knowledge and intelligence they would ever retain."

"So they're smart?" Ken wondered.

"Yes, they aren't capable of forgetting anything, and can learn through observation, but they can't develop any new skills like humans do."

"Some of us don't *ever* learn," Ken taunted sarcastically.

"Right," Fr. Whitburn blurted out and smiled as he watched Ken laugh at his own joke. The young priest was grateful that their conversation wasn't getting too weird. He continued, "Humans are capable of finding wisdom. The most crucial point is that angels were given the freedom to love God as well. Or not."

"Ah, the fallen angels?" Ken replied and nodded with enthusiastic understanding.

"Yes, about one-third of the angels rejected God. Lucifer was the most powerful *and* most intelligent angel. When they turned their back on God, they were cast out of heaven and became demons."

"Okay, I'm no religious scholar, *obviously*, but that seems pretty dumb to reject God, doesn't it?" Ken joked.

"Well, yes," Fr. Whitburn answered and smiled, surprised by Ken's light mood about a serious subject.

"But why would they reject God? What would be the point of that?"

"*Pride*," the priest easily answered.

"Pride?"

"Yes. Lucifer and his legion of demons were jealous when God created humans. Angels and demons are spiritual in nature, compared to people who have a spiritual and material nature." Ken looked confused and Fr. Whitburn tried to clarify, "You have a soul, your spiritual part, and you have a body, a physical part. Demons don't have a physical nature. They're just spirits."

"Right, but why are they *jealous of us*?" Ken asked incredulously.

"God put us above the angels in His hierarchy. Angels were created to serve mankind. Lucifer didn't like that, so he rebelled against God and wanted to be on the same level as God."

"Father, forgive me if I'm confused," Ken huffed and added, "but it sounds like the demons should take up the issue with God."

"Yes, you make a good point," Fr. Whitburn answered and smiled. "They were banished from heaven and stripped of all their grace. The fallen angels despise us because we can attain salvation in heaven, and *they can't*. The bottom line, demons have redirected their rage against humans."

"But we didn't do anything to them. Certainly not an individual person," Ken argued.

"Unfortunately, that doesn't matter. Their animosity is channeled to tempt us to commit mortal sins, which is essentially a rejection of God."

"So they hate us and want to bring us down," Ken concluded, pleased with himself that he *got it*.

"Exactly. They watch us and wait for an opening to worm their way in and influence our lives."

"To make us sin."

"Yes, but they're more of an accomplice. We have *our free will.* We can choose God or choose sin. Most of the time, it's our decisions to act badly and less of the time where *the devil made me do it.*"

"We don't get off the hook that easily," Ken lamented and produced an easygoing grin. This time, he leaned back in his chair without his arms folded, but instead brushed his fingers through his short, dark black hair, which framed his rugged, good-looking face.

The young priest noticed Ken finally relax and appear content. However, the grin dissipated within a few seconds as Ken's next thought came out, "But what *about me*? Can you *help me*?" Ken asked as he hoped for an affirmation of his condition. He slightly bent over as a searing pain ripped through his head, as if an icepick slowly pierced his eye and punctured his brain. He brought his hand up to his forehead and rubbed it, to no avail.

Fr. Whitburn thought long and hard about this simple question, yet one with a complex answer. Ken appeared to be afflicted with something, although his behavior at the coffee shop was perfectly normal and in control. Maybe it was mental illness, but what if it's more? He couldn't deny what happened in the confessional room. That wasn't a mental illness outburst. But he was unsure of the situation. The one thing he was sure of was that *he* wasn't prepared to do any exorcism ritual.

Ken spoke again and brought him back into focus. "Father, do you think *I'm possessed*?" he whispered even though the coffee shop wasn't crowded, and no one was within earshot.

"I don't know," Fr. Whitburn answered slowly, and he could see Ken's face slightly twitch. Was he pleased or disappointed? Could he exhibit two opposing expressions at once?

"Well, what do I do now?"

"I need to talk to someone with more expertise."

"Can't *you* help me?" Ken pleaded as if he and Fr. Whitburn were lifelong friends.

"I don't have the required training, but don't worry, I'm not handing you over to some stranger. I'll stay involved."

"What are you going to tell them?"

"Please understand that anything we discuss or *occurs* in the confessional is confidential. It's one of the strictest principles of the priesthood. If you're comfortable, can I share what we discussed today at the coffee shop?"

"Sure, I need help," Ken asked, rubbed his temple, and ran his fingers through his hair and added, "let's get it done."

Fr. Whitburn nodded. He wasn't an expert, but he understood it wasn't going to be a quick process. Whether Ken had mental health issues to work through, or suffered from diabolic affliction, it was serious, and any solution would take time. There isn't a *one and done* silver bullet in either scenario. He hoped Ken had the fortitude to see it through.

He didn't want to discourage Ken, so he confidently stated, "I'll call this afternoon, and we will reconvene to talk about what to do next."

Two Hours Later

After exiting Interstate 25, Clement headed west on Baseline Road, Colorado Highway 7, in Broomfield past the Anthem neighborhood and into the town of Lafayette. He never tired of viewing the Flatirons, Boulder's most iconic rock formations, which would remain directly in front of him for the next thirteen miles until he arrived at his destination, an early dinner with Fr. Palermo.

They were meeting at a barbeque restaurant. He acknowledged Colorado had beautiful mountain views. But barbeque? It wasn't bad, *but it wasn't Texas barbeque.* He agreed, however, because Fr. Palermo picked the restaurant.

Clement pushed the button on his steering wheel to answer his cell phone in hands-free mode, "Hello."

"This is Fr. Whitburn from St. Benedict's parish. Do you have a few minutes to talk?"

"Yes, I'll be in the car for another fifteen minutes, so go ahead."

"I have a parishioner who believes a demon afflicts him. It isn't someone I know very well, but there *is* something going on. He also had a rather difficult confession," Fr. Whitburn stated.

"Have you met with him outside the sacrament of confession?"

"Yes."

"What can you tell me?"

"Sure, we had a follow-up meeting, and...hello?" Fr. Whitburn stated and looked at the phone receiver and realized the call was cut off, assuming it was on Clement's end, since the young priest was calling from his parish office on a landline. He redialed.

"This is Clement. I'm sorry, Father, the call dropped. I don't know why since I'm in the middle of suburbia."

"No problem," Fr. Whitburn assured him and filled in Clement on his discussion with Ken at the coffee shop. Ten minutes later, he wrapped it up by stating, "I'm not sure how to proceed."

"Okay, in this initial phase...hello," Clement said and realized the phone call dropped again. He shook his head in frustration, and twenty seconds later, his phone again rang.

"I'm sorry again, Father."

"It's fine...you were telling me about what I should do next."

"Yes, you will initiate a baseline of prayer with the parishioner along with a specific discipline of behavior for thirty days. He could suffer from extraordinary diabolical affliction or psychological issues and human character flaws. Either way, he needs to reconcile with God and His Church. There are detailed steps to follow, which I'll email you, and you'll send me weekly updates."

"That's perfect, thanks so much," Fr. Whitburn replied, grateful that the call's connection stayed intact.

The Next Day

"Ken, I don't know what we're dealing with, but there's one thing I know for sure," Fr. Whitburn started the conversation as they settled in their chairs at the Monarch Street Coffee House. He continued, "You need to come back into God's grace. You'll benefit tremendously by opening your heart to Jesus. You cracked opened the door a tiny bit, but much more is needed."

"Okay, but the other priest you talked to, can't we meet with him and get the show on the road?" Ken exclaimed, for he wanted to skip the details and fast-forward to the solution.

"I talked to a case facilitator, not a priest, and there are certain protocols that must be followed."

"I don't get it, can't we have a priest perform, you know, *an exorcism*?" Ken murmured and looked around the coffee shop for anyone eavesdropping. The place was busy, and three women were chatting at the table next to them. "Just get an expert priest to say a few prayers, throw some holy water on me, and then I'm good, right?" Ken pushed.

"*If it were only that easy*. We still don't know the root cause of your affliction, but like I said, let's get you in the right relationship with God first."

"I've carried this weight a long time. I simply *want it done*," Ken replied with a loud sigh and stared at the young priest, whose facial expression was not communicating what he wanted to hear. Ken was a man used to *getting his way*. A man used to *being in charge*, whether it was with customers on a job site or employees who needed a paycheck.

He didn't like being in the situation where he needed someone else.

Urgently.

The roles were flipped, and that didn't sit well with Ken. Anger welled up inside, and a thought flashed across his mind. *I'm going to show that priest.*

He didn't know the priest very well, but he could read people, think on his feet, and find a weakness in anyone, including a priest, and exploit it. *He doesn't know who he's dealing with.* Ken was about to return a typical snarky remark and arrogant attitude. He opened his mouth to deliver a stinging insult to the man trying to help him, but the priest's next question left him speechless.

"Do you want to make it to heaven *or not*? It's that simple," Fr. Whitburn laid out his cards. He figured Ken was a *bottom-line* kind of guy, so why not cut to the chase?

"What?" Ken stammered, for he wasn't expecting *that* question. He never seriously contemplated what would happen to him after he dies.

"There's no quick fix for whatever is going on with you, but putting that aside for a moment, it all depends on *you*. It starts and ends with your relationship with Christ, but only if you *choose it*."

"I guess," Ken unenthusiastically replied.

"You *guess*? I think God deserves a little more eagerness than that, don't you think?" Fr. Whitburn chastised him in a jovial manner.

Ken had two choices for a response. Become insulted and lash back, or realize his answer *was lame*. The two seconds before his response wasn't a long time, but prolonged enough for Fr. Whitburn to develop a smirk. Ken's heart filled with a moment of grace.

"Okay, I have to admit, my response was pretty weak," Ken answered and laughed at himself, something he hadn't done in a long time. "But you have to understand, I don't normally think about religion."

"I get it, I really do. But there's no time like the present. And I'm totally serious. You need to make your *salvation* a top priority." That statement was pretty hard to argue against, even for Ken. "I'll be with you every step of the way," the young priest shifted his tone to be more supportive.

"What do I have to do?" returned a dejected Ken, for he still greatly desired the immediate solution.

"The protocol, it's a plan, a *blueprint* for you."

"All right, a blueprint. I know what to do with that," Ken stated and nodded, his energy level rising.

"For thirty days, we are going to get you into a life of prayer and discipline. We'll assess after that," Fr. Whitburn explained, and Ken's face communicated a thirty-day program was longer than he expected but soon morphed in to understanding. Ken relaxed and silently agreed. Fr. Whitburn knew that thirty days was only the beginning, for he hoped Ken would make long-lasting changes.

"What's the *plan*?" Ken asked.

"Here is what you need to do," Fr. Whitburn replied and slid a piece of paper across the table. He gave Ken a minute to read it and took a sip of his coffee.

"Okay, 6:00 p.m. I can start tonight," he told the priest with confidence.

Later That Day, 5:55 p.m.

Ken reviewed his *homework* assignment. The detailed instructions were laid out in a simple format. Simple doesn't equal *easy*. Ken felt depressed seeing the long list of difficult and unfamiliar items. He previously never developed prayer habits or discipline and became overwhelmed as he tried to figure out how to fulfill the requirement for *thirty straight days*:

- Angelus prayer, three times per day at 6:00 a.m., noon, and 6:00 p.m.
- Auxilium Christianorum prayers also at 6:00 a.m., noon, and 6:00 p.m.
- Psalm 130 prayer at 6:00a.m., noon, and 6:00 p.m.
- Confiteor prayer at noon.
- Act of Contrition prayer at 6:00 p.m.

Discipline and devotions:

- Media fast, no social media, internet, games, or television.
- Gregorian chant 24/7 at low volume, Benedictine monks of Domingo de Silos.
- No reading other than daily Mass readings.
- Burning of blessed candles to dispel night terrors or evil presence(s.)
- Sacred art and images should replace secular magazines.
- To be prayed and followed by all present in the household in which the petitioner lives, especially spouses, parents, and siblings. This wasn't applicable to Ken, as he lived alone.
- Ask family members to pray for Ken, such as his mother.
- Weekly confession with Fr. Whitburn.
- Weekly reporting to Fr. Whitburn.

The priest explained the purpose of sticking to the time-of-day schedule. When God created the heavens and earth, He sanctified the days of the week. Christ, through his passion, sanctified the hours of the day. Ken took a deep breath, rubbed his temples, loudly exhaled and started, "*The Angel of the Lord declared unto Mary. And she conceived of the Holy Spirit.*"

Eight Days Later, 6:12 p.m.

Ken sent his weekly summary to Fr. Whitburn and was pleased to report that he'd diligently followed the protocol. He went to confession. It lasted only seven minutes because Ken was not ready to tell the young priest *everything*. He sensed the priest knew he was leaving out something, but Fr. Whitburn didn't push him, much to Ken's relief.

The young priest knew not to press Ken too hard, fearing he'd give up, which was an accurate assessment. Ken struggled but so far managed to fulfill the requirements.

He'd finished the 6:00 p.m. prayers, but instead of feeling better, he was coming out of his skin. The prayers were *way too long,* and the discipline was becoming unbearable. It felt more like punishment. No games, internet, or television. Come on, man!

Ken spun himself up, agitated, and felt like something was going to pop. There was pent-up energy that needed to be relieved. He reviewed the priest's instruction sheet. He didn't see anything which prohibited a visit to his favorite watering hole.

O'Connell's Tavern and Grille was one of Ken's favorite places to unwind after a long day. The proprietor catered to hardworking blue-collar locals. Real men, mostly in the construction trade, and a few hardened women who weren't afraid to spark up an arc welder or drive a truck and swear like a sailor. The kind of women who could hold their liquor, never ordered a strawberry Daiquiri, and could be featured in a Toby Keith music video.

The owner, a native of Worcester, Massachusetts, Eddie O'Connell ditched Boston's progressive politics over twenty-five years ago. He didn't own a blender to make *girlie drinks*. Or serve anything made with grapes. Diversity was celebrated by offering two types of beverages: beer or Irish whiskey.

Denver morphed into the Massachusetts he left behind, and his pub no longer fit into the city's yuppie vibe. The establishment was a dying breed. But don't tell that to O'Connell, who ignored the reality that he was surrounded by wine bars and hipster breweries. Both the building and proprietor were *too old school* and *so last century,* but defiantly thrived in Denver's new technology culture. The place was packed, and several patrons ordered O'Connell's specialty, lamb stew.

Ken parallel parked on the street a block away and recognized the double "W" logo on the truck in front of him as one of his contractor competitors, Walter Wilson. They rarely crossed paths because Ken's customers were typically small and medium businesses, where Walter catered to building custom homes. They weren't enemies, but they never socialized as *friends*. Their few previous encounters grated on Ken's nerves.

Despite finding Walter arrogant, they avoided confrontation due to infrequent interactions. Ken settled his emotions and vowed not to engage with Walt. He ordered a double shot of whiskey, a bowl of stew and sat at the bar by himself.

Three hours and five shots later, Ken noticed Walter and one of his employees leaving the establishment, headed in Ken's direction. Like in a predictable movie, Ken could tell that Walter didn't notice him at first, and then their eyes locked. Ken's stare was blank, not threatening, but nowhere near friendly. Walt recognized him and couldn't care less.

Walt's employee made a joke and gave him a slight shove to get his attention. Walt's reaction to the small push was slow, forcing him to take a step sideways, and his shoulder bumped into a waitress clearing a table.

The tray wobbled, and it was uncertain if she could prevent the contents from spilling on someone. But the old gal had strong arms from years of carrying food and saved the day. Disaster averted. Walter mumbled an apology, and the waitress responded with, "Don't worry about it."

Ken was far away, and the tray tipping would have been someone else's mess. It was over before it even started, and within seconds, Walter and his employee were out the door. Ken couldn't quite put his finger on it, but the situation irritated him.

The balding, ugly, and rotund man got lucky.

Nothing happened to the pompous idiot!

And perhaps that irked him the most: someone who didn't deserve luck got lucky. Where's the justice in *that*? Someone whose actions should have had consequences came out unscathed, like nothing happened. Where was God's justice with *that*? Walter simply got away with it, and it got under Ken's skin in a bad way.

He'd been praying to God for days, but He *did nothing for him*. Yet, Walter gets *taken care of*. Where's the *fairness in that*? Did Walter pray every day? *I bet he didn't,* Ken fumed to himself. *He's probably one of those hypocritical Christians.*

Ken riled himself up and directed his anger at God. Who was going to be strong enough to *right the wrongs*? Who would make sure an irresponsible guy like Walter, who was clueless about his behavior, got called out? Who was going to...but Ken was interrupted before he could finish *that* thought.

"You want another?" asked the bartender, who momentarily distracted him.

He processed the meaning of the question and answered emphatically, "Yeah."

Forty minutes later, Ken decided to call it a night. He grew tired of listening to bits and pieces of nearby conversations, people *droning on and on* about stupid, meaningless topics. Is that all these people did, complain about every little thing in their boring and useless lives? He was sick of it. He slapped down enough cash to cover his tab, plus a generous tip, and quietly headed out the way he came in, alone and tired.

Ken didn't notice it at first. Someone drove down the street, and the oncoming headlight lit up the front of his truck. He spotted that the metal surrounding his blinker was crushed. The truck's grille and some of the front bumper got dented too. No one left a note on his windshield, and whoever was parked in front of him was long gone.

He instantly became infuriated.

Walter Wilson did this to him, and he was going *to pay*! If God would not apply justice, then Kennedy Flowers would. He jumped in his truck, gunned the engine, and sped off.

Twelve minutes later, Ken aimed his bright lights directly at the front entrance of Walter's small business office. He took a deep breath, solely focused on *settling the score*. Justice must prevail, and Ken would not let Walter win. He left the truck lights on, opened his door, and found exactly what he needed in his truck bed. A two-inch by four-inch piece of pine about the length of a baseball bat.

As he approached the office door, he confirmed the inside was dark and unoccupied. The top half of the door was a heavy-tempered glass but would not be a match for Ken. He channeled his inner Todd Helton and, without hesitation, swung the piece of wood as if he were looking to hit the ball out of Coors Field. The glass shattered, and the inertia from the swing caused Ken to lose his grip, and the piece of wood flew past the glass and into the office.

That gave Ken an idea.

He carefully put his arm through the newly emptied space in the door and carefully twisted the deadbolt, slowly opened it and went inside. His work boots made a crunching sound as he stepped on the broken glass. He fully absorbed the sharp evidence of his handiwork and felt strong and powerful.

Ken wasn't a man to be messed with. He noticed a framed picture of Walter and a one-dollar bill, dated a dozen years ago to commemorate the beginning of his business. Ken easily swiped the picture off the hook, and it fell to the floor with a *clunk*.

Next, he eyed a four-drawer filing cabinet and tossed the piece of wood onto a nearby desk. Ken cracked his knuckles, placed his hands on the cabinet, and let out an animalistic growl as he mustered enough strength to push the heavy cabinet over. It crashed down onto the floor with a loud clanking noise.

He spewed a guttural and primal scream of dominance. His heart pounded, and he breathed in deeply. He sought to continue the conquest. He swiped everything off the desk in front of him, including the two by four, and was about to destroy the computer and monitor on the nearby workstation when he was interrupted.

The purpose of an alarm system is to notify the police of a disturbance. The advantage of a silent alarm is the possibility of catching someone in the act. Sergeant Lamine Cortese and his partner Jesse Mullenax arrived at the scene to find an intruder in a small office suite. They cautiously and silently entered, saw Ken, and Sergeant Cortese commanded, "Police! Don't move."

Ken was in shock. *The police?* He slowly raised his hands in the air and slightly turned his neck to notice his makeshift bat on the floor.

"Don't even think about it," instructed Sergeant Mullenax.

Eleven Days Later

Ken stared at his phone screen and read the third text in the last three days from Fr. Whitburn: *I'm concerned about you. Are you okay? I didn't receive your weekly progress report on the daily prayers and discipline. You also didn't come in for confession. Please call me.* Ken looked at the screen, swiped left, and deleted the message.

Although his boots weren't visibly scuffed, Ken spent a lot of time digging in his heels. Even after he was arrested and spent three days in jail before he could arrange bail, he wasn't sorry for his actions. He only regretted not having enough time to cause more damage. Walt deserved a lot more destruction.

Why am I the only one willing to get their hands dirty?

Why am I the only one willing to right a wrong?

Why am I the only one willing to do the hard work around here?

Certainly not God.

I've been reciting all these prayers, and has God listened?

He sits up there on his lofty throne, letting bad things happen to me!

God's forgotten about me.

He doesn't want to save me.

Ken didn't realize a wicked smile formed on his face as he remembered smashing the door. *Too bad it wasn't Walter's head.* Walt pressed charges and told the prosecutor to throw the book at him. The arrest may have slowed him down, but *he wasn't* finished with his nemesis. When Walt wasn't looking, when he expected it least, Ken would be ready to pounce, he promised to himself.

He'd figure out a way to hurt him *really bad*. Or better yet, destroy him. Maybe he could find a way to ruin his business. Could he also burn down his house without getting caught? Walter had three young daughters. People drive crazy around here, and *accidents happen*. If one were hit by a truck, even at a low speed, *unintentionally, of course*, it could be enough to put her in a wheelchair for the rest of her life. Would it be enough for Walter to see the *errors of his ways?* Ken wondered.

Or perhaps his wife might trip and break her pretty little face? It would be a damn shame if something bad happened to her. What if she went *missing?* Or maybe, *just maybe,* he'd drug Walter and take some compromising pictures and post them all over the internet.

Ken was clever like that.

It wasn't enough to hurt Walter; he wanted all those around him to suffer too. It would be his new mission in life: make Walter's life miserable. Ken salivated with anticipation and glee. The only remaining question in Ken's mind was which one he'd do *first.*

Fourteen Hours Later, 3:01 a.m.

The dimly lit bulb dangled from the ceiling, and the tall shape slowly walked out of the shadows. He slapped the only source of light, and the single bulb swung and bounced the blackness in all directions. It's as if the room became filled with a legion of mysteriously dark figures surrounded by boundless shades of gray.

The illumination faded, consumed by the oppressive hues. He took another step onto broken glass, and the sharp scraping on the concrete reverberated and dominated the senses, *that is,* until one noticed the smell of dampness and rotting flesh. A nest of bloodied dead rats and maggots perfected the eerie presence in the basement.

It matched Ken's spirit.

Menacing.

Wicked.

Or was it *diabolic*?

Perhaps *fiendish*?

Better yet, *unholy*.

Either way, Walter *was screwed.* He was duct-taped to a small wooden chair with his mouth covered. But not his eyes. He wanted Walter to *see* everything that's coming. He squirmed to get free, but Ken made sure there was *no escape.*

Ken dropped his large toolbox, and the metal container made a loud, sharp gnawing noise when it kicked up the basement's dust. First, he pulled out a pair of pliers. Walt's eyes darted around the room, looking for someone to help him. No one was coming to save him, and Ken's slow and methodical pace had the desired effect.

Walt was desperate.

And petrified.

Walter could barely move his hands, so his fingers were vulnerable. Ken held the pliers and put them in front of Walter's face, whose eyes followed Ken's movement to his right thumb. Ken squeezed, and Walter let out a pain-induced scream. Without warning, Ken dislocated his thumb from the socket with a quick twist. Walter struggled in agony.

But the worst was yet to come. Walter's heart filled with pure fright and severe dread. He recognized the look on Ken's face.

Ecstasy.

The Next Day

"Honestly, I wasn't sure if I was going to hear from you," Fr. Whitburn said as they settled at a table in the coffee shop.

"I'm sorry I blew off your texts. I was going to figure it out on my own. Well, that was the plan until..." he trailed off.

"Until?"

"Father, I was so enraged, I got arrested last week for trashing someone's office," Ken admitted.

"What? Someone you knew?"

"Yes. I hate to admit it, but I lost control," Ken conceded.

"Did anyone get hurt?" Fr. Whitburn inquired.

"No. The actual damage in terms of dollar value wasn't that much, so the criminal offense wasn't as bad as it could've been. But then there's the DUI."

"Oh no."

"Yeah, I'm embarrassed. It's clearly a low point in my life," Ken replied and ceased making eye contact with the priest.

"Yes, you've put yourself in a bad spot."

"But that isn't the *reason* I wanted to talk to you."

"Oh, what is it?"

"Father, my night terrors are getting worse," Ken muttered in a quiet, defeated voice.

"Tell me about them," Fr. Whitburn suggested, and Ken described his nightmare about Walter in the basement.

"It was so real. But the most terrifying part was that I took such pleasure in torturing Walter. I know I'm not a saint, and I've done some bad things, but I'm not a sadistic person."

"I'm sorry that you are having these experiences."

"That's not me. I'm not a psycho from a *Criminal Minds* episode. I need your help."

"I can only offer one suggestion."

"Forget it, I know what you are going to tell me," Ken dismissed the priest and waved his hand as if a fly was buzzing around him.

"How well are things working out for you *on your own*?" the young priest purposefully returned his comment with a snarky tone and a gaze of annoyance. "If you want God's help, you have to open your heart," he added, but softer.

"I don't know if it's in my nature," Ken countered.

"We humans were built to love God."

"Well..."

"We can talk all day, but ultimately, you need to make a choice. Do you want me to sugarcoat it or give it to you straight?"

"Please," Ken answered and gestured for the priest to continue.

"You either want to walk with Jesus *or not*. You either want your heart to fill up with the Holy Spirit, or you don't, but *it will* fill up with *something else*," Fr. Whitburn told him in a measured tone. A priest can only do so much. The heart and soul must be willing to embrace Jesus.

"I don't know if I have it in me. It's not that easy," Ken complained.

Fr. Whitburn cocked his head slightly and pursed his lips in a facial expression that Ken couldn't quite accurately determine. It wasn't disappointment. It wasn't aggravation. It wasn't disbelief. It was the unexpected shock of *Ken's capitulation to apathy*.

The next words from the young priest hit home.

"Are you going to sit here, look me in the eye, and convince me you*'re afraid of hard work*?" the priest pressed, who believed support and kind words weren't enough. Ken needed a bucket of cold water thrown on him. Would it wake him up?

"Well," Ken stuttered, for he never thought the solution to end his affliction would require *hard work*.

"Standing still isn't the answer. You need to step in a particular direction, with purpose and zeal. Now isn't the time to be timid, is it?"

"Well, no...," Ken answered, but couldn't formulate a valid excuse.

"It's totally up to you, and I'll be here to help. I don't know you that well, but I can tell you're a guy who likes to be in control, right?"

"Yes," he agreed.

"Then take control of the situation! Control your life with prayer and discipline," he exclaimed with vigorous gusto.

"I suppose I can do that," Ken answered and tentatively nodded his head in agreement. The young priest knew Ken wasn't completely convinced.

"Make your choice. You're not weak. God gave you free will, *so use it*," Fr. Whitburn stated with an *oomph*. Like a classic move from a *Dale Carnegie* course, he threw down the challenge.

Ken let the words sink in. Normally, Ken would react negatively if he was *challenged,* but this was different. The priest had nothing to gain, and it was Ken who would benefit, possibly with the greatest reward of all time.

"You came to me for a reason. Deep down, you know you need Christ. Now is the time to show your strength and flex those muscles, and I'm not talking about the ones on your biceps."

"I know what you mean. I'll do it," Ken stated nervously, making the most bold and important decision of his life. Somewhere deep inside, hidden in a small corner of his heart, a thirst for Christ existed.

"You need to fight complacency. Resist the desire to quit. Use that strength of yours. I never said it'd be easy, and some days will be harder than ever. You'll step forward and backward. It took a long time to get in the spot you're in, so it will not turn around overnight. You can't expect that."

"That makes sense."

"Fight *the good fight,*" the young priest encouraged with passion. He knew Ken liked a good brawl, and he was hoping to put it in terms that would resonate. This battle was for ownership of his soul, and if Ken would not participate, he'd probably lose it.

"If you think it will help, let's meet every other day for the next thirty days. No more email," Fr. Whitburn offered. *Now* was the time for support and kind words.

"Yeah, I would appreciate that."

"We need one more person in your corner, someone who can pray *with* you and *for* you."

"Who?" Ken asked, perplexed as to who else could help him. He didn't have many close friends.

"We need to bring in the calvary. The big gun," Fr. Whitburn blurted out, and a broad smile took over his face. It was infectious, and Ken felt confident in his future.

"Okay, so who's that?" he repeated the question.

"Your mother."

Thirty Days Later, August 2018

"I've been getting the weekly updates. I'm glad Ken completed the entire thirty days," Clement stated.

Fr. Whitburn was sitting across the desk in the small office. "Yes, there were times I didn't think he'd finish, but to his credit, he fought through the temptation to quit."

"That's common, where it's right on the edge of being overwhelming. Thanks for supporting Ken throughout the process. I'm sure it helped, and even with the smallest movement of Ken's will, God provided grace. No one can do this on their own. You said his mother was praying for him?"

"She prayed twice per day to Ken's guardian angel for his intercession," the young priest explained and added, "his mother is worried about him."

"Her concern is warranted. She should continue. Guardian angels are much more active when someone requests their help, so I'm sure it made a difference," Clement noted.

"She also joined Ken for many of his daily prayers, helping him stay on track. It's the nights which were the most difficult for Ken."

"I saw that in Ken's report," Clement commented, and Fr. Whitburn placed a two-page report on Clement's desk. "It's time to get down to business and perform an analysis. As I mentioned previously, after the thirty days, if the situation gets better, we're essentially done. If there was diabolical oppression, he should be free from that. If it stays the same, perhaps it's a mental health problem. However, if it gets worse, well, there could be something more."

"You've seen the reports. Ken's situation decidedly became worse."

"Yes, let me review," Clement stated and examined the two-page report prepared by Ken. He focused on some of the more pertinent sections.

Day 1, Headaches that lasted all day and became worse during the prayer recitation.

Day 4, Ken *lost* the list of daily prayers, both on his computer and the copy he printed out. Fr. Whitburn resent another copy via email.

Day 6, More intense headaches.

Day 7, Ken lost the prayer list again, and when he went to print another copy from his email, his computer crashed. He came to Fr. Whitburn's office to retrieve another printout.

Day 8, Ken wakes up and can't find the prayers he left on his dresser from the night before and later finds it crumpled in a ball and hidden in a box underneath his bed.

Day 8, Ken's truck breaks down on his way to weekly confession. Fr. Whitburn picks him up, and they perform a roadside confession while waiting for the tow truck.

Day 11, Ken discovers his kitchen cabinets infested with cockroaches forcing food to be thrown out. It took hours to clean up the bugs. He previously didn't have a cockroach problem.

Day 13, More intense headaches.

Day 14, Ken reports an overwhelming wave of hopelessness at the noon prayer recital. He breaks down crying, and only because his mother was present were they able to finish.

Day 16, Ken is woken up in the middle of the night by the sound of someone pounding on his front door. He goes to check, but no one is there.

Day 17, Again, he's woken up in the middle of the night by the sound of someone pounding on his front door, but no one is there.

Day 18, Ken experienced blurred vision at the 6:00 p.m. prayer session and couldn't read any parts related to the Virgin Mary. His mother was with him and helped him finish saying his prayers.

Day 20, Ken is so tired at the noon prayer session that he falls asleep, and his mother had to constantly wake him up so they could finish.

Day 23, Ken experienced a nightmare. Although he can't remember the details, he knows it was about vengeance. He's filled with fright and turns on all the lights in the house, but the light appears muffled and shadowy, and he's unable to fall back to sleep.

Day 25, Ken has another nightmare, and this time he remembers torturing someone. The dream in Ken's own words:

It starts out like usual, where I have someone tied up in a chair. This time, I have a sledgehammer in my hands, and I lift it up and bring it crashing down on the person's knee. She screams in agony, and the force from the blow causes her to fall over. I can't tell who I hurt because the light is dim.

I feel a presence behind me in the small basement room. Someone or *something* is with me, and I sense a hot foul breath on my ear. I don't hear a voice, but thoughts pop into my head, *"You know you like it, the power you wield. I will bring you more power, more glory, and you'll decide justice. Worship me, and I will make you unstoppable."*

I freeze in fright and indecision. It felt good to dominate, but far in the corner of the room, I see a light, and it gets brighter and *whoever* I tortured is wailing and begging for me to stop. The light comes close enough to reveal who I've hurt.

My mother.

The nightmare ends abruptly. I wake up and literally spring out of bed, and my hand smacks the digital clock on my nightstand. I'm breathing hard and wonder if I'm having a panic attack. I sit in silence for several minutes trying to compose myself. I turn on my bedroom light, and that's when I notice it.

The digital clock I knocked over is still on the nightstand, but it's upside down. Memories of the nightmare pound my brain, and I see the clock tells me the time: 3:17.

As it's upside down, it seems to spell a word: *Lie*.

Day 26, Ken makes it to confession and is highly agitated because he's reliving the nightmares during the day and can't stop thinking about his dreams of vengeance.

Day 28, More intense headaches.

Day 29, Ken reports that he'd rather be in a mental institution than perform the daily prayers.

"You told him to continue, correct?" Clement asked.

"Yes, but I'm worried about him."

"Diabolical affliction seeks to confuse the person, so that would be an easy excuse to stop doing his prayers and behavioral discipline. Based on the report, I think we need to go to the next step. I'm worried that Ken is in a serious situation."

"Phase 2?"

"Correct. This involves identifying impediments to grace and any defects in the petitioner's understanding and/or practice of their faith."

"He's confusing justice and revenge," Fr. Whitburn surmised.

"Absolutely. What draws a demon to a human is a particular vice that they share and are psychologically compatible."

"Vengeance and mercy are the opposite of forgiving those who trespass against us," the priest stated and clarified. "He continues to see himself as a victim of other people's actions, so he believes he's justified, but then other times, he recognizes his behavior is sinful, and he's remorseful."

"There's a battle going on inside him for the truth of what's right and wrong," Clement explained and added, "he's clearly struggling with temptation. The antidote is growing in grace and virtue, which is easier said than done."

"I agree, we meet for coffee often, and one minute he wants to apologize to someone from his past, and two minutes later, he's *proud* about putting other people in their place."

"And *their place* is below him, of course."

"Exactly, but since I met him, the nightmares are becoming more vivid and dark."

"If there is a demon involved, it's been agitated over the last thirty days. It will react by making Ken uncomfortable. Well, more than that, to frighten him so he gives up and steers away from God."

"He persevered for the last thirty days, so there's a part of him choosing Christ, but from what you've told me, there are forces obstructing his spiritual growth."

"I agree," Clement said with the voice of experience, "and those forces are fighting hard. They will not give up easily."

"What's next?" the young priest asked.

"I want to meet him."

PART 2: *A PRICK OF CONSCIENCE*, FIVE DAYS LATER

The alarm sounded off with an annoying buzz at exactly 4:30 a.m. Clement drew back the blanket and rolled out of bed, fully awake. He's quiet, not wanting to disturb his wife, and immediately got dressed. Ten minutes later, he entered his home office, checked email, and waited for his coffee to brew. There's always a new challenge working for the Archdiocese of Denver. When you're the case manager, consulting on multiple cases of demonic influence, *boredom* is a word rarely uttered.

Fifty-eight-year-old Clement discovered eighteen emails that came through during the night. The job kept him busy, fielding questions and updates from priests all over the country. He goes through each email methodically and started with the one that's sat in his inbox for six hours. The devil may not need to sleep, but Clement does and knows well that anything can happen in the middle of the night. Unlike poorly made movies, real exorcisms don't take place at midnight, but that didn't stop the inquiries and requests for advice.

But then again, real exorcisms are a rare occurrence: 90 percent get resolved before ever starting an exorcism rite. Many cases are instead a mental health issue, ranging from depression to bipolar, and he refers most cases to a counselor. If a case is diabolic oppression, it can be resolved through deliverance prayers and behavior correction.

Some think that their inability to stop sinful behavior is the work of the devil. Clement has witnessed disturbing behavior and habitual sin, so he knows better than most that people are their own worst enemy.

There are plenty of temptations to contend with, such as the age-old ones of greed and lust, and the modern world has made it easier to sin. He's seen the world dismiss God and turn more secular, telling people to find *their own truth* and their own unique spirituality by embracing *their desires*. Society's advice about the path to happiness is *to do whatever you want*.

Hogwash.

Why be disciplined when you can get instant gratification? Secular society tells people not to blame themselves for their actions, but to blame God. Defying God doesn't destroy Him, it destroys yourself. Modernists long for a narcissistic society. Correction, we're already there. Blame is never pointed inward. Modernists never confess to almighty God that they've sinned through their own grievous fault. They encourage people to do what *feels good*, and no one has the right to tell anyone otherwise. Such logic occurs when society cancels God.

The devil must be happy, that is, if demons could experience happiness. They willingly rejected God and were cast out. There's no chance of redemption for demons, which is the opposite for angels who can't sin. Once an angel has chosen God, they don't change their mind. Demons, on the other hand, are bitter because they know heaven isn't within reach. They don't have a snowball's chance in hell, so to speak. Demons are infuriated about their situation because their happiness is an absolute impossibility.

Demons are forever consumed in their hatred for us, seeking to bring us down to their tormented existence. That's why they observe us and hope to find a weak moment. They know us by our sin and want us to also reject God. Hell isn't a place but rather their *state of being*.

He reads another email, a request for deliverance prayers. Those are designed to free a person from demonic influences. Such conditions are more common than a complete possession, and any Christian can recite deliverance prayers. Many prayers invoke the intercession of saints or our Blessed Mother. However, only a priest can perform the exorcism rite.

He retrieved a strong cup of no-nonsense black coffee and, as he returned to the office, glanced at a framed pennant from his alma mater, Texas A&M. There are several photos of his three children and eight grandchildren hanging on the wall, and he reflected for a moment and thought, *I'm truly blessed.*

It's been quite a journey, growing up in central Texas, marrying his college sweetheart Valerie, and spending his early career aspirations with a large ranching operation. Long days, unpredictable weather conditions, and volatile price markets filled the years. A hard life, to be sure, but greatly satisfying.

Eventually, his analytical and detail-oriented mind wanted something more, so he went to law school at age twenty-nine. He had no desire to practice law, never took the bar exam, but used the acquired skills in his career.

Clement's strong life of faith began when he was a child and fondly remembered his grandparent's reading and talking about Bible scripture. His children inherited Clement's unwavering faith and devotion.

One day, his parish priest asked him to pray for another parishioner. He gladly accepted the ministry and prayed the Rosary with a family.

A year later, he was asked to join in prayer by a different priest, Fr. Palermo, who also happened be an exorcist. This continued for years, and he supported the priest during several exorcism rites. After one session with the exorcist, Clement made a comment that would forever change his life.

"Father, whenever you bring up the Blessed Mother, I see the same reaction, regardless of who you are helping. It's a predictable pattern." His methodical mind was in overdrive, thinking back to previous sessions. He saw correlations and connections. The demon's behavior got to a point where Clement was no longer surprised.

He was invited to a spiritual warfare conference but didn't attend any seminars because he was working on difficult cases with Fr. Palermo. The two had many late-night discussions on the process of performing an exorcism. It quickly became apparent that they needed new and better protocols to train priests. They both sought to increase the priest's effectiveness.

To develop a new exorcism manual, an analytical approach was needed, and Fr. Palermo asked for Clement's help. It took years, and by this time, Clement's children were grown up, which provided him with additional time to work on this project. It became apparent to Fr. Palermo that this was a full-time job, and so in 2015, Clement became an official employee of the diocese as a case manager, working directly for Fr. Palermo. His job was to review, document, analyze, and vet any situations before Fr. Palermo got involved.

He eventually read his last new email from Fr. Whitburn confirming their meeting with Kennedy Flowers.

Later That Day

"I'm glad to meet you," Clement replied and extended his hand. Ken grabbed it and shook it firmly. He also greeted Fr. Whitburn, and they settled into the diocese office's small conference room.

"Thank you for seeing me. But you're not a priest, right?" Ken asked.

"Correct, I'm a layperson. I conduct the initial meeting, gather information, and see where it takes us. I understand you've been reciting the deliverance prayers for the past thirty days."

"Yes, and the specific discipline requirements. It's been tough to stay off the internet and television," Ken stated with an easygoing laugh.

"That's common." Clement smiled and understood. Whether or not diabolical affliction was present, most people had the habit of spending too much time staring at a screen. He followed with a question. "Were you able to adhere to all the protocols?"

"Yes, and the last thirty days were the most difficult of my life," Ken explained. "I thought I would feel better when it was complete, but it's worse."

"Your tenacity to finish the program is commendable," Clement said with full sincerity and noted Ken's comment about feeling *worse*.

Ken's diligence demonstrated his choice to embrace Jesus. But most cases Clement dealt with didn't progress in a straight line. The path was winding, sometimes went backward or around in a circle. Battles would be won and lost on the path to redemption, and he wasn't expecting Ken's situation to be straightforward.

"I've received Fr. Whitburn's weekly reports, so I have a little bit of background information on you, but why don't you tell me in your own words? Start with where you grew up, your participation in the church, and the events that led up to this meeting."

"Sure. I grew up in Colorado along with my sister, who now lives in Florida. I'm almost thirty and own a construction company. I was married but divorced a few years ago. No kids."

"Tell me about your religious life," Clement coaxed.

"I stopped going to church when I was about eleven," he said, and his eyes darted away, then continued, "my mom went, and she tried to get me to go, but I refused. Last month when I saw Fr. Whitburn, it was the first time I stepped into a church in a very long time."

"So that begs the question. Why go to confession? Why did you come back to the church?"

"My mother. That, and because I've run out of ideas," Ken exclaimed.

"Please elaborate."

"I have these headaches. I've been to multiple doctors and taken different medications. Nothing has helped."

"That could be caused by lots of different reasons. Why do you think it's something not medically related?" Clement asked.

"I've had the headaches for years. But it's the nightmares. They're getting worse and have amped up over the past month."

"Tell me about them."

"Okay, so maybe this will sound farfetched, but I have nightmares about people stealing from my business or sabotaging a project that I'm working on. I fly into a rage. I mean a truly *uncontrollable* rage where I want to kill the person responsible. Well, it's more than that."

"What do you mean?" Clement asked and made a notation in a small spiral notebook.

"First, I knock the person out, and the dream suddenly shifts to a dark basement," Ken stated and added, "I don't know how I get there, but a person is already tied up."

"These people in your dream. Are they strangers?" Clement asked, while Fr. Whitburn was quietly observing.

"That part is bothersome. They're people I know, customers, suppliers, friends, or family members. One of them was even my mother. When the dream gets to the part in the basement, that's when it *starts*."

"What exactly?"

"The suffering," Ken admitted and paused a moment. Clement gestured for him to continue, so he did, "Usually, I start with breaking a few fingers. I mimic the actions in every movie I've ever seen where there's a torture scene. Breaking fingers or cutting off body parts with a hedge clipper. Sometimes I wake up, but if I don't..."

"What happens then?" Clement asked gently, for he could sense Ken's anxiety level rising.

"It always ends with the rat bucket from *Game of Thrones*."

"I've never seen that show," Clement told Ken, who seemed surprised at first. But he's a no-nonsense type of man, so Ken shouldn't expect anything frivolous in Clement's choice of entertainment.

"It's set in medieval times, and someone is being interrogated, but he won't talk. A rat is in a wooden bucket, and it's strapped to the prisoner's body. The bucket is lit on fire, and the rat tries to escape. The only way out is to burrow *into* the person's body. It's gruesome," Ken explained.

"It is. And you do this in your dream?" Clement asked for clarification.

"Yes. I usually remember them although I frequently wake before the end."

"Was there a business deal that went badly with the people in your dream?" he asked.

"At first, yes. I've had some projects go south where I got screwed over, and they were the first ones I dreamed about torturing. It started years ago."

"But the nightmares continued?"

"Yes, now it happens every night, sometimes with people I get along with. They always die in the end. But that's not the worst part."

"Why not?" Clement asked and wondered how it could get worse than what Ken described.

"When I wake up, I'm terrified."

"That's understandable."

"Not because I tortured and killed them, but because I *really, really enjoyed it,"* Ken admitted.

Fr. Whitburn gasped in horror, but Clement was steadfast, for he truly had *heard it all before*. He scribbled some additional notes and looked at Ken directly and noticed that he no longer appeared contrite.

"Are you afraid you might act this out in real life?" Fr. Whitburn spoke up.

"Father, the one thing that pisses me off is when someone crosses me. I *make them wish they never did me wrong,*" Ken quipped and involuntarily flashed a wicked grin. "I've never come close to killing anyone, but I'll admit, I usually try to crush that person, career wise, social standing, or the occasional beat down."

"You enjoy exacting revenge?" Clement asked.

"Oh yeah, I make my *enemies pay*. I won't be denied," Ken freely bragged and puffed out his chest with boastful vengeance, daring either Clement or the priest to challenge him. The air in the room seemed to shift along with Ken's attitude.

Clement wasn't impressed. Nor scared. He slightly adjusted his glasses, soaked in all of Ken's admission, and then got the discussion back on track. He asked, "But you're concerned that you may take it too far?"

"Yes, but it's more than that. It's not as simple as needing anger management skills. I'm afraid I might do something when I'm not really *me.*"

"What do you mean by *that*?" Clement asked to see where Ken was coming from.

"It's not just the headaches. I don't want to sound *crazy*, but I haven't felt alone with my own thoughts for a long time. Just *my own* thoughts."

"You're hearing voices?" Fr. Whitburn asked in a non-accusatory way.

"Not like a voice in my head telling me to hurt someone. Don't look at me like I need to be locked up," Ken spit out, frowned, and stared down the priest.

"We're not here to make any conclusions or diagnose you," Clement said in an even tone. "It's important that we understand your experiences as accurately as possible. Please continue," he suggested with all the indication that Ken was his top priority. That resonated.

"My head is never quiet. It's *always noisy.*"

"Thank you, that's a significant detail," Clement responded, purposely stroking Ken's ego. "You indicated it's been that way for a while. Can you recall when it started?"

"My head hasn't been right for five or six years. The nightmares started getting worse a few months ago."

"Did something happen in your life that might have initially triggered such a condition?" Clement asked and noticed Ken's boastful attitude dissipate. For now.

"Hmm, that's a good question," Ken responded calmly and took a moment.

"Think about what was going on in 2012 or so," Clement suggested.

"I started dating Dolly, and I'd been working construction for a few years. I had a falling out with old man Hank, the guy I used to work for. I hated that guy. Still do, actually."

"Did you *make him pay*, as you described earlier?" Clement queried.

"Oh yeah. Not only did I figure out that he was cheating *me out of money*, but I discovered he lied on his tax returns for years. He was in a car accident that broke his leg and hip, and he could barely get around, which is a problem in the construction business," Ken recalled and grinned.

The *attitude* was back.

"Did you cause the accident?" Clement inquired evenly.

"I wasn't in the other car, if that's what you're asking, but I might have had a *little something to do with it*," Ken boasted and smirked. He had a secret, and once again, the air in the room shifted with Ken's attitude.

"Tell me how you did it," Clement asked with raised eyebrows, feeding Ken's ego with his apparent impression of Ken's *power*.

He took the bait.

"My new girlfriend, Dolly, and I put a curse on Hank. She was really into séances, tarot card readings and fancied herself as a modern-day witch. She was obsessed with television shows and movies about black magic. I thought it was mostly a load of you know what," he bantered but held his tongue and refrained from using profanity.

"Did you take part in any of these occult activities?" Clement asked in a measured tone.

"Not until I wanted revenge on Hank. We found all kinds of cursing rituals online, and I swear we used every one of them."

"How many?"

"At least a dozen," Ken snickered, leaned back in his chair, and folded his arms in defiance.

"Was it a ritual?" Clement asked.

"Oh yeah. Dolly found step-by-step instructions on YouTube and some other witchcraft sites. She was familiar with all of them."

"And you fully participated?"

"Sure, I wasn't into it like she was, but yes, I would assist her with the séances. She was always contacting her dead mother. But when I found out that Hank shorted me on a few paychecks, she suggested doing a *curse*. I thought it was a brilliant idea."

"You cast a spell on the man you worked for?"

"He was the first one," Ken admitted.

"And you wanted to curse Hank?"

"Absolutely. I *hated him*," Ken told them, and his face hardened, and Fr. Whitburn sensed a sudden *chill in the air*. Clement either didn't notice or care, for he continued with the assessment.

"How many others besides Hank did you and Dolly ritualistically curse?"

"At least another five or six people. Sometimes we had to perform the ceremony multiple times for the same person."

"And the purpose was always revenge?"

Ken paused a minute and rubbed his temple and said, "Yeah, it was on someone who did me wrong. Dolly wanted to help me. It was the justice my enemies deserved."

"Did you take any other action to get your revenge besides the spells?"

"*Of course*. I didn't want these people thinking it was merely *bad luck*. I wanted them to know *it was me* that ruined their life," Ken gloated.

"You wanted them punished," Clement stated the obvious but was interested in Ken's reaction.

"Oh yeah," he responded and nodded his head and stared at Clement with soul-piercing eyes. "I wanted them *to suffer*," he provoked without remorse.

Clement leaned back in his chair and scrutinized Ken's movements and nonverbal cues as he obviously relived the moments of his revenge. There was only one plausible reaction. There was only one possibility, so he quietly replied, "I believe you."

"That's all I thought about. *Payback time*," Ken added and smiled. He was on a roll.

"You went out of your way to hurt them?"

He leaned forward, purely for emphasis. "I *delighted* in coming up with ways to get back at them. I'd focus on it day and night," Ken bragged as a warrior would savor a conquest and leaned back again and relaxed in the chair after making his comment. He was *very* pleased with himself and didn't notice a rotten egg smell permeating the room.

"I appreciate your honesty. Would you mind elaborating on what you did, apart from the curses and spells?" Clement asked with genuine curiosity.

"Sure, old man Hank wasn't that old, probably a dozen years older than me. After his accident, his wife was stuck taking care of him. I showed up at his house as the dutiful employee to give him updates. But I was more interested in gaining his trust, so I first offered to take over his books, and that's when I discovered his little tax scheme. It wasn't an accident that he was ripping off the IRS for years."

"So you blackmailed him?"

"That would've been too easy. I tipped off the IRS, but I knew they'd be slow to set up an audit, so I had some time. I started giving discounts for customers that paid in cash."

"And you would pocket that, right?" Clement guessed.

"Well, of course," Ken answered with a perturbed tone, rolling his eyes and continued his bravado. "I charged the supplies for the project to Hank's business account, and I collected the cash, so from Hank's perspective, every project lost money. Between his medical bills and a tanking business, it didn't take long for him to run out of money."

"To be clear, this action was on purpose. Premeditated, so to speak. I'm not trying to condemn you. I merely want absolute clarity," Clement stated, and Ken nodded with his cocky attitude.

"Oh yeah. But that wasn't the best part!" Ken announced triumphantly and folded his arms with a pleasure that only a man who's achieved his goal *and then some* could project.

"Go on," Clement responded without emotion.

"Hank and his wife weren't getting along before all this, and she wasn't *real* happy with Hank practically being an invalid who required constant care. With the business going south, there weren't any funds to hire a nurse. He had a difficult time getting to the bathroom on his own," Ken informed them with a hearty laugh. "She was left doing all the dirty work. Literally!" he roared with the cruel pleasure one finds in the misfortune of another. Ken couldn't help but smile or contain his amusement.

Clement and Fr. Whitburn were not so amused, and the young priest coughed from the lingering stench in the small room.

"*What*?" Ken asked with feigned shock. He knew full well that they wouldn't approve of his actions. But he didn't care, for he was having way too much fun reliving the story. "For a woman like Anne, being Hanks's nursemaid got old, *real fast*. Even though Hank never left the house except for a doctor's appointment, she was a lonely woman, if you know what I mean," he cackled.

"You seduced her."

"Correction. She wanted to be f——," Ken sneered, but Clement raised his hand to stop him from finishing his sentence. Ken complied and grinned from ear to ear. He was quite proud of his accomplishment.

"Okay, I get the picture," Clement told him.

"I never mentioned *that* part to Dolly, of course, although somehow I think she knew."

"That wouldn't surprise me."

But Ken wasn't finished. He had one more tidbit to throw into the mix. "When Hank found out, it was one of the best days of my life," Ken snorted, amused by his words. "Yup, one of the best days!" he repeated, and couldn't contain a deep, guttural laugh.

Ken must have noticed that Clement and Fr. Whitburn's body language communicated beyond a normal disapproval at Ken's actions. *It revolted them.*

"Hey, I was the victim here," he defended himself and pleaded his case. "We only cast spells on our enemies!" Ken reasoned. Doing more harm as a remedy of being wronged wasn't a winning strategy. And the degree of Ken's mistreatment was certainly up for debate.

Clement's patience was thinning. There wasn't a reason to continue giving Ken time to relish his glorious revenge. His actions were disturbing, and his purposeful cruelty and delighting in his sin made matters worse.

"My girlfriend was only trying to help me," Ken argued. "And trust me, she had power. She even put a *love potion* in my coffee so I'd ask her out," he said, laughing some more and followed up with, "that's how we met. She worked as a barista."

"I understand, and I appreciate you being forthcoming so we can see the full picture. But let's get back to the core question. When you started casting spells, is this the time when you felt different?" Clement asked, and Ken's facial expression immediately changed.

The boastful man in front of Clement and Fr. Whitburn was gone.

"Yes."

"What happened with your girlfriend?"

"We got married. Then divorced. It was an ugly split," Ken admitted.

"How is your relationship now?" Clement inquired.

"We haven't spoken for over a year. I hate her, but she *hates me more,*" Ken spit out. The boasting was replaced with a new emotion.

Fear.

"What are you not telling us?" Fr. Whitburn piped in.

"I think she put a spell *on me* after we broke up," Ken answered.

Clement and Fr. Whitburn paused to let that tidbit sink in. The case was getting more complicated. They sat in silence for a long full minute. "Let's get back to your spiritual life. Why did you decide to go to confession last month? You hadn't been to church in years, right?" Clement asked.

"Yes, I know. It goes back to our conversation about getting nowhere with doctors and therapists. Nothing got me back to my old self. But what got me worried was that I was having a difficult time remembering what the old Ken was really like. I became desperate, and my mother convinced me to talk to a priest. At first, I brushed off the suggestion as a waste of my time. No offense, Father," Ken jested and looked at Fr. Whitburn, who waved off his halfhearted apology.

"So this decision wasn't on a whim?"

"No, my mom's been bugging me about it for months. I also started, but *only occasionally,* to feel a little bad about stomping on my enemies. So I finally agreed, mostly to get her off my back," Ken explained.

"Help me understand your thought process. Why go to confession? You don't seem remorseful," Fr. Whitburn discerned.

"Well, not really."

"Confession doesn't work unless you're sorry for your behavior," Clement pointed out.

"I get it. I thought talking to a priest would, well, maybe bring clarity about right and wrong. *Maybe* I went too far. I used to always get mad if somebody slighted me. I was always a little bit of a hothead, but not to this level."

"Someone who was so obsessed with revenge," Clement added for clarification, and Ken nodded his agreement.

"Right, I thought by making them pay, I would feel better about it."

"Did you?" Clement inquired.

"Yes and no," Ken huffed in frustration, for he was worried that Clement wouldn't take him seriously if he sounded wishy-washy. He took a deep breath and continued, "At the time, yes, I was absolutely ecstatic that my enemies were miserable. But it's been a few years, and now it seems like a hollow victory. I took a step backward when I vandalized Walter's office. I want to get back to the guy who lost his temper, maybe got in a fight, but then *let it go*."

"Not the man that's full of a rage that won't dissipate."

"Yes, that's it exactly!" Ken replied excitedly. "Sometimes I briefly thrived on that anger, as if something was propping up that attitude. Then I'd beat myself up for being so preoccupied with anger. But I *do* know better."

"You must be so tired," Clement commented in an offhand manner, but it resonated with Ken.

"Yes, you get me! It's so draining to be angry all day long. I wanted to drop it, but I couldn't."

"It's like continuing to punch a guy that's already knocked out," Clement surmised.

"You're spot-on. I'm embarrassed to tell you guys, but I've literally done that."

"Hatred for your enemies has consumed you to the point of exhaustion," Clement added.

For the first time in a long while, Ken was truly contrite. "I guess I've done some pretty bad stuff."

"The fact that you are seeing the ills of your ways is the first step," Clement replied. "But you also need to show metanoia, which means demonstrating physical and tangible efforts to change your ways."

"Yes, you're saying I need to *walk the talk.*"

"Exactly."

"I want to *get right* with God, and that's why I thought a priest could help. Someone to tell my sins," Ken stated, and they were silent for a moment.

"I think a priest can help," Fr. Whitburn spoke up.

"Ken, do you mind if I confer with Fr. Whitburn for a few minutes and discuss what to do next?"

"Sure, that's fine."

"Wait here," Clement told him and motioned for Fr. Whitburn to follow him to his office.

***

"Did this go as you expected?" the young priest wondered as he closed the door to Clement's office.

"Yes, we covered a lot of areas. For me, the purpose of the meeting was to dig deeper about the nature of his sin and to identify his impediments to grace and any defects in Ken's understanding of his faith."

"So you think something is going on here?"

"Yes. I am seeing some indicators. First, there was the difficult initial confession. Second, there are his nightmares about torturing people which stemmed from actual cruel acts of vengeance."

"He wants more than respect. He wants to be feared, and he enjoys bragging about his sin," the young priest added.

"Correct. He wanted to shock and get a rise out of us."

"And don't forget the rotten egg smell," Fr. Whitburn exclaimed.

"Yes, I noticed it too."

"And the thirty days of prayer and deliverance, Ken struggled with that."

"Right, and the evidence is consistent with demonic oppression and obsession. The nightmares, computer and car problems, strange noises and material goods getting lost with no reasonable explanation. Individually, that doesn't mean much, but collectively, it makes me want to dig deeper," Clement suggested.

"The simple deliverance prayer rattled something," Fr. Whitburn pointed out.

"That could be a demon rebelling against Ken's action, trying to discourage or frighten him from continuing. However, I'm not prepared to come to any conclusion," Clement stated, and the two men paused for a moment.

"Participating in the occult must have opened some doors," Fr. Whitburn stated.

"Yes, and it doesn't matter that it started through his girlfriend. He took part and exacerbated the situation. He willfully committed sins to pile on the misery of his perceived enemies."

"Yet, some part of him knows it's wrong, like he has competing thoughts and emotions. He's comfortably sitting on a nail."

"And after his marriage ended, the witch cast a spell on him," Fr. Whitburn added.

"That wouldn't matter so much if he was in a state of grace. If he regularly attended church and atoned for his sins, the spell would be ineffective."

"But that wasn't his lifestyle."

"Right, practicing the occult opened the door, and his cruel revenge possibly invited demonic influence, which would have reinforced his sin and beliefs contrary to church teaching," Clement observed.

"Sometimes we're our own worst enemy," Fr. Whitburn replied.

"And the second worst enemy is the *world's temptations*. In his case, it started with unfairly getting a financial windfall."

"Greed, along with purposefully coveting his neighbor's wife."

"All originated from hate and anger," Clement replied.

"Yes, somehow his girlfriend got attracted to the occult, and he got sucked in," said Fr. Whitburn.

"The reason the occult is so dangerous is that someone is trying to get power that is not yours to get. They're not seeking the power of Christ, but instead from a dark force. In Ken's case, he potentially made it easy for the demon, since he was already weighed down with sin."

"God wasn't a part of his life. That surely didn't help."

"If so, he might have been able to resist," Clement agreed and continued, "being away from the church will make it easier for a demon. If you're not filled with the Holy Spirit, something else may fill up the space. The demons look for any opening, and performing witchcraft spells and curses can get a demon's attention."

"It didn't sound like he was trying to invite the devil in," Fr. Whitburn countered.

"No, but that isn't needed. A curse is an inverse blessing. Demons look for sin, and Ken opened the door a crack, so if they found him, they won't stop until they destroy the person."

"That affected more than only Ken."

"Correct. Ken could damage other lives besides his own. Demons prefer someone who can expand the wreckage," Clement surmised.

"His admitted short temper was exploited, and it didn't stop after his marriage ended," Fr. Whitburn added.

"Absolutely, Father, if there is a demon, its personality is compatible with Ken. He relishes hurting others in a hateful and malicious way. It matches the intense hatred that demons have for mankind."

"The demon's personality?" Fr. Whitburn asked, and his brow creased.

"Yes, each demon is a unique spiritual being. They have characteristics and minds of their own."

"That makes sense, but I never thought of them as having personalities," Fr. Whitburn replied.

"I've observed many exorcisms, and they're all a little different. Ken unwittingly gave his demon ammunition to exploit his behavior."

"That kind of information in the hands of the enemy must be devastating, right?"

"No doubt. Something could easily influence Ken, so he concludes that he's a victim. In his mind, he'd be justified in getting revenge. But on the other hand, it could all be the consequences of Ken's choices or convinced himself that he's possessed by a demon," Clement theorized.

"How will you know?"

"At this point, I'd only be speculating, but there are signs of spiritual affliction. Rejoicing in human misery caused by deliberate sin, that's exactly what a demon would do. And that sin disgusts them, even though they are influencing such behavior. They hate themselves for being part of it, but that is their fallen nature. It's truly diabolical," Clement explained with his expertise.

"He continued to follow along until the sin became second nature, as if it was hardwired into Ken." Fr. Whitburn pointed out and added, "Marrying the witch reinforced the behavior, so it became part of his personality and actions."

"That's a good observation. It's a deep level of depravity that's ingrained, which will make it more difficult to help him."

"Unfortunately, humans are capable of great sin," the young priest stated.

"Yes, even without diabolical influence. We can easily make a mess on our own. Either way, he needs help, but we'll step in if a demon has taken an active interest in Ken," Clement volunteered.

"What about his physical signs?" the priest asked, redirecting the assessment.

"Bodily affliction is common, but obviously, all kinds of things can cause headaches."

"So what do you think?"

"With his sin of wrath, the anger is foremost, but he's also shown a heavy dose of pride and lust," Clement analyzed. "Based on Ken's testimony, I can see why a demon might be drawn and latch onto him."

"His choosing to sin?"

"Yes, the devil's temptation is making the sin appear attractive even though he knows it's wrong. Overcoming that is a way for the soul to strengthen in grace and virtue, but Ken is far away from turning it around."

"But he somehow found the courage to go to confession."

"Yes, and that's *so important*. I see Ken experienced a prick of conscience. He recognized that he's greatly sinned, and if someone wants to make amends, such as going to confession, the demon is going to notice and attack the person or manifest itself."

"It doesn't want to lose control," Fr. Whitburn replied.

"Right. It will lash out. The good news is that if there's a demon involved, the mere fact that Ken stepped into a church and has recited the prayers for the past thirty days shows he wants to get rid of any demonic influence."

Fr. Whitburn paused to process everything Clement explained. After a few moments, he opined, "He didn't seem to suffer from a mental illness when we talked to him today."

"I agree. He was lucid, and I didn't detect any signs of schizophrenia or bipolar, but I'm not an expert. He had moments of regret and boasting about his sin. There's an inner conflict going on, that's for sure."

"What's the next step?"

"I want him to get a physical and psychological examination. Let's not jump to any final conclusions," Clement advised.

Part 3: *Squatter's Rights,* Thirty-two Days Later, September 2018

Fr. Louis Monte Palermo didn't enter the priesthood intending to become an exorcist. His heart was on fire for the Lord, and by the time he graduated high school, he clearly heard the calling to serve God. Twenty-one years later and fifteen as a parish priest, he met with the bishop, who formally appointed him as the first official exorcist priest in the diocese. He immediately departed for training in Rome for an apprenticeship.

Five years into the assignment, he asked Clement and his wife Valerie to help pray during a solemn exorcism rite. As the cases were resolved, he and Clement developed a working rhythm, and the experienced exorcist relied more often on Clement's observation and counsel.

After years of working together, the two men determined three things with absolute clarity. The volume of potential exorcism cases required more priests. Second, a step-by-step process needed to be developed and documented. And finally, such training should be delivered to a set of select priests.

Most priests learned from a more experienced one, and training skills and knowledge passed from one generation to another were inconsistent. A handful of new exorcists wasn't a solution to cover the thousands of annual inquires and requests, proving that there simply weren't enough qualified priests in the United States to handle the caseload.

Like other priestly duties, certain protocols needed to be followed, and Fr. Palermo knew that improved methods and practical training would significantly help new exorcists to become more effective. Most importantly, it would greatly benefit the congregation.

Deliverance and protection prayers started the first phase. The next required Ken, the petitioner, to undergo a medical and psychological assessment. Only after a strict evaluation and review would a priest consider performing the final phase, a solemn rite, or the *exorcism*, in layman's terms.

"Let's review the case file," Clement announced. He coordinated a meeting to discuss Ken's examination results and to determine the next steps. Fr. Palermo, Fr. Whitburn, and Clement settled into the small conference room at the diocese office.

"Please do," Fr. Palermo stated, met eyes with Clement, and gave his full attention.

"I have the medical report here. Ken has blood pressure slightly above normal, but not enough to warrant a prescription. Heart rate and breathing were healthy for his age. The rest of his blood tests came out normal. Thyroid, glucose, and cholesterol were all within range. They gave him a full drug test, and the results were negative."

"I'm not surprised. Ken seems pretty fit," Fr. Whitburn commented.

"The doctor also took a chest X-ray, checked his eyes, reflexes and looked for any physical anomalies. There weren't any."

"Okay, no physical issues. The psychological exam?" Fr. Palermo asked.

"Ken spent a few hours with our approved psychiatrist, who didn't have any serious concerns. He previously sought treatment from several therapists and a psychiatrist. They prescribed him different drugs over a period of two years, but that ended last year. The drug test didn't detect any prescription or illegal drugs in Ken's system, so his experiences aren't attributable to any medication side effects."

"He stopped seeing those mental health professionals because the treatment was ineffective," Fr. Whitburn added.

"What prompted Ken to seek help?"

"He first sought medical doctors because of the headaches. They performed a series of tests but couldn't find any anomalies. Next, he went to the psychiatrist and later a therapist. He had mood swings and *didn't feel like himself*, so he assumed it was more of a mental health issue rather than a physical malady," Clement answered.

"But nothing improved?" the experienced priest asked.

"Correct."

"You said he stopped talking to a therapist over a year ago, correct?" Fr. Palermo inquired.

"Yes, and like my Scottish grandmother used to say, *you can't talk your way out of the situation you behaved yourself into*," Clement quipped.

"Exactly, and this brings us to his actions and beliefs," Fr. Palermo replied and motioned for Clement to continue.

"He practices habitual sin, mostly vengeance, but also greed, lust, and a cruel enjoyment of inflicting pain on others."

"How do you know he doesn't have a sadistic personality and isn't simply a *bad guy*?" Fr. Palermo challenged.

"Yes, I thought of that possibility too. I think his personality is absolutely predisposed to react with vengeance. He's succumbed to ample moments of temptation and embraced his sinful lifestyle. I believe the pivotal moment was when he became involved in the occult."

"People don't take the dangers of the occult seriously enough, thinking it's just fun and games to see an astrologist or palm reader. The risks ratchet up if someone *plays* with a Ouija board, cast spells, or gets into witchcraft," Fr. Palermo added, and an unmistakable look of frustration formed on his countenance.

The midforties-year-old priest quietly yawned and refocused his dark brown eyes. His matching brown hair only recently showed a touch of gray. The stocky man shifted in his chair, unsuccessfully attempting to relieve some hip pain, and apologized, "Sorry, I was up very early this morning."

Clement understood that Fr. Palermo's yawn was not a sign of disinterest, so he continued, "Ken was introduced to the occult by his girlfriend, whom he later married. They bought the lie created by modern society, which has watered down the importance of faith and religion, positioning the occult to appear real and advantageous."

"It's upside down. People engage in the occult for answers in their life instead of a relationship with Christ. They portray deeply religious people as superstitious," the experienced priest added.

"I think they're broken and feel unloved, maybe even believe they're unworthy of love, so they deny God and look for another source of affirmation," Clement replied.

"That's because the occult, including Satanism, has only one rule: do what you want," Fr. Palermo asserted.

"It doesn't require following a moral code, like the Ten Commandments, but allows the individual to make up his own rules, which essentially puts you on par with God," Clement concluded.

"Which, of course, is exactly what the demons want, for humans to reject God and focus on themselves. Is that the situation with Ken?"

"In my opinion, yes."

"You've spent the most time with him. Do you agree?" Fr. Palermo asked the younger priest.

"I'm not an expert, but Ken has consistently elevated himself above God and became the authority of vengeance. In his mind, he had every right and justification for his actions," Fr. Whitburn told them.

"A demon would take advantage and reinforce his behavior," Clement kicked in.

"All of his sins trace back to pride. *Pride* is why the fallen angels originally rejected God. Okay, so back to my original question, how do we know he isn't merely doing evil acts versus being diabolically afflicted?" Fr. Palermo asked with skepticism.

"We're not sure. On the negative, he's been attached to heresy in mind, heart, word, and deed. On the positive, Ken's been out of the occult for a few years," Clement cautiously asserted.

"You wouldn't have brought this case to me if you didn't suspect *something*, so I feel there's a *but...*," Fr. Palermo expressed and smiled, for he knew Clement wasn't one to waste his time, so there was meat on this bone.

"*But* he toiled during his thirty days of prayer and discipline, and based on his testimony, there are signs of diabolical oppression and obsession. I believe he's struggled internally and experienced a prick of conscience, a moment of grace which enabled him to embrace Christ when he entered the church for the first time in a decade and attempted to make a confession with Fr. Whitburn."

"He's trying to restore his relationship with Christ, *but...*" Fr. Palermo stated, expecting one of the men to finish his thought.

"But the demon won't let him," Fr. Whitburn said.

"We're uncertain he's possessed by a demon," Fr. Palermo concluded and added, "however, I *am* certain that Ken's obstructed from receiving a flow of grace. Something is occupying his house. I want to meet him in person and determine if any *squatters are exercising their rights over him.*"

***

St. Benedict Medal Perimeter

Vade retro Satanas;	Get behind me Satan;
Nunquam suede mihi vanas!	Never give me vain thoughts!
Sunt mala quae libas;	The cup you offer is poison;
Ipse veneno bibas!	Drink it yourself!

Three Days Later

Ken nervously fidgeted in the chair, this time in a larger conference room in the diocese office, along with Fr. Palermo, Fr. Whitburn, and Clement. Ken was sweating profusely, even though the air conditioner was working properly.

"Thank you for coming in, Mr. Flowers," Fr. Palermo greeted him formally and extended his hand.

"You can call me Ken," he tensely replied, shook his hand quickly, and added, "that is, if you want to."

Clement was somewhat surprised by Ken's overly respectful and submissive attitude. *Would the aggressive and boastful Ken return?* he wondered. Meetings such as this were always unpredictable, so Clement wanted to immediately get on track and review the facts.

"Fr. Whitburn and I have fully briefed Fr. Palermo. He's up to speed," Clement stated in a businesslike manner.

"Well, gentlemen, I'm afraid I have wasted your time," Ken stated with an awkward smile. Fr. Whitburn's jaw dropped in shock, for that was the last thing he expected Ken to say.

"What do you mean?" Fr. Palermo gently asked, also surprised.

"I know I've been saying for months that I'm possessed," Ken started and whispered the last word *possessed*. "But I don't believe it anymore."

"The real *safe space* is with us, and with God. You can tell us anything," Fr. Palermo gently told him.

"There's nothing to tell. I'm not possessed," Ken stated wryly.

"Why do you say that?" Clement inquired with genuine interest.

"Well, I'm embarrassed to say, but it's pretty simple. I've got schizophrenia," Ken announced, and his eyes darted to briefly focus on each of the men and lastly landed on Fr. Whitburn.

"Many times, people will confuse mental illness with demonic possession," Fr. Palermo pointed out.

"Yes, I think that's exactly what happened. Again, *I apologize*."

"Have you recently been to a doctor?" Clement pressed.

"Yes," he lied. "That's when I was diagnosed with schizophrenia. The *supposed* demon talking to me, the voices in my head. Bad dreams and hallucinations, it's all part of *my disease*."

"What hallucinations?" Clement asked.

"Thinking that I caused other people harm with spells and curses," he said and again whispered, "*I know it's not real.*"

"You're saying you didn't recite curses on your enemies?" Clement questioned for clarity.

"Oh, I did, along with Dolly, the witch. But thinking they worked, that was *delusional*."

"I see," Fr. Palermo interjected without any emotion, and Ken felt obligated to continue.

"I have anger management issues, that's real, so I think I should see someone to help me in that area. My moment of rage, like when I got arrested, that wasn't me. It was my *alternate personality*."

"You mean as part of a multiple personality disorder?" Clement inquired.

"Yes, that's right, so I need treatment. But not from *a priest*. No offense," he apologized to the young priest, who became frustrated and felt stupid in front of his more experienced colleague.

"But everything you've been doing the last couple of months," Fr. Whitburn pleaded, but Ken interrupted him.

"I know. I came to you for help, but I've been diagnosed properly. It's a relief, knowing I'm not possessed. I'm merely having a mental health crisis, that's all," Ken replied flippantly, rubbed his temple, and wiped the sweat from his brow.

Clement thought to himself, *It's not adding up. The psychologist's report would have detected signs of schizophrenia. This seemed more like Ken's demonstration of how to use the Google search engine.*

Fr. Palermo was unfazed and unemotional. He studied Ken's nonverbal cues, then replied, "Thanks for your explanation. You look a little stressed and overheated. How about some water?"

"Sure, that would be nice," he answered.

Fr. Palermo stood up, opened the door to the conference room, poked his head out, and asked his assistant for help, "Cold water please."

"I'm glad that someone knows how to help you," Clement submitted, and Ken smiled with relief.

The gentlemen watched through the glass wall as Kathy approached, carrying a tray of four glasses of water and a half-filled pitcher. She deliberately placed the tray in the middle of the round conference room table and turned the tray exactly ninety degrees.

Kathy placed the first glass in front of Fr. Palermo, one next to Clement, then Fr. Whitburn, and finally the last glass was placed in front of Ken. She left the pitcher on the tray and promptly left without saying a word. Fr. Palermo thanked her as she was leaving the room. She turned, smiled, and carefully pushed the door closed.

"Ken, I wasn't expecting schizophrenia to be the root cause of your distress," Fr. Palermo told him.

"Me neither, but boy am I glad about it," Ken replied with a little too much enthusiasm for someone with a serious mental disorder.

"I'm happy for you," the experienced priest replied, smiled, and took a long pause before mentioning. "There *was* some evidence to support a diabolical affliction."

"No need to worry about that now," Ken responded, agitated and wanted the meeting to be over as quickly as possible.

"There's an easy way to tell if you're demonically possessed," he blurted out as Ken went to pick up his glass of water.

"Oh?" Ken answered, trying his best to react nonchalantly to the priest's statement.

"*Holy water*," Fr. Palermo stated with authority, and Ken stopped moving his arm. The water glass was a mere few inches from his mouth. He put the glass down and wiped additional sweat from his brow.

"Hollywood gets that part correct. Demons *will react* to holy water," the experienced priest said in a serious tone with expressionless eyes. "Even if one droplet touches the body of a demonically possessed person, the reflex is involuntary."

"I get it, like in the movies," Ken stated and examined the glass.

"Ken, I'm sorry if I implied that your glass contained holy water." Fr. Palermo smiled and laughed. "It's not a test, I assure you. I only asked Kathy to bring in water because you looked parched."

"I'm not thirsty," Ken stated.

"Well, it *is* a little warm in here. I assure you that your glass is merely cold refreshing water. It's not blessed, I promise," the experienced priest said in an easygoing manner.

"Well, a priest wouldn't lie to me, right?" Ken anxiously smiled and picked up the water glass.

"Certainly not. I was referring to the small fountain in our lobby. *That water* was blessed. It's holy water," Fr. Palermo replied.

"Okay, yes, I noticed it when I walked in. I didn't mean to make such a big deal about it," Ken half apologized.

"No problem, I'm glad you figured out what's been ailing you, and now you can get better."

"Right," Ken stated and slowly brought the glass to his lips, paused, and said, "Bottoms up." He leaned the glass forward, cautiously opened his mouth, squinted his eyes, and barely allowed a few drops to touch his tongue.

Brace for impact.

Nothing.

Ken smiled and looked at the other men in the room, let out a small nervous laugh, took a full sip of water, paused, and then gulped three quarters of the remaining liquid. He leaned back in his chair with an air of satisfaction.

"I'm sorry we couldn't help you," Fr. Palermo said and placed his hand on the top portion of his own glass, which *was* blessed, *barely* allowing his index finger to touch the holy water as he lifted the glass and casually took a sip. He stood up, and with eyes fixed on Ken, he put out his hand and joyously added, "The best of luck to you!"

Ken stretched his arm to shake Fr. Palermo's hand.

The reaction was unmistakable and instant. Ken's eyes lit up like a volcanic eruption spewing molten lava into the atmosphere.

"Arrgh!" he bellowed and writhed in pain, pulling his hand back so hard and fast that he smacked himself in the forehead. The temperature in the room instantly dropped twenty degrees, and his eyes looked bloody and bright.

"Get away from me, you foul priest!" the voice bellowed, and the walls of the conference room vibrated.

The glass pitcher *disintegrated* and spilled onto the conference room table, as if it were dropped from one hundred feet above. A small shard of crystal stuck in Fr. Whitburn's forehead, and a trickle of blood dripped into his eye.

There was no doubt.

There was no question.

Ken was no longer in control.

The demon manifested itself.

Part 4: *Tell Me Your Name*, Eight Minutes Later

"What happened?" Ken asked, momentarily confused.

"What's the last thing you remember?" Fr. Palermo inquired cautiously and noticed Ken gaze at his surroundings for recognition. He didn't find any.

"Where am I?"

"You're in my office," he explained. Ken was seated in front of his desk, and Fr. Palermo was in the other guest chair.

"Well, let's see. I drank some water and stood up to leave. Hmm, and now I'm here," Ken answered slowly and rubbed his temples, trying to focus.

"We shook hands to say goodbye, and my finger had a drop of holy water. I don't know how to sugarcoat this, so I won't. A demon inside you exposed himself when our hands met," the experienced priest explained. There's no easy way to inform someone that they're possessed.

"But how did I get to your office?" Ken asked and rubbed his temple.

"The demon reacted and started cursing at me for several minutes. After realizing what happened, the demon retreated, and we brought you to my office and calmed you down."

"The demon's gone?" Ken asked incredulously and added, "So it's over?" he asked, now alert.

"Unfortunately, no. It merely confirms my suspicion," Fr. Palermo told him calmly with a measured tone. Demons hang on tight, and the priest knew it was going to be a battle.

The reaction varies when Fr. Palermo has confirmed to someone that he or she was possessed. Some respond positively, happy that the source of their problem wasn't a mental health crisis. Gripping fear can take over if one recognizes that their brain isn't functioning properly. He remembered one person shouting for joy, saying, "Thank God I'm not crazy!"

On the other hand, some have the opposite reaction—of pure fright and panic once they realize a *demon* has significant control. The fear of the unknown usually compounds people's reaction. What will happen next? In all cases, the situation was delicate and required an immediate interpretation of the person in front of him. He needed to provide comfort and guidance with a confident plan. However, he can't do it alone.

"I knew all along that something wasn't right with me. I suspected, but wow, it's hard to fathom what it means," Ken replied and stared at the ceiling, feeling the weight of the world on his shoulders.

"You're still *you* inside, but unless the demon is removed, your soul is in serious jeopardy. That won't happen unless you want to be rid of it."

"Well, of course, I want it gone. Why would anyone *not* want to remove a demon?" Ken asked incredulously, with a tinge of frustration.

"When someone is completely attached to their sin or doesn't want a relationship with Christ. Demons can *only* be exorcised out if someone truly wants them gone. That means changing your life and striving for virtue. Otherwise, they won't leave, or *they can return*," the priest told him, and Ken's eyes opened wide, flooded with emotion. Fr. Palermo wanted Ken to make his own conclusions. He leaned back, signaling Ken to take his time.

"Everything you said, it stirred something in me, but it's hard to make the leap to trust you."

"You need to trust Jesus. Be not afraid," Fr. Palermo replied with a frequent line from the Bible.

"It's not in my nature to *trust*," Ken explained and frowned, still processing his situation.

"It's scary, I understand. We can work on your fears and doubts. There are prayers specifically to ask Jesus to help open your heart," Fr. Palermo told him, providing some hope. "It's perfectly reasonable to ask for the strength and ability to say *Jesus, I trust in You.*"

"It is?"

"Yes. Many people pray for help, for lots of different reasons."

Ken contemplated his situation and eventually spoke, "Yes, that's something I need."

"It'll help, I assure you. Everyone has moments of doubt and confusion, especially when we experience traumatic events. You won't be alone through the process."

"I never quite understood it until now," Ken exclaimed and nodded, his energy level rising.

"What?" Fr. Palermo asked, genuinely confused.

"I never figured out why my mother is always so happy and at peace," he gushed excitedly and announced. "It's her relationship with Jesus."

Fr. Palermo beamed with joy. He finally got it, and Ken's next words were the exclamation point!

"I want what *she* has."

The Next Day

Colorado is known for majestic mountains and snow-capped peaks. Those mountains are far from the eastern plains of Weld County. Ken nervously fidgeted in the car while Fr. Whitburn zipped down the state highway toward the convent. The priest involuntarily touched the slight cut on his forehead from the day before. It would leave a tiny scar, a permanent reminder of how the devil can impact our physical world. God occasionally permits demons to wield their power and influence. It's a mystery that no priest fully understood.

Ken's solemn exorcism rite, day 1, was about to begin. They entered the aging convent where an empty room was allocated to Fr. Palermo and his team.

"Good morning," Fr. Palermo greeted Ken, who nodded and immediately looked away and shuffled his feet. His heart rate rose, and he suddenly felt warm. He tugged at his shirt to let some of the heat out. Ken looked as uncomfortable as you would expect for his first session with an exorcist priest.

"You're nervous. That's to be expected. Let's discuss our plan, shall we?" Fr. Palermo asked and led him into the kitchen area. Ken declined an offer of coffee or water. He wasn't thirsty, and his stomach was in knots for the last eighteen hours, so food was the last thing on his mind.

Ken half expected that when he entered the convent, some sort of *drama* would explode, and his head would swivel around a few times, and he'd immediately projectile vomit pea soup like Linda Blair. But for the moment, all was calm. That didn't mean it wouldn't turn into a Hollywood-type script, but for now it all seemed so *businesslike*.

Ken watched the priest's every move, and as he came closer, Ken silently handed him a signed document, the legal liability waiver.

"How does this work?" Ken asked.

"Let's set expectations," Fr. Palermo smiled and gestured for him to sit at the dining table. Ken sheepishly complied and folded his hands as if waiting for his death sentence to be read by a judge.

The priest explained, "We're at the convent because it's best to do this on sacred ground. Plus, it's quiet, and we'll have our privacy. Your safety is our primary concern. We have specific protocols to perform, which were approved by the bishop and is similar to the integrity and formality of receiving a sacrament."

"Okay," Ken answered, but didn't have further thoughts because like many experiences in life, it's hard to understand something until you go through it.

"I'm going to lead a series of deliverance prayers. Fr. Whitburn will assist me, and we'll have Clement and two others in the room. They'll pray too, and this will probably agitate the demon, so you may need physical restraint."

Ken didn't know what to say, so he went with, "I guess that's okay." He anxiously took in a deep breath, for his understanding didn't provide any comfort.

"The demon will have no choice but to react. We'll probably go for a few hours and take some breaks. It's physically demanding, both for you and us," Fr. Palermo explained and observed the distress on Ken's face. As an experienced exorcist, this wasn't a surprise.

"Have faith," Fr. Palermo stated and placed both hands on Ken's shoulders to reassure him.

"I trust you."

"I don't have any special powers."

"What?" Ken gasped in panic mode.

"Jesus is doing all the work. Have trust in Him," Fr. Palermo calmly clarified with complete confidence. Ken studied the priest's face, full of assurance, and this bolstered his faith. It was in God's hands now.

Ken nodded with cautious hope and replied, "Yes, of course."

Fr. Palermo rose out of the chair, the signal that it was time to start. He guided Ken down the hall and into a small bedroom. It was a simple room with a tiny table, dresser, twin-size bed, and a few chairs. Clement and two others were already waiting for them. The prayer team had prepped the room by covering the windows, bringing the proper vestments, ritual books and removing any unnecessary objects.

This is it, Ken thought to himself, and that's when it hit him, *I'm possessed by the devil*. The gravity of the situation flooded him with a mix of emotions. His initial instinct was to *run*. He needed to get away and forget everything that had happened since he entered the confessional booth with Fr. Whitburn.

How can I be possessed?
What was I thinking?
These people are nuts!
Or maybe I'm crazy too!

Or maybe this was a way for the demon to escape by putting fear and doubt in Ken's heart. He felt the inner struggle, and another thought popped into his mind. *You want to be free, don't you?*

There wasn't time to have the debate inside his head, as the decision was made for him.

"Let's begin," Fr. Palermo asserted, bringing Ken back into focus. "Let's start with you and Fr. Whitburn saying the Our Father prayer."

Fr. Whitburn was also nervous, it being the first time he assisted the exorcist priest. He silently asked God for help, *Don't let me make a mistake!* After the slight pause, he made eye contact with Ken, nodded, and they both said, "Our Father who art in heaven, Hallowed be Thy name."

Fr. Palermo joined in for the last line, "And lead us not into temptation, but deliver us *from evil.* Amen." He nodded at Clement, who led the Litany of Saints prayer along with his wife Valerie and another assistant, Dean, a former EMT and police officer.

"Lord, have mercy. Christ, have mercy. Holy Mary, Mother of God, pray for Ken. Saints Michael, Gabriel, and Raphael, pray for Ken," they said in unison and would continue to pray while the two priests worked.

Fr. Palermo brought a crucifix and removed it from the velvet bag and placed it in front of Ken's face, which also forced the demon to see the sacred object. His eyes rolled back into his head, for the demon could not stand the sight of Christ. Ken fell onto the mattress and curled up in a fetal position. He started slithering like a snake.

Fr. Palermo stood in front of Ken who arched his back, and his pupils became thick and red while his iris turned black with total darkness. *The demon was in control.*

"In the Name of Our Lord Jesus Christ, through the merits of the Most Holy Virgin Mary, through the intersession of Saint Michael, the Archangel, the Holy Apostles Peter and Paul and all the saints, I break every occult of black magic between you and Ken."

"Get away, priest!" the demon hissed and twisted Ken's spine, so his upper body was at a ninety-degree angle, and his head bobbed sideward like a cobra ready to strike.

Fr. Palermo was unfazed and continued, "I bind every power of this spirit, and I command you to leave Ken."

"I will not leave."

"Tell me your name."

"You have no idea who you're dealing with, weak priest."

"Tell me your name."

Ken fell to the floor and tried to slither away from Fr. Palermo; Clement and Dean ceased praying and grabbed Ken by the shoulders and lifted him onto the small bed. Fr. Whitburn and Valerie leaned down on Ken's ankles to restrain him.

"Get off me! You have no power. You're a fake priest," the demon bellowed and stared down Fr. Whitburn.

Fr. Palermo quickly interjected and told Fr. Whitburn to continue praying.

"You're a cheater. What kind of man plagiarizes his seminary essay application?" the demon mocked and laughed hideously, which gave Fr. Whitburn chills. Its dark eyes attempted to mesmerize the young priest.

"Focus," Fr. Palermo shouted.

"You should've *never* been accepted to the seminary. Everything you've done as a priest *is a lie!*" the demon stated with piercing authority.

"Tell me your name."

"He's mine, and I won't let him go!" the demon growled and spit at the priest. The room dropped in temperature, and Ken exhaled a foul sulfur stench. Dean coughed, and Clement had to look away and attempted to find fresh air as he kept pressing down on Ken's shoulder.

"Tell me your name!" Fr. Palermo repeated in a rising voice. He wasn't going to be sidetracked.

"He rejected God and let us in, so we have a *right* to be here. We own him!" the demon said in a raspy voice while looking at the ceiling.

Like a lawyer from hell, the demon was arguing its case. There was some truth to its claim. Ken *had* opened the door to the demon and accepted a series of invitations. It's no wonder they claimed a heart that abandoned God.

Fr. Palermo picked up on the clue that the possession was plural and inched forward to lock eyes with the demon. "In the Name of Jesus Christ, I break any unholy ties, links, and bondages between Ken and all evil sources and spirits," Fr. Palermo recited and sprinkled holy water on Ken.

"Arrgh!" Ken screamed with a loud baritone voice that vibrated the walls.

No man's voice could be that low and deep. It was *unnatural.*

"Give up, priest. He's not worth it."

"I order you, demon, in the name of Jesus Christ, to repeat these words, *You are my Creator and I adore you!*"

"Never!"

"I command you," Fr. Palermo stated but was interrupted by the screeched wail of the demon.

"Your sister is pregnant. I will abort her child, and she will blame *you*, useless priest!" the demon threatened.

"By the power of Christ, I compel you: Tell. Me. Your. Name!"

"Lucifer."

***

> For he had said to him, "Come out of the man, you unclean spirit!" Then Jesus asked him, "What is your name?" He replied, "My name is Legion; for we are many." He begged him earnestly not to send them out of the country. Now there on the hillside a great herd of swine was feeding; and the unclean spirits begged him, "Send us into the swine; let us enter them." So, he gave them permission. And the unclean spirits came out and entered the swine; and the herd, numbering about two thousand, rushed down the steep bank into the sea, and were drowned in the sea. (Mark 5:8–13)

***

"I seriously doubt that he's possessed by Lucifer. Demons lie all the time," Fr. Palermo stated in the hallway, out of earshot of Ken, who was resting in the tiny bedroom while being monitored by Dean.

Fr. Whitburn couldn't wait to explain himself and blurted out, "The application, I had help writing it."

"There's no need to elaborate. The demon is trying to exploit your weakness. You don't need to go into the details."

"I confessed about this a long time ago," he stressed.

"That's all I need to know," Fr. Palermo stated, and his hand waved off the young priest's need to continue. "Two days ago, my younger sister announced she was pregnant with her third child. After this session, will you two help me pray for her and the unborn child?"

"Of course," Clement answered, and Fr. Whitburn nodded in silence.

"The demon may possess Ken in the name of Lucifer, but he is trying to impress us by claiming to be the most intelligent and powerful demon," Fr. Palermo returned to the issue at hand.

"So if it's not Lucifer, then who?"

"I'm not 100 percent sure, but I suspect who the higher-level demon is, but it's yet to reveal itself. He wants us to be scared of Lucifer and give up," Fr. Palermo replied.

"He's trying to boast," Clement added.

"Exactly. I think *he is* a higher-level demon, but not Lucifer," Fr. Palermo speculated, but didn't see recognition on the face of his priestly counterpart, so he explained, "he wants us to think he's important. Just like there are nine choirs, or levels of angels, the inverse is true too. Most of the low-level demons will diabolically influence a person, but a higher-level demon is required for possession."

"I think there are some secondary demons lurking around," Clement predicted.

"I agree. The stronger demon has recruited lower-level ones which have probably been oppressing Ken for years."

"Why wouldn't the stronger demon want us to know his name so he could brag about it?" Fr. Whitburn asked.

"I can see why you'd think that, but once the possessor has been revealed, he's easier to command and control," Fr. Palermo answered.

"Yes, that makes sense."

"A demon is the inverse of the original angel that was created for a specific purpose. In Ken's case, his sinful behavior relates to vengeance," Fr. Palermo continued.

"The lower levels are the entourage," Clement added.

"And the *entourage* must be demons of lust and greed, Ken's other vices," Fr. Whitburn expressed as it started to click for him.

"Yes, that's my guess," Fr. Palermo affirmed.

"And they can't change, so a demon of gluttony doesn't one day decide to be a demon of lust," Clement explained, and Fr. Whitburn nodded with understanding.

"Let's go back in," Fr. Palermo instructed, and the two men followed him. Dean and Valerie were on watch as Fr. Palermo proceeded cautiously with the demon, avoiding harm to Ken and others.

"I don't remember anything," Ken told them and appeared lucid.

"Don't worry about that. Let's go a bit longer, and we'll debrief afterward."

"I understand," Ken said reluctantly.

Fr. Palermo got down to business, reciting, "O Glorious Queen of Heaven and earth, Virgin Most Powerful, thou who hast the power to crush the head of the ancient serpent with thy heel, come and exercise this power flowing from grace of thine Immaculate Conception."

"Not her!" the demon cried out.

"Shield us under the mantle of thy purity and love, draw us into the sweet abode of thy heart and *annihilate* and render impotent the forces bent on destroying us."

The lightbulb on the ceiling burst and shattered but remained encased in the glass fixture. The small light on the desk also exploded, and most of the glass bounced off the lampshade and fell onto the tabletop. Although the room's two window blinds were closed, it allowed some light, casting muted color tones.

Ken's presence attracted and *absorbed the shadows.* "Get these other people out of the room. I want you on my own, Pa-ler-mo!" the demon snarled.

The demon was fighting back and seeking to intimidate. Fr. Palermo knew the demon's playbook and had no intention of backing down, engaging or bantering with the demon. He dismissed any thought of asking the others to leave the room. Not because he was scared to face the demon alone, but many times, a demon could control a human's body with superhuman strength, similar to someone hyped up on drugs. Left alone, the demon could physically overpower the priest.

"Tell me your name."

"You have no power over me."

"*Tell me your name,*" he repeated with a cool head.

"Cast a spell on me to make me leave. *I dare you!*"

"Tell me your name," he repeated, undeterred.

"Leave us alone, *worthless priest*. You can't have him," the demon groaned in a nasty, throaty, and raspy tone.

"Hail Mary, full of grace," Fr. Palermo recited but was interrupted.

"Ken doesn't want me to leave. We've been together for *so long,*" the demon hissed, clearly agitated.

"The Lord is with thee. Blessed art thou amongst women and blessed is the fruit of thy womb, Jesus."

"You can't break me!"

"Holy Mary, Mother of God, pray for us sinners, now and at the hour of our death. Amen."

"Give up, priest. Don't those old bones need a rest? How's that hip of yours?" the demon taunted and laughed at his own cruelty and sarcasm.

"Tell me your name," Fr. Palermo repeated. For once, the demon didn't respond, seeking to bait the priest. Suddenly, the room went eerily quiet.

"It's okay, it worked. The demon is gone," a voice that sounded like Ken pronounced. Fr. Palermo wasn't buying it, especially after Ken uttered, "You can stop praying now."

"Lord Jesus Christ, Sovereign King enthroned in Heaven, in Thy love and mercy establish a perimeter of protection with Thy Precious Blood around Ken, me, and all those here, blocking the empowerment which flows from the insidious movement of Satan or any demonic enthronement, abominations in Thy sight," Fr. Palermo stated, and when he ended, there was *complete and utter silence.*

***

"I'm worn out," Ken stated and wiped the sweat from his brow. Fr. Whitburn handed him a towel, and he wiped his face. "What happened?"

"The demon manifested itself, but you did great. The *real you* is there, deep inside. Keep asking Christ into your heart," Fr. Palermo stated while they rested at the kitchen table.

"Honestly, I'm scared. I don't know which part of me *is me* and what part is *something else.*"

"The demon can't hurt you. Be more afraid of the sin."

"Yes, I get that," Ken responded, but wasn't comforted at the moment.

"The demon has influenced your intellect and willpower over time, so it will require some time."

"I know, it's not *one and done,*" Ken nervously jested and looked at Fr. Whitburn, recalling their conversation about finishing it up in an afternoon. His smile lightened the mood.

"Breaking away from any kind of sinful behavior is *never easy,*" Fr. Whitburn added.

"How long are we talking?"

"I won't sugarcoat it. Months, most likely," the experienced priest relayed.

"Wow," cringed a dejected Ken. That meant he'd be in limbo for what seemed like an eternity. How would he know which thoughts were his own? What actions were his alone? His forehead creased, and his jaw clenched, noticeable to both priests.

"I know you're frustrated. We won't abandon you."

"I still don't understand how this happened to me. *Why me?*"

"We'll never know the complete story. This may be *your path* to Christ. Granted, it is not the easiest, but you can be stronger than ever at the end."

"Do you believe that?"

"Absolutely. I've seen it happen many times."

"Really?"

"Yes, *many times*," Fr. Palermo reiterated and paused a moment while Ken formulated his thoughts.

"I do feel different. I don't know how to describe it other than *my life* seems to be more in focus."

"Tell me how you see it," Fr. Palermo encouraged.

"The past couple of years have been chaotic," Ken conceded.

"That's good."

"Huh?"

"You saw how your life was disordered and focused on the wrong behaviors."

"Right. It took years to admit I needed help to change my life around."

"The demons blurred your senses, twisting what's right and wrong, so it's not black and white but rather infinite shades of gray," Fr. Palermo replied, teaching the subtleties of the demon's diabolical playbook.

"Yes, sometimes I would become consumed with revenge and lose focus on everything else. I felt a temporary high when I punished my enemies, but..." Ken trailed off.

"But you also knew the source of euphoria was malicious," Clement added.

"Yes, that described my struggles and competing desires."

"It's a battle for the airwaves of your mind," Fr. Palermo replied, eyes focused on Ken, providing silent and compassionate encouragement.

"Like the devil on one shoulder and the angel on the other, whispering in my ear," Ken observed.

"Something like that. To the extent that we participate in sin, we become more compatible with the demon and incompatible with God. You can't pursue both simultaneously. Similar to your job, you can't be present at two construction sites at the same time."

"That makes complete sense." Ken nodded, grasping the concept. It's a lot easier to fight an enemy when you see what's happening on the battlefield, and in this case, the battlefield was Ken's mind, heart, body, and soul.

"Before you came to Fr. Whitburn, you were struggling with this on your own and kept it a secret. This implied permission to the demons," Fr. Palermo noted, and he didn't want to deter or mute Ken's progress, so he quickly added, "however, there's a remedy."

"The exorcism?"

"Not exactly. The most important discovery is we've figured out your impediment to grace, seeking vengeance over and over again. When you embrace virtue just as passionately, that's when we'll get close to the end. We made a lot of progress today."

"We did?" Ken asked, surprised. "Is it good enough? Can we stop?"

"Unfortunately, no. We don't stop halfway. There's no such thing as a partial exorcism. This is the first time the demon exposed himself and has given us valuable intel. The more we know about the demon, the more effective we can fight."

"Intel, like a military strategy?"

"Exactly. We will start up again in a few days. You need to rest, and I'll provide a set of prayers to recite in the meantime."

Thirty-Seven Days Later, October 2018

At fourteen sessions in, Fr. Palermo was frustrated with the slow progress. It was hard to fight off dejection. It was difficult being a full-time exorcist priest, and he was frequently lonely. Many of his brethren priests didn't understand what he did.

No one denied the existence of demons, but many priests understood them only at the theoretical level, whereas Fr. Palermo was at the practical level, like an officer on the battlefield. The one bright spot was his new friendship with Fr. Whitburn, whom with he carpooled to the convent.

He believed the entourage demons remained, and until those were dispelled, it would be difficult to rid the demon that possessed Ken. They were putting up a fight and probably called for reinforcements. Perhaps if he explained the situation to Ken, he'd respond positively.

Ken was already there and greeted the priest, "Good morning, Father."

"Ken, how are you?"

"Good, and I'm following all your instructions."

"Excellent. Let's chat before the others get here," he suggested and joined him at the table. "The demon continues to claim he's Lucifer."

"Is that why the resistance is so strong?"

"Maybe, but a Lucifer possession is extremely rare, so I believe he's lying. I also think there are multiple lower-level demons present."

"The entourage, as you've described."

"Yes. The low-level ones are less intelligent and are the first to be expelled."

"Okay."

"All angels augment the flow of grace in some way, so as the opposite, the demons will seek to obstruct the flow of grace. Some lower-level angels were created to bring comfort and aid, and so the inverse is to deliver discomfort and destruction through temptation and confusion," Fr. Palermo explained.

"Well, they certainly did that to me," Ken proclaimed.

"They flocked to you the way buzzards circle a dying animal."

The priest's blunt assessment touched a nerve. Ken stood up abruptly with enough force to slide his chair backward and bump into the nearby cabinet. His hands gestured wildly and exclaimed, "Well, that really pisses me off."

"Ken?" Fr. Whitburn piped in, concerned.

"I'm sick and tired of having this *entourage* around. I want them out of my head, out of my body, and out of my spirit!" he griped with an *oomph* but maintained control of his emotions. The experienced priest didn't react and motioned for Ken to return to the table. He retrieved the chair and sat back down.

"I feel your energy level, that's good," Fr. Palermo complimented.

"Where's that crucifix?" he asked and added, "I don't care if I'm blinded forever. I'm going to make that demon see *what I see*." Ken was on a roll.

"That's why we use it. Christ on the cross is the epitome of His love for us. It's Jesus with his working clothes on," Fr. Whitburn chimed in.

"I'm sorry I got a little upset. I just want to be *me* and left alone with my own thoughts. Is that too much to ask?"

"I like your enthusiasm, but we need Clement and the rest to be here." A few seconds later, Fr. Palermo's phone rang; it was Clement. He was only a few minutes away. The next five minutes seemed like a long time.

"Your pursuit of virtue, hence the flow of grace, is key," Fr. Palermo continued.

"Over this past month or so, I'm slowly getting there. Choosing virtue *is hard*."

"It is for everyone," Fr. Palermo acknowledged. "Do you want a life of virtue?"

The priests expected an immediate reaction with an emphatic declaration. Ken looked down and was truly deep in thought. His lips slightly moved from his quiet prayer, and after a long forty-five seconds, he gritted his teeth, breathed a loud sigh, and answered with a serious affirmation, "Yes."

When Clement arrived with Valerie and Dean, no words needed to be spoken, for he'd already beaten himself up for being late, and he apologized as soon as he entered the convent.

"Let's start," Fr. Palermo stated without giving Clement and the others a chance to get settled. "We're going to begin with the Litany of Saints." They moved to the same small bedroom, and all recited the prayer. Fr. Palermo took out of his bag the crucifix and a twelve-inch statue of the Virgin Mary. Ken's eyes once again rolled back into his head.

"*Tell* me your name," Fr. Palermo started in right away.

"Go home, pathetic priest."

"Tell *me* your name."

"Die, priest!"

"Tell me *your* name."

"I have a friend in the room. A real sinner."

"Tell me your *name*!" Fr. Palermo emphasized.

"I can help you get justice, Clement! You know you want to."

At that moment, Clement realized that he wasn't in a state of grace. He got a late start and was speeding down the state highway, which wasn't his usual habit. He muttered under his breath when he saw the red and blue flashing lights behind him, which of course put him even further behind schedule.

If that wasn't bad enough, he then got stuck behind a farm truck going ten miles under the speed limit. His blood was boiling when he passed the driver and honked his horn. Not a mortal sin but enough to catch the attention of the demon.

Fr. Palermo turned and asked, "Clement?"

"I'm sorry, road rage."

"Don't tell it to me. Go and confess to Fr. Whitburn." Both men left the room without a word.

There was another small bedroom on the other side of the narrow hallway where they could have some privacy. After

Clement confessed his sins to Fr. Whitburn and they completed the sacrament, he added, "I want to apologize to you too for being late. I have a great amount of respect for you. You're assisting Fr. Palermo in ways you can't even imagine."

"Thank you for the kind words. I'm flabbergasted by the way the demon called out our sin."

"Yes, they'll use any means to thwart the process and make it about the people in the room, especially priests, if they can get to them," Clement stated, which reminded them about how the demon previously knew about Fr. Whitburn's seminary application *mistake*.

After a long pause, the young priest commented, "Fr. Palermo obviously knows what he's doing. I don't see any fear in his eyes."

"I agree. This demon knows he's up against a good priest, a pious man. Only those with high integrity can be an exorcist," Clement pointed out with the implication that Fr. Whitburn was asked to assist because he was also a dedicated and devout priest.

"Looking back at seminary now, the exorcism rite isn't talked about much. This is the definition of *getting your hands dirty*."

"Very much so. It's not pie in the sky theoretical biblical study. Not that there's anything wrong with that," Clement stated.

"For me, being new to this, it's solidified my faith beyond what I could've imagined, and I'm blessed for that."

"Being part of these proceedings usually changes us. I'm sure the demon is frustrated that the experience has brought you closer to God. It's certainly made a difference in Ken's life."

"He'll never be the same," Fr. Whitburn concluded, and the two returned to Ken's room and immediately noticed Fr. Palermo smiling.

"I *think* we're rid of the entourage," he exclaimed and added, "Ken's resting for a moment."

"What was the final push?" Fr. Whitburn asked.

"I started reading scripture. The demons know it's true, and *they can't stand it* and wish they didn't believe it. Ken seemed different, and from what I can tell, the lower-level demons were tormented enough, so they gave up and left. Jesus will do with them what He wants."

***

Fr. Whitburn sat quietly while they finished lunch. He prayed silently, *Please God, give me the strength and wisdom so I can be your instrument.*

Ken broke the silence. "I remember a little bit this time," he said and looked around the table.

"Tell me more," Fr. Palermo coaxed.

"I heard you praying. It was distant and muffled, but it was definitely you."

"That's a good sign."

"The exorcism rite tortures the demon with *the truth.* They've rejected God, and they don't want to hear that Christ has defeated them on the cross. I believe the entourage is gone."

"Don't say it. There's more work to be done, right?" Ken teased, fully aware of the answer.

"This is a significant step forward. Whatever is happening, God is allowing through providence."

"I get it. This is my penance for rejecting God," Ken stated without emotion and followed up with, "I'm not upset or feeling sorry for myself. I think this is part of God's plan for me."

Fr. Whitburn noticed a shift in Ken's attitude, on the right path, and he jumped into the conversation to point out, "Christ will rescind any rights the demon has over you, and your part of the fight is critical. You have one of the best weapons."

"Virtue. I understand it. Now I have to *do it.*"

"You'll fall short, like every other human, and no one expects perfection. You're a strong man, and you can choose to be humble. It's not an either/or situation," Fr. Whitburn declared.

"You've been afflicted for years, hearing both the temptations of the devil and the voice of Christ, the voice of truth, which doesn't have an expiration date," Fr. Palermo declared and posed the most important question in Ken's life, "which voice will you follow?"

One Hour Later

"Please, kill me and put me out of my misery," he begged in Ken's voice. The demon would rather have Ken dead than liberated. His arms flailed about and looked for a weapon to inflict harm. If a knife was available, he'd have slit his own throat.

"Restrain him," Fr. Palermo reminded his team, and Clement and Dean leaned down upon each of Ken's shoulders with all their weight.

"Tell me your name," Fr. Palermo commanded.

"Let this poor soul be rid of his body. Put him out of his misery."

"Tell me your name," Fr. Palermo repeated.

"Let him die!" the unnatural voice bellowed.

"The power of Christ compels you."

"TELL!"

"ME!"

"YOUR!"

"NAME!"

"Arrgh," the demon screamed in rage, and the walls vibrated as if they contained a speaker from a rock concert. The base pounded, moved the air, and reverberated through everyone's body.

"I am Invictus."

Finally, Fr. Palermo thought to himself.

"Now leave us alone, foul priest."

That's not going to happen, Invictus. The priest had a nickname for this demon, *My Way*. Demons don't have a gender, but they have a disposition. They can be passive aggressive, sneaky and manipulative. Invictus's trait was the opposite: intimidating, domineering, with an *in-your-face* forceful style. This demon is a bully and chose vengeance instead of justice because he's appointed himself as *the enforcer*.

"Leave this man, serpent."

"Ken wants me here. He loves *my power*."

"In the name of Jesus Christ, I command you, *Invictus,* to leave this man and go to the foot of the cross."

Instantly, Fr. Palermo felt the temperature in the room drop, and a foul smell engulfed them, forcing the priest to pause and cough from the repugnant smell of rotting flesh. The stench of *death* is repulsive and forces an interior shudder, and an average person's first instinct is flight, not fight.

Fr. Palermo was expecting the distraction from the demon, and *his* reaction was to *fight*. "Ken is a child of God and belongs to no one but God. Dark forces have no dominion. No right. No authority."

"I hate you, priest!"

"Through the love of our Lord, Jesus Christ, I command you to leave."

"He wants me, not you, vile priest!"

"St. Joseph, Terror of demons, pray for us."

"I am not afraid of your saints," the demon shouted in agony and pain.

"The Lord is the light and my salvation, *whom shall I fear*? The Lord is my life's refuge; *of whom should I be afraid*? When evildoers come at me to devour my flesh, these my enemies and foes themselves *stumble and fall,*" Fr. Palermo stated with complete authority.

There wasn't a notion of *flight* in this priest. Ken was breathing heavily, whimpering and drooled over himself. The priest noticed a change and waited several moments.

"What, what happened?" Ken cautiously asked, now in control of his faculties. The foul smell evaporated, and the temperature returned to normal.

"How do you feel?" Fr. Palermo asked, and Ken looked at Clement and Dean, who were holding him down. His eyes met with Clement who realized the demon had subsided.

"You can let him go," Clement instructed Dean, and both men released Ken, relieved to end the physically demanding work.

"I'm okay, I think," Ken responded and sat up in the bed.

"Do you remember anything?"

"Just a little. I remember you praying, but it was quiet and muffled, like your hand covered your mouth. I can see by the look on your face *something* happened. Was there a breakthrough?"

"We know who we're dealing with. Invictus, the demon of *revenge*."

"I'm sorry I've put you all through this," Ken instantly apologized.

"Don't be. We want you to be liberated from any diabolic affliction."

"I thought it might be tough for me, but I didn't know it would be so grueling for everyone else."

"It goes with the territory," Fr. Palermo admitted, and the others nodded, for they assisted in many other exorcisms. Even Fr. Whitburn was now considered an experienced veteran in spiritual warfare.

Two Days Later

"Thank you for seeing me," Veronica Flowers told the priest as soon as she settled into his parish office.

"You've been very supportive of Ken during this process. It's been helping."

"That's good. For years, I've watched my son slip away, powerless to get through to him. I don't know *half the things* he's done over the past few years, but I'm sure it's been bad."

"You're praying to his guardian angel and the protection prayers. You attend adoration in the chapel when we meet with Ken, correct?"

"Yes, each time," she replied and looked away. The fifty-year-old woman's face dropped slightly, accentuating her sad eyes. She repositioned herself in the chair, trying to ease the back pain, and adjusted her simple and modest flower-patterned dress.

"I'm sure this has been difficult for you," Fr. Whitburn stated tenderly. "I didn't realize when I first met Ken that he was your son. I know you attend mass regularly."

"I'm sorry, Father. Both my kids have fallen away from the faith," the thin tall woman admitted. "I guess I failed them."

"Don't be too hard on yourself. I'm sure you did the best you could," he offered.

"I don't understand it. I've always been faithful, but both of my children have turned away from God. It's heartbreaking."

Like Merle Haggard would tell you, *Mama tried; mama cried.* It was a trend far too common in many families, parents helplessly watching their children fall away from the church, fooled by the modern world's message of self-love.

"Unfortunately, your experience isn't unusual," the priest lamented.

"We attended church as a family, that is until..." She trailed off and drew in a deep breath. "Has Ken talked about his father?"

"Only that he died of cancer when Ken was young."

"He was eleven. Neil was a family man, faithful and a good dad to the kids."

"That must have been a difficult time. Tell me about him."

"We started dating as seniors in high school. We'd clicked right away and had similar values. We went to the prom, and wow, he looked so good in a suit and tie," she said and smiled, reliving the moment. "Most of his friends were embarrassed to dance and look silly, but not Neil. He knew I loved music, and he danced with me, awkward as it was," she laughed, recalling his two left feet.

"An unforgettable evening," Fr. Whitburn commented. Veronica agreed, and the priest sensed she wanted to explain further, so he returned the smile, and she continued,

"He paid the band $20 to play my favorite song, *Nothing's Gonna Change My Love For You*. That's the night I knew we'd be married someday. Yup, that was *the night*. The summer after graduation, he proposed to me by climbing up a ladder and singing that very song through my bedroom window after he asked my father for permission. It was magical, and we were married within a year. Soon after, we had Ken."

"I can see you loved him deeply," Fr. Whitburn acknowledged.

"Very much. We had a good life. He worked construction with one of his Knights of Columbus brothers, although Ken will never admit that he followed in his father's footsteps," she added, and her facial expression turned sullen. "I'll never forget the *dread* in the pit of my stomach the day Neil spit up blood."

"Oh no."

"Stomach cancer. I still don't understand how someone gets that," she stated and wiped a tear from her eye. "I miss the simple ordinariness of our lives. It's sad when the love of your life is no longer there. All the things that *might have been*. I'm left with the emptiness."

"You're still hurting," the young priest stated with empathy.

"If I could only get another five minutes with him," Veronica wished, looked down, and tried to control her erratic breathing.

"Time doesn't heal all wounds. When you're alone, the sadness is amplified," he acknowledged in a tender manner.

"Yes, and every now and then, I still grieve," Veronica nodded and further explained, "I wasn't consumed with sorrow. I was too busy raising the kids. Even after they grew up, I wasn't interested in dating."

"I'm sorry. It's obviously painful to talk about," was all Fr. Whitburn could offer, clearly recognizing the anguish as raw as it was almost twenty years ago.

"It's okay. We had several great years. It wasn't a perfect marriage, but we were happy. This is why I wanted to meet with you."

"What do you mean?"

"Ken won't talk about his father or childhood, at least with me. I assume he hasn't provided details to you either. I thought it might help to know some of his background."

"Tell me whatever you're comfortable with."

"Ken never grieved. He took it personally and felt abandoned. Not that it's Neil's fault."

"When a child loses a parent, it's hard to see that."

"I know, but he was never the same, so maybe it explains everything that's happened to Ken."

"How so?"

"He was so angry at his father for leaving him. He wouldn't talk to him in those last few weeks. We all sensed the end was near for Neil, and little Kenny refused to interact with his father. He didn't visit him in the hospital and said such hurtful things."

"He was acting out, and I assume he held on to the negative feelings," Fr. Whitburn surmised.

"Completely. Ken was resentful for his father leaving him, and the behavior became worse when the money got tight. Neil had a small insurance policy, and after the doctor's bills and funeral expenses, there wasn't much left over. It was tough on me to keep the household together."

"I take it he didn't turn to God," Fr. Whitburn remarked.

"The opposite. Whatever hatred he had for Neil, it was doubled toward God. As a child, the situation was hard for him to understand. He channeled that hatred into teenage rebellion."

"Did he question God's existence?"

"Not at all. He needed to direct his wrath. He perceived Neil's death as God's unjust punishment, so he racked his brain on ways to rebuke Him. It was the age-old reaction of wondering how a loving God, a just God, could do this to a good father, but more importantly, how could God take away a father from a young boy?"

"There isn't some grand orchestration to make bad things happen to good people."

"I know. We live in a broken world," Veronica added.

"Becoming closer to Christ through suffering is a tough concept for people to understand, let alone embrace."

"It's more difficult for a child."

"I agree, and I'm sure it seemed senseless."

"Yes, when Neil died, I admit, it tested my faith," she testified.

"Yet, you didn't lose your love for Jesus."

"I asked Him for strength and comfort. I allowed Him to prop me up during the worst period of my life."

"By allowing Him to carry you."

"Yes, that's how I survived, but Ken, well, he reacted by lashing out."

"He got into fights at school and railed against authority, including mine. Ken graduated high school as an angry young man. He felt God, the universe, and life in general dealt him a bad hand."

"Yes, your son absolutely experienced every parent's nightmare, not being able to take care of your child and watch and help them grow up."

"He had let go of most of his anger by his midtwenties, but then he met Dolly."

"The witch."

"Yes, she was alluring, and they moved in together soon after they met. From what I can see, most of his problems were either self-inflicted or he made something out of nothing. She became controlling and tirelessly schemed plots for *his revenge*. She spun him up and kept him constantly angry. After they eloped, he told me they cast spells on his enemies. Dolly scared me, and I didn't see much of Ken during the early years of his marriage."

"She had a tremendous influence over Ken," the young priest conceded.

"Definitely. I once questioned her witchcraft beliefs, and she became enraged. Soon after, she cut me out of his life. He never wanted to upset Dolly, and she discouraged Ken from seeing his family and friends. She seemed to have control over him, and the few times I saw him, he was obsessed about ways to dish out *his version of justice*."

"That's consistent with what Ken told us. He mentioned they had a difficult divorce. What's your take on why the marriage didn't last?"

"She had several affairs with other men and a few women. I think her own anger at God motivated her behavior. She would make both subtle and *not-so-subtle* comments about how she intentionally snubbed God with her actions. She never got into any of the details, so I don't know what started her thinking that way."

"She embraced a sinful lifestyle to rebuke God," Fr. Whitburn surmised.

"Yes, that fits her personality. She aborted a child, and that upset him, although he wasn't sure the baby was his."

"That must have added to his anger."

"Absolutely. She wanted to join a cult and moved to Portland, Oregon, but he refused to go with her. I didn't find out any of this until after she left," Veronica explained.

"There must have been a turning point because he eventually came to me for confession."

"I thought once she was out of his life, he'd improve, but he continued getting angry about everything. It got worse both mentally and physically. I think his constant headaches and nightmares convinced him he was dying, and somehow, I eventually persuaded him to see you."

"Ken's grown tremendously in his faith since I met him. He's opened the door and invited God in. There is something else you can do for Ken."

"Anything. What is it?"

"Pray to St. Joseph for his intercession. He was the gentle head of the Holy Family. Ask him to obtain God's blessing for your son. It's part of the St. Joseph Novena."

"Yes, Father, I will start that today."

"The demons fear St. Joseph because when he makes a petition to Jesus, it's paternal and that's unique. The demons know it's a special relationship, and it terrifies them."

"Yes, when you explain it that way, it makes perfect sense."

"Excellent. You've provided some context and insight. I appreciate it. Do you mind if I share this conversation with Fr. Palermo and Clement?"

"Not at all."

The Next Day

As promised, Ken arrived at the park at 8:00 a.m. Clement was already in the parking lot and noticed him. He got out of his car and walked toward Ken, carrying a tote bag.

After greeting each other, Ken replied, "Okay, I still can't figure out why you needed to know my shoe size before we got together."

"Because I wanted to give you this," he answered and handed the bag to Ken. "Fr. Whitburn blessed them yesterday."

Ken opened it and retrieved a pair of used sneakers. With a quizzical look, he stated, "I appreciate the gift, but I'm not a jogger."

"They're trail running shoes," Clement clarified.

"Um, thanks." Ken gestured with hesitant confusion.

"You've come a long way since we met, but there's more to be done."

"Let me guess, these are for me to walk the narrow road," Ken stated with a hint of sarcasm.

Unfazed and unamused, Clement illuminated, "Now is the time to run toward Christ. You've done a good job running away from your demons. But what are you running toward?"

"So it's a metaphor?"

"Maybe. Running shoes help you chase."

"You mean to chase Christ?" Ken asked seriously and nodded to answer his own question.

"They're used. Not because I'm frugal, which I am, but because it gives you a chance to literally walk in someone else's shoes. Vengeance is less likely when you see the other person's point of view. Run in their shoes for a while, and maybe you can use them as a reminder," Clement further explained.

"Yeah. Thanks."

"Besides, it's a healthy way to release some energy," Clement stated and quickly said his goodbyes. Ken watched him get into his car and drive away.

He walked over to a nearby bench and sat down alone. Ken regretted his flippant attitude, so he decided to say a few prayers. He closed his eyes and recited several prayers to ask to open his heart to Jesus.

Afterward, he opened his eyes and looked at the shoes. They didn't appear *too* worn. Clement added new cushion insoles, and Ken remembered his last run. It was in high school gym class.

He hated running and wondered if he'd previously mentioned it to Clement? From Ken's observation, everything that Clement did and said had a deeper meaning, so this wasn't simply a casual gift to encourage exercise.

I guess I could go for a run, just a mile or two, Ken thought to himself and was soon trying on his *new* pair of shoes. It was a perfect fit. The weather cooperated too, at a comfortable fifty-five degrees. He noticed a trailhead at the edge of the parking lot.

So he ran.

And ran.

His feet and legs were a little tired, but Ken happily pushed through the pain. After realizing he was several miles away from the park, he turned around.

The movie theme to *Rocky* popped into his head, the scene where Rocky Balboa goes for a run. Ken picked up his pace, and he subconsciously started throwing a few punches into his movement. *Gonna Fly Now, Flying High Now.*

Endorphins were pumping through his veins as Ken likened himself to Rocky, an underdog who had to fight for everything. He was the *ultimate underdog* battling the devil.

Ken understood he wasn't alone, but he was the lynchpin, and Jesus wasn't going to complete the removal of the diabolical affliction to his body, mind, and heart unless Ken was right with God. What did Clement mean by *there's more to be done*? He was saying all the prayers and following the instructions. *Wasn't that enough*?

Apparently not, and Ken became frustrated with his situation and imagined throwing his *punches* at the devil. He thought back to Clement's comment, *walk in someone else's shoes and run to Christ.* It wasn't enough to avoid vices.

It was as if a dam was spilling over. Ken was flooded with emotions as something fused inside his brain and heart. Ken threw a few more punches as he ran down the trail. He'd been *fighting* to get his life back, but that was only the first half. Getting rid of his demons wasn't the end goal.

He threw more air punches so hard that he almost pushed himself off the slim path. He put two and two together and saw it so clearly. The demons were in his way! They were standing in the middle of the road that led to Christ. For the first time, he desired *to truly be with God.*

As if on cue, the song was ending in his head. The trail led to a steep incline, and he envisioned Rocky running up the steps of the Philadelphia Museum of Art. Ken sprinted to the top of the hill and triumphantly thrust his arms in the air and slowly turned around. He wasn't merely *ready* to love Christ. He *wanted it.*

Ken panted and breathed deeply from the physical exertion. He looked around and saw up ahead the trail paralleled the street and was only a quarter mile from the park. He walked the remainder, and a few minutes later, he approached his truck. As he opened the door, he noticed a car in the far corner of the parking lot, taking up two spaces. An older man pulled the spare out of his trunk, about to change the flat rear tire.

Normally, he'd laugh at the old man's misfortune. Ken watched him for a moment and saw him retrieve something from the car's passenger side. He appeared to be reading a small book, probably the owner's manual. The old Ken would mock his obvious struggle and lack of knowledge. But today, he saw an opportunity to do something for someone else.

He walked toward the man. "Hey, do you need some help?"

"Oh, I don't know, maybe. I'm not very good with cars," the man replied and laughed at himself.

Ken inspected the flat tire and saw a three-inch piece of sheet metal lodged in the tread. "This tire is damaged and may not be fixable."

"Hmm," the old man responded.

"I can help you. I'm Ken," he said and stuck out his hand.

"Thank you, young man. My name is Joe." The old man smiled. He was a skinny fellow with curly gray hair and a thick beard.

"Do you have a tire iron and a jack?" Ken asked, and the old man went fishing to the bottom of his trunk. He moved some things around until he found what he was looking for and showed Ken.

"These will do," Ken replied, and the old man handed him the tools. Ken found the proper location to place the jack and proceeded to slowly lift the car's back end.

"KF Construction," the man said, referring to Ken's sweaty shirt. "Is that your company?"

"Yup, although it's only me. I had to let my employees go and haven't been working much because of a few things going on in my personal life," Ken admitted, which was the understatement of the year.

"I was a carpenter myself, but I'm retired now," the man told him as Ken started to remove the lug nuts.

"That's nice. Were you on your own?"

"Yes, I mostly built custom shelves, furniture, and staircases."

"How do you like retirement?" Ken asked, making small talk.

"Oh fine, although I'm just as busy as when I was working. The Lord has shown me many ways I can stay useful." Ken continued to unscrew the lug nuts and removed the flat tire.

"I greatly appreciate your help," he thanked as Ken started putting the spare tire into place. The old man handed him a lug nut.

"Sure. What keeps you so busy in your golden years?" Ken asked as he imagined his own retirement, sitting on the recliner, cold beer in hand and watching as many sporting events as possible.

"I donate my time to fix up old churches, that and volunteering at a youth mentoring program."

"Good for you," Ken casually commented, more focused on tightening the final lug nut.

"We're always looking for more mentors."

Ken got the hint. The old man was recruiting. "I don't know. Like I said, my life's a little chaotic right now."

"I understand. Let me pay you for your time," he offered.

"Nah, you don't need to."

"Are you sure? I don't mind. I've got fifty bucks in my wallet," he proposed as Ken lowered the jack and removed it from underneath the car.

"Don't worry about it. Donate it back to your nonprofit."

"I'll do that. I know exactly who it will help," he exclaimed with a smile and took back the jack and tire iron from Ken.

Three Days Later

It was another grueling session. Ken's memory was fuzzy about the events over the past few hours, but he was keenly aware of how tired and sweaty he was. Everyone else was exhausted too, except for Fr. Palermo. Ken returned to full consciousness and saw the priest smiling. *That* hadn't happened before, and the next few words seared into Ken's brain. "The demon is desperate. We're getting close."

"What does that mean?" Ken asked with cautious optimism.

"The reinforcements aren't coming. The demon is on his own, and his control is slipping."

"How do you know?"

"He was compelled to admit that *she* was coming soon," Fr. Palermo explained, beaming a smile.

"How soon is *soon*?"

"We don't know exactly, but it's time for you to take an important action. You need to repair your relationship with those you've hurt. It's not enough to be sorrowful for your sins."

"I understand, and that's fair, although in a way, I'm looking forward to it. Is that strange?"

"It depends. How do you mean?"

"I want to make amends and show everyone that I'm a changed man. If they want to punch me in the face, I'll let them."

"It may surprise you how people react to honesty and contriteness," Fr. Palermo suggested.

"We'll see. I'll report back," Ken stated and helped Clement and the others pack up their material. Ken placed the crucifix in a soft padded bag and studied the figurine. It no longer hurt to look at such a sacred object.

Ten minutes later, they were saying their goodbyes, and Ken started the hour-long drive back to Denver. The display on his truck lit up, showing an incoming phone call.

"Hello, is this Mr. Flowers?" the voice on the other end inquired.

"Yes," he responded with some confusion as the caller sounded like a child.

"I wanted to thank you for the baseball mitt and bat. Oh, this is David."

"Maybe you have the wrong number. I'm not sure what you're talking about," Ken slowly answered, trying to figure out who this kid was. It'd been a long time since someone called him *Mr. Flowers*. He heard a clank, and a few seconds later, another voice came through the speakers in his truck.

"Hi, Ken. This is the guy you helped with the flat tire. Your money went to equipment for a kid in the mentor program."

"Ah, okay, now I understand."

"David called to thank you personally."

"Gotcha. That was nice of him. How old is he?"

"He's twelve. Go on ahead, I'll be out there in a minute," the man instructed and clarified. "I was telling David to go outside. I'm going to throw the baseball around with him.

There aren't too many days left before it'll be too cold to play catch."

"Try to break in the new glove," Ken added.

"It's used, but it fits him properly. He's had a rough go of things lately. His father."

"Oh?" Ken asked, his interest peaked, knowing that the old man was looking for an opening to recruit him again. Ken decided to accommodate him.

"David's father died last year. He's been acting out, as you might expect. His mother brought him to the program to try to make a connection with a good male role model."

"I see," he stated in a somber reality. His memories flooded back to his own childhood.

"Well, I don't want to take up any more of your time. I'm sure you're busy."

"Yes, but how did you get my number?" Ken asked, unsure why he wanted the conversation to continue.

"KF Construction. Your website had a phone number."

"Right, of course."

"Thanks again. You made David's day."

"I was glad to do it," Ken answered, feeling happy for bringing a moment of normalcy to a kid's life.

That got him thinking. He'd already made a list of the people that he wronged. Ones that he treated unfairly, and let's face it, unjustly. Ken became overwhelmed with guilt, and a tear formed and dribbled down his cheek. Ken wasn't much of a crier, but he looked back at all the many cruel and despicable acts he did. And that doesn't include his thoughts and emotions. Hate and anger filled so much of his life, and everyone else suffered because of it.

He originally planned to first apologize to Walter. But instead of heading to his office, he had a higher-priority apology to make.

PART 5: *THE OLD ENEMY*, ONE HOUR LATER

"Ken, come in. What a nice surprise," Veronica Flowers expressed happily.

"Mom, did I catch you at a bad time?"

"No, I returned from adoration at the church about a half hour ago."

"Thank you so much. I know it's helping," he pressed in a strained voice.

Memories of the last difficult conversation he had with his mother filled his brain. He remembered pacing up and down in her living room as he contemplated how to tell his mother he was possessed by the devil. He quickly added, "Can we sit and talk?"

"Sure. You look upset," she reacted with concern. "Did something go wrong today?"

"No, it was good. That's not why I'm here. Well, not exactly," Ken awkwardly explained and headed into the small living room at his mother's house.

His mother scrunched her brow in confusion, and Ken took a deep breath and said, "I need to make reparations to everyone I've hurt."

"Yes, that makes sense. It's an important step."

"Exactly, that's why I'm starting with you."

"Me? Don't be silly," she laughed.

"I do. I've probably hurt you the most."

She projected a quizzical look. She forgave her son many times and didn't believe she was owed an apology. Her heart didn't hold resentment. Although the last few months were difficult for her son, she witnessed Ken grow in his faith, which *always* brought warmth to her heart and a smile to her face.

She was grateful to be part of his team and hadn't felt this needed by her son in over a decade. As Veronica was about to argue with her son, he uttered a name Ken hadn't mentioned in ages. "Dad."

"Oh. What about him?"

"I'm so sorry," Ken replied and grabbed his mother's hand, clearly distraught.

"Honey, I'm sorry too. Your father died at such a young age."

"I thought that if he loved me more, he'd have the strength to stay alive."

"He fought against the cancer with everything he had," Veronica croaked, upset by Ken's bluntness.

Ken noticed his mother's reaction. He touched her hand gently and continued, "I know he did. I want to explain what I was thinking back then. Unfortunately, I interpreted his death as a rejection *of me*."

"He loved you and your sister very much. You know that, right?" Veronica asked.

"I do. Getting cancer wasn't his fault. But at the time, I could only see myself as an abandoned child. I didn't want to *be that kid* whose father left him."

"Anyone would be traumatized," his mother defended.

"That's true. But I was selfish and filled with so much resentment."

"I'm so sorry you went through it. You were only a child, hurt by circumstances beyond your control."

"Yes. I wish I would have reacted differently. I can't change the past. After he died, I hated him. *Intensely*," Ken continued.

Veronica's face went ash white and contorted, trying to hold back the tears.

"Mom, I'm not saying this to upset you. There's more to the story."

Veronica quietly nodded, unable to speak. Ken grabbed her hand to comfort his mother.

"I hated God too," he admitted and looked down for a moment. "It's now so obvious how this changed my life, especially the way I interacted with people. I believed since I was treated unfairly, I could do the same to others."

"It *was* unfair," she countered.

"Yes, but instead of leaning on Christ to help me through it, I directed my wrath at Him. I made the wrong choice. You saw it all, and I took it out on you too. I abandoned God, but He never abandoned me. I've finally come to realize it after all these years."

"It's going to be okay."

"You know, Mom, I finally believe that. All you did was love me, and what did I do? Dump it all on you. I treated you *so* badly. Can you ever forgive me?"

"Oh, honey, I already have!" she exclaimed.

"How did you do it? You weren't resentful."

"It's not God's job to prevent suffering. He wants to be there to hold our hand through the difficult times. He'll take our burden if we let Him."

"Unfortunately, that's not what I did."

"Asking God for the strength to carry on got me through it. I never stopped believing that God loved me. Your father dying wasn't to punish him *or us*."

"I understand. The only place without suffering is heaven," Ken proclaimed, and his mother nodded in agreement.

"The more we love God, the more comfort we'll receive. Bad things simply happen sometimes. Many people find that inadequate, but blaming God *never* brings you comfort," Veronica said solemnly, and they were silent for a moment.

"I'm experiencing that now. We have to trust in Jesus even when we can't comprehend what's happening around us," Ken added, and his mother nodded, her heart filled with joy. Her prodigal son had returned.

"Do you want some tea?"

"Sure, I'd love some," Ken answered and followed his mother to the kitchen.

"There's a quiet, strong peace in you, I can tell," his mother told him.

"I feel it too. There's one more thing," Ken announced.

"I don't know if I can take any more of this," she said in jest, getting Ken to smile and laugh.

"This might be the most important part. I forgive Dad. I know it's dumb. Obviously, it wasn't his choice to die. When I think of Dad now, I remember the good times. I expected my childhood to be filled with happiness, and when he died, it left me with hatred and bitterness. The reason I came here today is to tell you I *don't* feel that way anymore. The resentment and blame, *it's gone.*"

St. Benedict Prayer

Crux Sacra Sit Mihi Lux	May the holy cross be my light
Non Draco Sit Mihi Dux	Let not the dragon be my guide

Three Days Later

Moving on and leading a better life seemed like an inadequate plan. Perhaps his suffering was something he should embrace, his connection to Christ's suffering on the cross. Ken contacted everyone on his list in person, including Walter and Hank. His daily headaches and discomfort continued, but he sensed the demon was being tormented as Ken recovered his own conscience and strived to be an instrument of God's love.

There isn't neutrality in one's spiritual life. You're either moving toward Christ, or you aren't. Everything one does, it's either feeding your grace or its poison. It's so simple, yet many fail to pursue their path to salvation.

Ken arrived early at the convent for another session with Fr. Palermo and the team. He wanted to spend thirty minutes praying. Soon everyone arrived, and forty-five minutes later, Fr. Palermo was citing the Umbrellino Prayer. "Invictus or any other evil spirits here are rendered deaf, dumb and blind. Render them unable to communicate and strip them of all weapons, armor, power, illusions and authority," Fr. Palermo calmly stated.

Ken started shaking violently, making it difficult for Clement and Dean to hold him. Besides keeping Ken safe, they were responsible for ensuring the exorcist priest wasn't harmed.

"In the name of Jesus Christ, I command you to hold the medal of St. Benedict and read its inscription."

The *old enemy* made its last stronghold attempt. Moving at the speed of thought, he attempted to call for demonic reinforcements, but none presented themselves. Ken continued to shake and cough and was having difficulty breathing. He hacked up blood, and Valerie quickly retrieved a towel to wipe his mouth. Ken's stomach and diaphragm were heaving, and he coughed again with the sound coming from deep within his body.

"He's mine. He's *always* been mine!" the demon screeched.

Many Christian soldiers in medieval times sang as they went into battle. Not known for being a crooner, Fr. Palermo surprised Clement when he broke out in song and belted out, "Hail, Holy Queen enthroned above, O Maria. Hail, Queen of mercy and of love, O Maria. Triumph, all ye cherubim, Sing with us, ye seraphim, Heaven and earth resound the hymn: Salve, salve, salve Regina!"

"Stop, you miserable retch!" the demon begged.

Fr. Palermo continued singing, and when he finished immediately proclaimed, "This man is a child of God. In Jesus's name, I command you to look at the statue of the Virgin Mary for three minutes *and then leave*," Fr. Palermo stated.

"Never!" Ken's face contorted in such a way that his lips seemed to disappear, leaving his teeth bare, covered with blood and gnashed at the priest. Ken's mouth opened wide and kept expanding beyond what was physically possible.

Father Palermo wasn't distracted by such parlor tricks and stated, "In the name of Jesus, your authority over Ken *has been revoked*!"

It was then that Ken coughed violently once more, and on the base of his tongue appeared a large four-inch metal padlock.

"Go to the foot of the cross, and He will dispose of you as He sees fit," Fr. Palermo raised his voice and retrieved the unlocked object from Ken's mouth. The demon's lock over Ken was broken. Fr. Palermo took this as Christ's triumph over the demon.

Instantly, silence filled the room. Not in an eerie way, but rather with great reverence. Clement looked into Ken's eyes as the most telling sign; they looked normal.

Ken felt a complete sense of calm along with God's presence, as if He was engulfing Ken in His light. It was like no other experience in his life.

Descriptive words are inadequate.

The demon wasn't merely expulsed; it was extracted.

Liberation was attained.

Thirty-Two Days Later, December 2018

"I think that about does it." As Ken finished cutting a piece of pine for an interior room wall frame, Walter said, "Your debt's been paid." Ken had worked for Walter for free to make up for the damage he caused at his office.

"Are you sure?"

"Yes. You do nice work. I'll admit, when you first came to apologize, I didn't believe it."

"You had every right to be suspicious," Ken joked.

"Although I didn't know you very well before, I sense you've changed," Walter observed.

"I'm not going to downplay or make excuses for my behavior. I want to make amends and live a better life."

"Well, I appreciate it, and over the past few weeks, you seem very genuine about it. Dedicating your life to Christ is how you described it, which is great, and I hope it continues," he stated with a hint of doubt and was expecting an uncomfortable rebuttal.

"I finally allowed myself to open my heart to Him, and it's changed every aspect of my life. But I understand the cynicism. Will the new behavior last, right?" Ken asked and stacked the dozen pieces of wood he had previously cut.

"Exactly," Walter responded, although not fully convinced. He's seen numerous people make a bold behavior change only to quit in a few months.

Walter had several employees addicted to drugs and later enter a rehab program. He wanted to be a catalyst for change and redemption by giving employees a second chance, but he often felt disappointed if they showed up to a job site under the influence. Walter was a little skeptical that Ken might disappoint him, too.

"Anyone can fall back into a lifestyle of sin," Ken acknowledged. "I was a vengeful person, and it consumed me. I trashed your office in a rage."

"Yeah, and I wasn't the guy who backed into your truck!" Walter teased.

"I know. Again, I'm sorry about that. It's easy to talk a good game about *finding religion,* but actions speak louder than words."

"True, and that's a daily lifestyle, not simply talk, as you mentioned."

"Each day will be a new challenge, but because I've developed a deep relationship with Christ, I'm optimistic. I'm not alone."

"You have a realistic outlook, and I respect the new Ken," Walter commented, impressed that Ken realized that each day would present a challenge.

"Thanks. A big part of that is rejecting the unholy trinity: *me, myself, and I.*"

"You got that right! It's difficult to put others first and be a man of character," Walter agreed and nodded at Ken.

It felt good to make amends with Walter. "I'll put the tools away and head out," Ken told him. He had enough time to go home and change. There was one more important meeting later that day.

A few hours later, Ken arrived at the Monarch Street Coffee House. Clement was in line getting his beverage and waved Ken over to him. A few minutes later, the two men were relaxing at their table.

"Fr. Whitburn and I sat at this very table when we first met in June. I'll never forget *that awkward* conversation," Ken stated.

"It must seem like a lifetime ago," Clement observed and laughed.

"It sure does."

"Did you have your court date?"

"Yes, for the DUI. Since it was a first-time offense, there won't be any jail time."

"That's good. Is that why you wanted to meet?" he asked, immediately getting down to business.

"There's more. You mentioned that you'd be phasing out. Before you do that, I wanted to thank you for the running shoes."

"You're welcome. You're right, going forward, you'll meet with your spiritual director. He'll answer questions and provide guidance. You'll no longer interact with the ministry team."

"Yes, that's what Fr. Whitburn told me," Ken stated.

"In many ways, life will get back to normal, such as rebuilding your business. But your spiritual life is another matter."

"For sure, that's not the same as before," Ken agreed.

"You'll need to continue pursuing a life of virtue. You made a dramatic conversion. The ministry team helped, but ultimately, it was always going to be determined by you. Sometimes diabolic possession is allowed for the purpose of building a union with God. It's a way to turn evil into good and it's a mystery we don't fully understand."

"I don't *like* that I went through everything the past few months, but I felt it was necessary to save my soul. As you said many times before, don't fear the demons. Fear the sin and the destruction it causes."

"So you were listening!" Clement poked fun at Ken.

"I was *always* listening, but not always following," Ken joked back. "My life was a train wreck back then."

"The diabolic creates chaos in the neatness of life," Clement quipped.

"That's a perfect description of what I experienced."

"I'm so happy for you," Clement said with stoic sincerity.

"The fundamental difference is that I see myself and my actions with greater clarity. I own my own thoughts and don't mind being by myself in silence. Although sometimes my mind drifts and I wonder if it's *really* over."

"Don't allow doubt to linger. Yes, it can happen, being repossessed, but it's when the person falls back into their sinful ways or returns to the occult."

"One possession was enough, trust me," Ken laughed, and Clement was pleased to see him so relaxed and at peace.

"Seriously, though, stay on the right path, and you'll be *more* than fine. We all struggle with sin. It's normal," Clement explained, a concept that Ken already understood. However, sometimes we all need to be reminded of the truth.

"I know. I'll be talking to Fr. Whitburn regularly."

“Good. He’ll keep you on track.”

“All I can do is to be faithful and trust in God’s grace and providence. I’m not afraid of the future,” Ken concluded.

Clement looked at Ken thoughtfully and, after a few seconds, stated, “God has a plan for you. Now go out and figure out what that is.”

“I already have.”

Five Months Later, April 2019

“Extend your arm a little more. Keep your index and middle finger on the laces,” Ken instructed. The boy threw the baseball, and Ken moved up a few feet to catch it.

“Take a step with your left foot and move your body forward as you release the ball with your right arm,” Ken continued and added, “it’ll help you throw it far, like Joe DiMaggio.”

“Who?”

“Never mind. Google that name some time.”

The boy threw it again, and this time Ken didn’t have to move. “That’s better. You’re looking good out there.”

“Thanks,” David enthusiastically responded.

“Let’s each take a step back. You can do it.” Ken watched the boy put a little more muscle into the throw. It had the distance but was a few feet off to the right. Not a bad throw at all. Ken nodded, and David returned a smile.

Ken began volunteering with the youth mentoring program a few months ago, and after an initial meeting, he and David hit it off. They met two days a week, and Ken enjoyed throwing the ball around with him. When Ken met the executive director at the ministry, he didn’t know of any volunteer named Joe. In fact, Ken never saw or heard from the old man again. It was strange. Or maybe it was something else?

Ken learned about David’s background and the tragic way the boy’s father died. They hadn’t talked about it yet. It would come up someday, and Ken would be there and share his own story.

The two didn't talk much at all. Sure, there were some conversations about school, sports, and favorite foods. But constant conversation wasn't necessary. Ken and David simply enjoyed baseball and hanging out. There wasn't a rush to get into all the emotional stuff, and David appreciated not being pressured to *spill his guts*. David would let Ken know when the time was right.

Ken's relationship with Christ was integrated into his lifestyle, and he sensed that David wanted to find out more about it. Ken planned to share in small doses over time how much he basked in God's love and glory. He would not force it, and he also needed to have a conversation with David's mother. His own sister too. Ken was confident his love of Jesus would be *contagious*.

Sometimes, simply being present with a good man is all a boy needs.

Sometimes, the *ordinary* moments of life will bond a boy to a father figure.

Sometimes, the ordinary moments of childhood are *most remembered*.

And sometimes, those ordinary moments of life can be the most joyous, and that's *extraordinary*.

Two Years Later, 2021

It starts with the *chase*. The wolves surround the prey and look for weakness, trying to isolate the creature from the herd. The prey may stumble and become overwhelmed. Or it may fight back and escape. But the predator doesn't give up easily, for it's hungry and singularly focused.

The lead wolf is intelligent and masterfully coordinates the group effort, targeting the *vulnerable*. The pack leader is looking for an opening, looking for an edge. It's their nature to hunt and devour. When the predator fails, it's not deterred. It may find a fresh prey, or it may return to the one it previously hunted. They continually look for the *wounded*.

At exactly 3:00 a.m., Ken woke up, experiencing pain on both his calves. He was sleeping on his stomach, and a great weight pressed down on his legs. It felt as if someone or *something* was standing on top of him. He audibly moaned from the pain and pressure and sensed himself sink into the mattress.

It stepped off his calves and placed both feet on his back so he couldn't move. The weight was too much. *Am I paralyzed?* Ken realized he wasn't dreaming; he was being attacked and terrorized. Was it punishment? Was it to instill fear? Compliance?

He was completely awake and comprehended the source of his distress. It was difficult to move his head to see what was on top of him. His back burned from the intense heat and weight. He strained his neck to find the source of his agony. He could only see the heel of a foot, skinless with *its flesh burning*.

It was diabolic.

Unable to speak, he thought to himself, *Get away from me, demon!* He panicked. Was it happening again? Trepidation gripped his body and mind. The weight and burning on his back continued. He was powerless to remove the source of his oppression. For a moment, his fear subsided when a thought popped into his head. Recite *the Hail Mary prayer*.

He couldn't remember the prayer! He'd say a few words and stop. *How could he have forgotten a prayer he recited a thousand times before?* He didn't know what to do, and his anxiety returned and was about to overwhelm him.

His brain was blocked.

On the fifth attempt, the words came smoothly, "Hail Mary, Full of Grace, The Lord is with thee. Blessed art thou among women, and blessed is the fruit of thy womb, Jesus. Holy Mary, Mother of God, pray for us sinners now, *and at the hour of our death.* Amen."

When he said the last word, the pain instantly ceased, and Ken breathed a sigh of relief. His terror was immediately replaced with a *complete and deep sense of peace.* The quick turnaround surprised him.

Calmness came over his entire self. His body and mind were fully relaxed. He instantly fell into a deep and restful sleep.

The predator *was denied.*

And the demon never returned.

Addendum

Seven Deadly Sins

	Vice	**Virtue**
1	Pride, arrogance, self-obsession, or vainglory	Humility or modesty which cures pride and self-love by removing one's ego and boastfulness, therefore allowing the attitude of service. Also includes bravery, faith, hope, reverence, and altruism.
2	Greed, wastefulness, or covetousness	Charity, generosity, benevolence, or love cures greed by putting the desire to help others above storing up treasure for oneself.
3	Lust or illicit sexual desire, power, or fame	Chastity, purity, or self-control cures lust by ruling over one's passion and leveraging that energy for the good of others. Also includes knowledge, modesty, honesty, and wisdom.
4	Envy, jealousy or avarice, materialistic	Gratitude and kindness cures envy by placing the desire to help others above the need to supersede them. Also includes loyalty, compassion, and integrity.

5	Gluttony, excessiveness, drunkenness	Temperance or moderation cures gluttony by implanting the desire to be healthy, therefore making one fit to serve God and others. Also includes self-control and honor.
6	Wrath, anger, and vengeance	Gentleness, meekness, compassion, and patience cures wrath by taking time to understand the needs and desires of others before acting or speaking. Also includes peace, fortitude, justice, mercy, and sufferance.
7	Sloth or laziness	Diligence, enthusiasm, sacrifice, and zeal cure slothfulness by placing the best interest of others above a life of ease and relaxation.

Diabolical Affliction and Influence

Demonic possession of a person is rare and is frequently confused with a mental illness. The three methods in which one can become possessed are:

Classic: usually a gradual progression through stages of oppression and obsession.

Partial: usually an invitation made to a demon in exchange for a favor (e.g., a pact with the devil).

Transient: rights are granted to demon by someone else, such as through a Satanic ritual performed on a child or an adult consecrating oneself to Satan.

A fractional possession does not exist although a demon may choose when and how it wants to manifest. Physical and behavior signs are presented below to the reader as a reference. Some occur more frequently than others, while some may not occur at all. The forthcoming table is meant to be informative, but certainly not an exhaustive list.

Level	**Possible Physical Signs**	**Potential Common Behavior**
Oppression	1. May commence with occult activities such as witchcraft, spells, curses, séances, fortune teller, tarot cards, or Ouija boards. 2. Lack of energy. 3. Dulled senses. 4. Failed technology (dropped calls, PC problems.) 5. Home infestation, such as unexplainable temperature changes, smells, noises, shadows, objects disappearing. 6. Unexplained behavior of animals and insects.	1. Withdrawn (especially from family, friends, and others religiously devoted). 2. Broadcast (tells story and may seek assistance from others in sinful lifestyle). 3. Associate with others who are like-minded. 4. Anger toward God. 5. Sees oneself as a victim and may seek vengeance. 6. Fear, anxiety, negative thinking, loneliness, despair, or depression.

Level	Possible Physical Signs	Potential Common Behavior
Obsession	1. Engage in activities to epitomize habitual and mortal (deadly) sin. 2. Change physical appearance (e.g., immodest, goth). 3. More prone to violence and fighting. 4. Self-harm and mutilation. 5. Diabolic activity permeates all parts of a person's life. 6. Actions become compatible with the demonic.	1. Reorder life to align with vices and isolate from others. 2. Urged to harm others. 3. Aversion to church services and sacred objects. 4. No longer seek forgiveness or redemption. 5. Resentment toward those seeking virtue, and belief that nothing is sacred. 6. Justification of one's actions, and blame others. 7. Intense and persistent attack on the mind with constant diabolic commentary. 8. Random and obsessive thoughts.

Level	Possible Physical Signs	Potential Common Behavior
Possession	1. Demon(s) invade body and seeks to control faculties, body parts, and organs. 2. Recoil and severe reaction to sacred objects or locations. (e.g., churches, statues, cross/ crucifix, holy water). 3. Strength beyond normal capabilities. 4. Ability to speak foreign languages not learned by individual. 5. Ability to know details of others for which no reasonable explanation exists. 6. Body contortions outside physical norms. 7. Levitation.	1. Emotional swings more rapid, intense, and extreme. 2. May exhibit signs of mental illness such as bipolar, multiple personality disorder or schizophrenic. 3. Isolate from most individuals, and relationships are pragmatic and utilitarian. 4. Gradual movement to demonic control is most prevalent.

ANGELOLOGY

Angels are spiritual, individual, and immortal creatures, with intelligence and free will. Their purpose is to glorify God without ceasing and serve God as a messenger of his saving plan (as defined by the *Catechism of the Catholic Church*).

Angels are spiritual only while humans are spiritual (soul) and physical (body.) Higher-level angels are more intelligent and were infused with more knowledge than the lower-level ones. Angels have their own unique personality and can exchange messages between God and humans. They can deliver our prayers and petitions to God. Angels can also deliver messages to one another through thought alone.

St. Thomas Aquinas explained that the nine levels are split into three hierarchies and are listed below, with the seraphim as the highest. The first hierarchy (7–9) are closest to God and remain in His presence. The second hierarchy (4–6) help guide the universe and are God's instruments in ordering all of creation. The third hierarchy (1–3) are the angels which are in direct contact with humans. The love of angels for God is limitless.

All angels were created with a purpose, and at the moment of their creation, they were instantly infused with knowledge and intelligence. At their creation to serve mankind, angels were given free will to glorify God. Those that rejected God became fallen angels or demons. As such, a demon's purpose is the inverse (opposite) of whatever they were initially created to accomplish or influence on humans.

The following is a summary of the angels and their missions:

	Level	Overall Mission
9	Seraphim	Created with one purpose: fiery love of God.
8	Cherubim	Have intimate knowledge and deep insight of God and continually praise Him.
7	Thrones	Choir of authority, humility, peace, and submission which is passed along to lower-level angels.
6	Dominions	Communicate the commands of God to lower-level angels and make known God's authority.
5	Virtues	Govern nature and the cosmos.
4	Powers	Defend humans and cosmos against evil forces.
3	Principalities	Guard and guide nations, kingdoms, states, cities, and groups and govern the souls and bodies of individuals.
2	Archangels	Includes archangels, who are specifically named in the Bible: 1. St. Michael, who battles demons. 2. St. Gabriel, who appeared to Mary and Joseph on separate occasions to deliver a message from God. 3. St. Raphael, who heals.
1	Angels	Includes guardian angels assigned to each individual and can assist with messages to God.

Prayers

Certain exorcism prayers are reserved only for priests, such as the Umbrellino prayer mentioned in this chapter. However, many different prayers can be recited by any Christian. Several prayers were included in this chapter, and the author has provided the complete prayers below.

For more information about deliverance, protection, devotion, and healing prayers, the author recommends: *Deliverance Prayers: For Use by the Laity* by Fr. Chad Ripperger, PhD.

Prayer to our Guardian Angel

Angel of God, my guardian dear
to whom God's love commits me here,
ever this day be at my side, to light, to guard, to rule, to guide.
Amen.

The Angelus Prayer

The Angel of the Lord declared unto Mary.
And she conceived of the Holy Spirit.
Hail Mary, full of grace,
The Lord is with Thee;
Blessed art thou among women,
And blessed is the fruit of thy womb, Jesus.
Holy Mary, Mother of God,
Pray for us sinners,
Now and at the hour of our death. Amen
Behold the handmaid of the Lord.

Be it done to me according to thy word.
Hail Mary, full of grace,
The Lord is with Thee;
Blessed art thou among women,
And blessed is the fruit of thy womb, Jesus.
Holy Mary, Mother of God,
Pray for us sinners,
Now and at the hour of our death. Amen.
And the Word was made flesh.
And dwelt among us.
Hail Mary, full of grace,
The Lord is with Thee;
Blessed art thou among women,
And blessed is the fruit of thy womb, Jesus.
Holy Mary, Mother of God,
Pray for us sinners,
Now and at the hour of our death. Amen.
Pray for us, O holy Mother of God.
That we may be made worthy of the promises of Christ.

Let us pray: Pour forth, we beseech Thee, O Lord, Thy grace into our hearts, that we to whom the Incarnation of Christ Thy Son was made known by the message of an angel, may by His Passion and Cross be brought to the glory of His Resurrection. Through the same Christ Our Lord. Amen.

Auxilium Christianorum Daily Prayers

Our help is in the name of the Lord.
Who made heaven and earth.

Most gracious Virgin Mary, thou who wouldst crush the head of the serpent, protect us from the vengeance of the evil one. We offer our prayers, supplications, sufferings and good works to thee so that thou may purify them, sanctify them and present them to thy Son as a perfect offering. May this offering be given so that the demons that influence or seek to influence the members of the Auxilium Christianorum do not know the source of their expulsion and blindness. Blind them so that they know not our good works. Blind them so that they know not on whom to take vengeance. Blind them so that they may receive the just sentence for their works. Cover us with the Precious Blood of thy Son so that we may enjoy the protection which flows from His Passion and Death. We ask this through the same Christ our Lord. Amen.

Prayer to Saint Michael, the Archangel

Saint Michael, the Archangel, defend us in battle.
Be our protection against the wickedness and snares of the devil.
May God rebuke him, we humbly pray;
and do thou, O Prince of the heavenly host,
by the power of God
cast into hell Satan and all the evil spirits
who prowl throughout the world seeking the ruin of souls. Amen.

The Lord's Prayer

Our Father,
Who art in heaven,
hallowed be Thy name;
Thy kingdom come;
Thy will be done on earth as it is in heaven.
Give us this day our daily bread;
and forgive us our trespasses
as we forgive those who trespass against us;
and lead us not into temptation,
but deliver us from evil. Amen.

Glory Be

Glory be to the Father,
and to the Son,
and to the Holy Spirit,
as it was in the beginning,
is now, and ever shall be,
world without end. Amen.

Litany of the Most Precious Blood of our Lord Jesus Christ

Lord have mercy.
Christ have mercy.
Lord have mercy.
Lord have mercy.
Christ hear us. Christ graciously hear us.
God, the Father of Heaven, have mercy on us.
God, the Son, Redeemer of the World, have mercy on us.
God, the Holy Spirit, have mercy on us.
Holy Trinity, One God, have mercy on us.
Blood of Christ, only-begotten Son of the Eternal Father, save us.
Blood of Christ, Incarnate Word of God, save us.
Blood of Christ, of the New and Eternal Testament, save us.
Blood of Christ, falling upon the earth in the Agony, save us.
Blood of Christ, shed profusely in the Scourging, save us.
Blood of Christ, flowing forth in the Crowning with Thorns, save us.
Blood of Christ, poured out on the Cross, save us.
Blood of Christ, price of our salvation, save us.

Blood of Christ, without which there is no forgiveness, save us.
Blood of Christ, Eucharistic drink and refreshment of souls, save us.
Blood of Christ, stream of mercy, save us.
Blood of Christ, victor over demons, save us.
Blood of Christ, courage of Martyrs, save us.
Blood of Christ, strength of Confessors, save us.
Blood of Christ, bringing forth Virgins, save us.
Blood of Christ, help of those in peril, save us.
Blood of Christ, relief of the burdened, save us.
Blood of Christ, solace in sorrow, save us.
Blood of Christ, hope of the penitent, save us.
Blood of Christ, consolation of the dying, save us.
Blood of Christ, peace and tenderness of hearts, save us.
Blood of Christ, pledge of eternal life, save us.
Blood of Christ, freeing souls from purgatory, save us.
Blood of Christ, most worthy of all glory and honor, save us.
Lamb of God, Who takest away the sins of the world, spare us, O Lord.
Lamb of God, Who takest away the sins of the world, graciously hear us, O Lord.
Lamb of God, Who takest away the sins of the world, have mercy on us.
Thou hast redeemed us with Thy Blood, O Lord.
And made of us a kingdom for our God.

Let us pray.

Almighty, and eternal God, you have appointed Thy only-begotten Son the Redeemer of the world, and willed to be appeased by His Blood. Grant we beg of Thee, that we may worthily adore this price of our salvation, and through its power be safeguarded from the evils of the present life, so that we may rejoice in its fruits forever in heaven. Through the same Christ our Lord. Amen.

Prayer Against Oppression

Most Blessed Trinity, by the authority given me by the natural law and by Thy giving these things and rights to me, which I have consecrated to the Blessed Virgin Mary, I claim on her behalf the authority, rights, and power over (insert name) income, finances, possessions, communications and anything else that pertains to the oppression. By the merits of Thy Sacred Wounds, I renounce any power or authority I conceded to any demon in relation to the oppression and I reclaim on Our Lady's behalf the rights, powers and authority over anything which I may have lost or conceded and I ask Thee to remove any demon's ability to influence or affect anything in my life. God the Father, humiliate the demons that have sought to steal Thy glory from Thee by oppressing Thy creatures.

We beseech Thee to show Thy great glory and power over them and Thy great generosity to me, Thine unworthy creature, by answering all that I have asked of Thee so that I might love Thee perfectly. I bind all demons of oppression, in the Name of Jesus, by the power of the Most Precious Blood, the power of the humility with which Christ suffered His wounds, and the intercession of the Blessed Virgin Mary, Virgin Most Powerful, Saint Michael the Archangel, The blessed Apostles, Peter, and Paul, and all the saints, and I command you to leave my income, finances, possessions and communications alone and go to the foot of the Holy Cross to receive your sentence, in the Name of the Father, and the Son, and the Holy Spirit. Amen.

Prayer Against Oppression (Additional)

Most watchful Guardian, glorious St Joseph, who wast so intimately familiar with the Incarnate Son of God, greatly thou didst sacrifice and suffer to protect the child Jesus, along with thy beloved spouse, Our Lady of Sorrows, especially in the flight thou madest with Him into Egypt; by this thy sorrow obtain for us the grace to keep far out of the reach of the enemy of our souls, by quitting all dangerous occasions, by driving back all demons of oppression so that we may be entirely faithful in our service to Jesus and Mary.

Mother Most Sorrowful, pray for us.
Virgin Most Powerful, pray for us.
Help of Christians, pray for us.
St. Joseph, Terror of demons, pray for us.
St. Michael, pray for us.
St. Padre Pio, pray for us.
Blessed Francisco Palau, pray for us.
All the angels and saints, pray for us.

Prayer Against Retaliation

Lord Jesus Christ, in your love and mercy, pour Thy Precious Blood over me, our family, friends and those with whom we work so that no demon or disembodied spirit may retaliate against us. Mary, surround us with thy mantle, blocking any retaliating spirits from having any authority over us. St. Michael, surround us with thy shield, so that no evil spirit may take revenge on us. Queen of Heaven and St. Michael, send down the legions of angels under thy command to fight off any spirits that would seek to harm us. All you saints of heaven, impede any retaliating spirit from influencing us. Lord, Thou art the Just Judge, the avenger of the wicked, the Advocate of the Just, we beg in Thy mercy, that all we ask of Mary, the angels and the saints of heaven be also granted to all our loved ones, those who pray for us and their loved ones, that for Thy Glory's sake, we may enjoy Thy perfect protection. Amen.

The Confiteor (I Confess)

I confess to almighty God
and to you, my brothers and sisters,
that I have greatly sinned
in my thoughts and in my words,
in what I have done,
and in what I have failed to do;
through my fault, through my fault,
through my most grievous fault;
therefore I ask blessed Mary ever-Virgin,
all the Angels and Saints,
and you, my brothers and sisters,
to pray for me to the Lord our God.

Act of Contrition

My God, I am sorry for my sins with all my heart.
In choosing to do wrong and failing to do good, I have sinned against you whom I should love above all things.
I firmly intend, with your help, to do penance, to sin no more, and to avoid whatever leads me to sin.
Our Savior Jesus Christ suffered and died for us.
In his name, my God, have mercy.

Prayers to Open Your Heart to Jesus Christ

Lord, touch my heart.
Touch me so that I may feel you in faith though my emotions remain dry.
I know you brought water from the rock, but have you ever dealt with a heart like mine?
Touch, breathe, sing life into this stone I carry in my chest!
Awaken the heart that sleeps.

I have witnessed your miracles and so I know that all things are possible for you.
Stretch out your hand and cure my blindness.
Reach out and shape flesh on these dry bones, lifeless without you.
Let me see your face, and I shall be saved.
Almighty, ever-living God, make us ever obey you willingly and promptly.
Teach us how to serve you with sincere and upright hearts in every sphere of life.
Through our Lord Jesus Christ, your Son, who lives and reigns with you in the unity of the Holy
Spirit, God, for ever and ever. Amen.
Lord Jesus, let my heart never rest until it finds You, who are its center, its love, and its happiness.
By the wound in Your heart pardon the sins that I have committed whether out of malice or out of evil desires.
Place my weak heart in your own divine heart, continually under your protection and guidance, so that I may persevere in doing good and in fleeing evil until my last breath. Amen.

Other books by the author

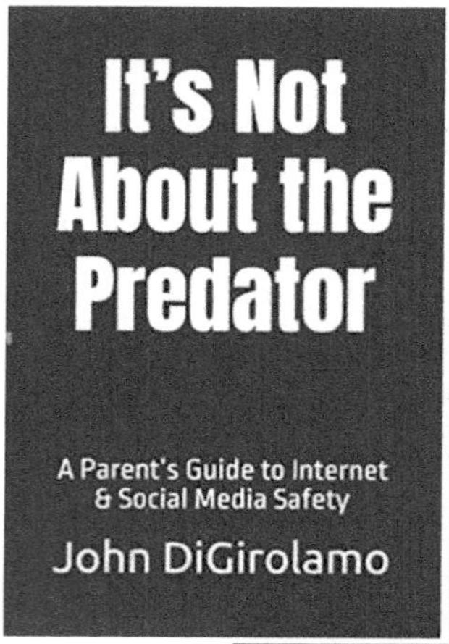

It's Not About the Predator: A Parent's Guide to Internet & Social Media Safety (2022) is a practical fifty-three-page booklet to help keep kids safe online. The book details the predator's playbook, grooming tactics, and specific proactive actions for parents. It also includes tips from an undercover police officer and how pornography feeds the predators. DiGirolamo wrote this book because many of the tactics used by predators engaged in human trafficking are similar to when someone exploits a child to obtain explicit pictures and extortion.

DiGirolamo also wrote the book *It's Not About the Sex* (2022) because he believes that human trafficking is one of the most underreported issues of our day that cuts across all economic, social, racial, and political boundaries. He focused on stories from rural and suburban America, seeking to shine a light on and create an awareness of the evils of human trafficking. The book features four individuals and their true experiences, from the perspective of an advocate, survivor, law enforcement officer, and a brothel madam's tale of redemption.

DiGirolamo previously wrote *It's Not About the Badge* (2021), a creative nonfiction book that profiles the human side of policing, featuring rural officers. After asking officers about a day on the job they would never forget, the book features compelling personal and professional stories of small-town police officers.

Photograph courtesy of Lyndsay Bertram,
reprinted with permission

ACKNOWLEDGEMENTS

I'd like to thank Deputy David Gomez, Dr. Catherine Wheeler, and Clement for sharing their experiences to make this book possible.

This book would not have been possible without additional input and testimony from Abigail Gnojewski, Tamera Gomez, Sarah VanDam, Debbie King, Sheri Olsen, Giuliana Day, Andrew LaRue, Rachael Nicole Miller, Joni Shepherd, Wendy Smith, Pat Knapp, Fr. James Williams, Sharon Beekmann, Wendy McMahan, and Kelly Cresswell.

I also appreciate my beta readers for their input and encouragement, specifically Geri Frost, Lynn Klopstad, Ted Montoya, Brian O'Connell, and Diane Williams.

And finally, to thank my wife, Kathy, for being my biggest cheerleader and first-line editor.

About the Author

John DiGirolamo is a critically acclaimed author, speaker, and antihuman trafficking advocate and is a member of the Christian Authors Network and Christian Indie Publishing Association. The author wrote *It's Not About the dEvil* to highlight three individuals who fight the good fight against modern evil.

He focused on distinctly different topics of online predators, abortion, and spiritual warfare. Yet, the reader will sense a common theme—the influence of evil in the world and some of the horrible acts one human can perpetrate upon another. However, by focusing on the personal stories of the triumph over evil, the reader may be inspired and hopeful for the future.

The author has been invited to speak at over forty different venues and can be contacted for a speaking engagement: johndtheauthor@gmail.com

Visit the author's website: https://itisnotabout.com/

The author has been interviewed numerous times about his books, and a complete list of interviews can be found: https://itisnotabout.com/interviews

John DiGirolamo is the Board President of Bringing our Valley Hope, Colorado, whose objective is to end human trafficking in central Colorado through education and survivor support. https://bvhope.org

DiGirolamo is the Board Secretary of the Chaffee County Patriots https://chaffeecountypatriots.org/

DiGirolamo also writes a newspaper column in the *Fremont County Crusader* and previously had columns in the *Sangre De Cristo Sentinel* and *Winter Park Times* and published a collection of short stories, *#12 Suicide.*

DiGirolamo is a retired CPA who worked in various management positions at both small and large technology companies and currently lives in Chaffee County, Colorado.